COMMON SENSE
MACRO-
ECONOMICS

COMMON SENSE
MACRO-
ECONOMICS

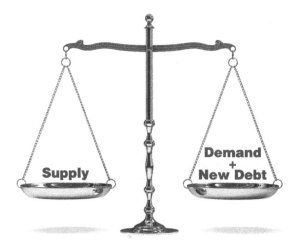

Ravi Batra
Southern Methodist University, USA

NEW JERSEY · LONDON · SINGAPORE · BEIJING · SHANGHAI · HONG KONG · TAIPEI · CHENNAI · TOKYO

Published by

World Scientific Publishing Europe Ltd.

57 Shelton Street, Covent Garden, London WC2H 9HE

Head office: 5 Toh Tuck Link, Singapore 596224

USA office: 27 Warren Street, Suite 401-402, Hackensack, NJ 07601

Library of Congress Cataloging-in-Publication Data
Names: Batra, Ravi N., author.
Title: Common sense macroeconomics / Ravi Batra, Southern Methodist University, USA.
Description: USA : World Scientific, 2020. | Includes bibliographical references and index.
Identifiers: LCCN 2020001795 | ISBN 9781786348395 (hardcover) |
    ISBN 9781786348456 (paperback) | ISBN 9781786348401 (ebook) |
    ISBN 9781786348418 (ebook other)
Subjects: LCSH: Economics.
Classification: LCC HB171 .B315 2020 | DDC 339--dc23
LC record available at https://lccn.loc.gov/2020001795

British Library Cataloguing-in-Publication Data
A catalogue record for this book is available from the British Library.

For any available supplementary material, please visit
https://www.worldscientific.com/worldscibooks/10.1142/Q0248#t=suppl

Desk Editors: Herbert Moses/Shi Ying Koe

Typeset by Stallion Press
Email: enquiries@stallionpress.com

Preface

John Maynard Keynes, perhaps the most celebrated economist in history, must be agonizing in his grave to see a world relying on negative interest rates for the sake of reviving the global economy and reducing the poverty of millions of people across our planet. Even in the middle of the Great Depression that he sought to end with his economic advice, Keynes could not imagine a future where nations would routinely run trillion dollar budget deficits just to grow their economies, or call upon their central banks to keep printing money to stimulate consumer demand. His analysis assumed that at most the interest fee could sink to zero.

After Keynes passed away in 1946, there have been several recessions, but never a depression. The worst slump occurred in 1981 and 1982, when the U.S. unemployment rate approached 11 percent, compared to 25 percent in 1933. Other areas such as Europe and Japan also experienced significant contractions in GDP in the early 1980s. Nations tried Keynesian polices of monetary and fiscal expansion, and always managed to avert a depression. No matter how bad the recession was, interest rates never fell below zero. But then came the Great Recession starting in December 2007, and soon global economies began to unravel.

Housing markets collapsed, banks were bailed out, share markets crashed, and the world feared the onslaught of a depression. Central bankers panicked and went on a money-printing spree. They even coined a new phrase — "Quantitative Easing (QE)." After several bouts of QEs from QE1 to QE2 and then finally to QE3, interest rates moved into negative territory. The world would never be the same.

Conventional macroeconomics now teeters on the brink of insanity. We need to inject common sense into macroeconomics, and that is where this book comes in. The book can be used as a text in macroeconomic principles as well as for advanced courses. Its focus is not on math and complexity of models but on simplicity. Equations are used only when they cannot be avoided, as in a nation's accounting system. It is a student-friendly work that explains complex economic problems through numerical examples, which are easy to comprehend. Specifically, the book innovates in the following ways:

(1) The purpose of studying macroeconomics is to raise the living standard of all, not just a privileged few.
(2) Contrary to popular belief, relentless monetary expansion to finance budget deficits actually makes the rich richer and the poor poorer, which is happening all over the world.
(3) Ethics and efficiency go together. For instance, lowering tax rates for affluent individuals and corporations while raising them for the poor and the middle class are unethical policies that hurt economic growth and generate poverty. Hence, such measures are inefficient, as they do not raise the living standard across the board.
(4) In order to raise everyone's living standard, government policies should generate competition and outlaw mergers among large and profitable firms.
(5) Inequality arises from monopoly capitalism, because then wages increasingly lag behind productivity and generate a rising wage–productivity gap. This rise in the wage gap is the ultimate source of almost all economic troubles and imbalances. While it is inherently unfair, it also leads to vast income disparity and wealth concentration, stock market bubbles and crashes, recessions and eventually depressions. It is the rise in the wage gap that preceded the Great Depression of the 1930s and more recently the Great Recession of 2008.

Hence, governments should not stifle competition and vigorously enforce anti-trust laws.

These are some of the ways in which this book is different from other texts. In short, *Common Sense Macroeconomics* relies on common sense and rationality, not on complexity of models designed to distract from the truth and hide reality.

About the Author

Dr. Ravi Batra, a professor of economics at Southern Methodist University, Dallas, is the author of five international best sellers. He was the chairperson of his department from 1977 to 1980. In October 1978, as a result of having dozens of publications in top journals such as the *American Economic Review, Journal of Political Economy, Econometrica, Journal of Economic Theory, Review of Economic Studies*, among others, Dr. Batra was ranked third in a group of 46 "superstar economists," selected from all the American and Canadian universities by an article in the leading journal, *Economic Enquiry*. In 1990, the Italian prime minister awarded him a Medal of the Italian Senate for writing a book that correctly predicted the downfall of Soviet communism, 15 years before it happened.

Dr. Batra has been written about in major newspapers and magazines, such as the *New York Times, Washington Post, USA Today, Time, Newsweek*, the *U.S. News* and *World Report*, and has appeared on all major networks, including CBS, NBC, CNN, ABC, and CNBC, among others. In 2009, Batra received the Pratima and Navin Doshi Award for his contributions to economic analysis.

In June 2015, the President of Iceland invited him to share his views about the eradication of poverty. His latest book is *End Unemployment Now: How to Eliminate Joblessness, Debt and Poverty Despite Congress*.

The following are some of the comments on Ravi Batra's work:

"Ravi Batra has made an outstanding reputation in the United States as an international economic theorists in the best Western tradition."

Leonard Silk, *New York Times*

"The forecasting record of this widely respected Southern Methodist University economist has won glowing praise from many pragmatic investment masters."

Tom Peters, *Chicago Tribune*

"Dr. Batra writes about his subject as clearly as if he were telling bedtime stories."

Christopher Lehmann-Haupt, *New York Times*

"The good professor has a formidable academic reputation and, from what I know, his forecasting record is impressive."

Barton Biggs, Morgan Stanley

"Batra [is] a scholar who has earned a considerable reputation as an expert on trade."

Albert Crenshaw, *Washington Post*

"His predictions in the early 1980s of low inflation, falling oil prices and a wave of mergers — mocked for years — have proved close to the mark."

Thomas C. Hayes, *New York Times*

"Ravi Batra was used to making tumultuous global forecasts and having nobody listen — then predictions started to come true."

Chip Brown, Associated Press

Acknowledgments

In completing this project I gratefully acknowledge help from the group of seven (G-7). First and foremost is my wife Sunita without whose prodding and inspiration this work might still be in incubation; Thor Theigrson, my former student and then an OECD economist, provided timely and useful research assistance; my son Rishee assisted me with the cover page; Essie Massoumi and William Barnett offered words of encouragement regarding the need for such a text; Satya Das read some chapters and gave useful suggestions. Finally, I am grateful to Natalie Watson, the editor for World Scientific Publishers for timely publication of this book.

Contents

Chapter 1

Introduction: Microeconomic Foundations and Common Sense

Ever since the late 1970s, when neo-Keynesian theories failed to tackle the twin ills of inflation and unemployment, macroeconomics has increasingly relied on individual behavior as the cornerstone of aggregate economic behavior and policy. The idea is that the actions and reactions of consumers, workers and producers crucially determine the movements in national, and ultimately international, markets. The analytical focus has thus shifted to examine what are popularly called microeconomic foundations of macroeconomics. This is the most important and salutary development in the subject since 1936, when John Maynard Keynes produced *The General Theory of Employment, Interest and Money*.

However, with the shift in focus has also come an increasing stress on technicality and mathematical models. Microfoundations do not seem to be good enough unless they have been derived from a sophisticated apparatus that frequently appears as artificial and far removed from the question under consideration. Macroeconomics now relies more upon the sophistry of the micro apparatus than the information available from unmanipulated facts of history. In the process, the subject has become unnecessarily difficult and inaccessible even to the vast majority of the educated population.

1

In plain English, "microeconomic foundation" is just another phrase for common sense, which neo-Keynesian thought had neglected when it sought to print money as a panacea for almost every economic ailment. For common sense we do not need complex models. All we need is to determine whether or not readers can identify themselves with the individual behavior presumed by a theory. Most students are rational and smart enough to see whether or not an idea makes sense, and if it does then it automatically derives from microeconomic behavior.

1. Common Complaints from Students

The stress on sophistry and technicality has created a disgruntled element in economics that is now raising pesky questions, which are rarely answered by standard texts on macroeconomic principles. In fact, the textbooks themselves generate the queries.

For instance, "Why do economists," asks a student, "make a distinction between demand and quantity demanded, or between supply and quantity supplied?" "So we can tell the difference between a movement along a demand curve and its shift, or between a movement along a supply curve and its shift," comes a teacher's programmed reply. "This is too technical," says the student. "There should be some good reason for this confusing potion." "Well, there is," replies the teacher. "You see, normally demand and supply of a good are affected not only by its own price but also by prices of some other goods. In order to isolate these two types of effects, we distinguish between demand and quantity demanded, or between supply and quantity supplied."

"But I don't understand, because the gain in separating the two effects pales before the monumental confusion that it creates for me and my class fellows," the student typically retorts. "If the price of a product falls, you say its demand is constant while its quantity demanded increases, whereas if income rises, the quantity demanded is constant, but demand goes up." "Yes, you've got it," says the teacher. "Don't you think this is confusing?" implores the student. "No, not at all. You should know by now economics is a difficult subject, and needs hard work and a higher IQ," replies the accomplished teacher, his face lit up with a sheepish grin.

"What about this?" continues the student, "A rise in demand lowers quantity demanded." "How did you get that?" shoots back the teacher. "If income rises," argues the student, "demand rises, and with supply constant, price rises and then quantity demanded falls. In other words, if demand rises, eventually quantity demanded falls. In the same way, if supply increases but demand is constant, the product price falls, so that quantity supplied also falls. Thus, quantity supplied decreases because of an increase in supply. You still think all this is not even a tiny-bit confusing?" The teacher, a bit on the defensive now, shrugs and says, "This is common practice among all texts, graduate or undergraduate, and they must have good reasons for it." "With all due respect Sir," blurts out the student, who is about to graduate with honors, "it sounds like gobbledygook or legalese to me."

The above paragraph is just one example of what is wrong with economics; it reveals a surface calm, but an undercurrent of growing discontent among students and some instructors, who are uneasy about the way economics is depicted in textbooks. Newspapers occasionally joke about economists and complain how far the subject is now divorced from reality.

I have been teaching economic principles for more than 15 years but have yet to find a student who was happy with my selected text. I have periodically changed my selections, varied the course content in accordance with current events and fads, but the end result has been more or less the same. Students in general find economics hard, boring and frequently devoid of common sense.

All this is surprising and somewhat disheartening. It is surprising because a good deal of research has been aimed at discovering the so-called microfoundations of various economic problems confronting society, and such foundations are supposed to bring the discipline closer to common sense and reality. But what appears as common sense to accomplished researchers appears to be gobbledygook to many students and non-economists.

It is also disheartening because economics could be a lot more popular than it is. The standard texts make it hard on the student, and unnecessarily so. Economics deals with human nature, and should be readily comprehensible, because everyone can relate to human nature. Instead students typically shun the subject and perform poorly when they do take it under duress.

Finally, I have decided to take matters into my own hands and write a principles text myself. The decision has not been easy, for the intellectual investment and time required to complete the task are no laughing matter. You have to be prepared to do the voluminous, boring and tedious work yourself in order to make it easy for others to understand.

I am starting out with macroeconomics, which, because of its rich policy and social content, is of particular interest to me, and in which I have recently authored a few articles articulating my concerns about the relevance and logic of popular economic theories (see references). Specifically, this book differs from others in the following ways.

2. Common Sense

Since economics deals with human nature, economic theories should be based purely on common sense, which suggests that only one or two explanations of observed phenomena should suffice. A lot of popular ideas seem to flout generally accepted notions of rationality; they are simply dogmas that are untruthful and have no historical legs to stand upon. At best they apply to exceptional cases, but exceptions should not count much in ideas claiming to derive from human nature.

For instance, it is an article of faith among macroeconomists today that low income tax rates on high incomes offer an incentive to save, work hard and invest, and thus stimulate economic growth. The late Professor Martin Feldstein of Harvard University and Michael Boskin at Stanford are among the influential exponents of this view. This idea is so common-place that a front-page article in *The Wall Street Journal* makes copious reference to it.[1]

First of all, does this theory make sense? People's incentive to work hard comes mainly from their incentive to eat, live in a house, get

---

[1] *The Wall Street Journal*, January 2, 2003. The article mentions Professor Feldstein as one of the chief exponents of this view.

education and healthcare, and, in general, to afford the necessities of life for their families. If the income tax rate goes up, few will stop working or trim their effort, unless they are independently wealthy. An exceptionally small minority of the fabulously rich may need a tax incentive to work diligently, but not a common person belonging to the poor and the middle class.

Even those with above-average incomes generally feel the need for hard work to maintain their lifestyle. Furthermore, if you lower the top income tax rate, then you have to rely on "regressive taxation," which raises taxes on the poor and the middle class, because the government cannot run free on air. The Boskin–Feldstein theory is thus one sided, ignores the State need for revenue, resorts to exceptions and is yet offered as a thesis applying to everyone.

A common sense proposition finds ready support from observed facts, but dogmas need the crutch of sophistry, statistical techniques and econometrics. Not surprisingly, the low-income-tax-and-high-growth hypothesis first relies on complex mathematical and econometric models, and then uses selective data. Econometrics is a wonderful invention to settle disputed theses. It has done a great job in investigating the theories of consumption, investment and production. But like any useful device, it is also subject to abuse. Mark Twain, the celebrated writer and a *New York Times* columnist, once wrote, "There are lies, damned lies and statistics." Today, he might say, "There are lies, damned lies and econometrics."

Mark Twain, of course, had mastered the art of exaggeration; yet there was a glimmer of truth in his parody of statistics. Today, when common sense and observed facts disprove a sacred economic idea, some scholarly experts resort to complicated models of econometrics to demonstrate that the observer may be blind. Let us take another look at the aforementioned gospel that only low income tax rates, but not other taxes, stimulate investment, the work effort and hence economic growth. Although the doctrine sounds self-serving and seems designed to further the interest of those paying high income taxes, it is the cornerstone of economic policy today. While it is most popular in the United States, it also goes unchallenged in many other nations such as Canada, Australia, Singapore, Japan and Europe among others.

3. High Growth with High Income Taxes

Yet history thoroughly contradicts the low income tax theology. All you need to explore its validity is one readily available fact: U.S. history reveals that *during the 1950s and the 1960s, economic growth was much stronger than in the 1970s, 1980s, 1990s and 2000s, even though the marginal income tax rate on top earning families, at less than 39 percent today, was as high as 91 percent in the past.* Anyone earning above $200,000, equivalent to more than a million today, had to pay this rate. In other words, when a millionaire paid as much as 91 cents out of their earnings above a million, then economic growth was much stronger than that observed since 1970.

There were some tax loopholes, and most people escaped the bite of the top rate. But even the effective tax rate, according to the Internal Revenue Service (IRS) figures, was as high as 75 percent. National output grew by 40 percent in the 1950s, by 44 percent in the 1960s and 33 percent in the 1970s compared to just 30 percent in the 1980s, 30 percent in the 1990s and less than 20 percent in the 2000s. Yet the top marginal income tax rate was 50 percent in the first half of the 1980s and just 28 percent in the second half, 70 percent in the 1970s, 80 percent in the 1960s, and as high as 91 percent in the 1950s. *Observed facts blatantly contradict the view that high income taxes hurt economic growth* and yet politicians today, Republicans and Democrats alike, backed by some economists, ardently preach this dogma.

These facts are undisputed and easily accessible from annual issues of *The Economic Report of the President* itself, and if someone comes up with an econometric model that uses perhaps the same data source and argues that low income taxes stimulate growth, then Mark Twain might call such econometrics "a damned lie." Econometrics, as mentioned earlier, is a great statistical technique that can be used to explore many economic and social hypotheses, but like any great device it can also be misused, and then it may breed unethical and self-serving policies and eventually poverty. Therefore, we should be careful about its use.

Even some econometricians, such as Thomas Cooley and Stephen LeRoy, realize that their discipline is subject to abuse. They lament that some macroeconomists behave like attorneys who vehemently argue their case in a court without full regard for the truth. In an article in *The American*

Economic Review, they write, "Particularly in macroeconomics ... The researcher has the motive and opportunity to represent his results selectively."[2]

4. Usefulness of Econometrics

Econometrics becomes useful when differences under observation are rather subtle. If the growth rates in the 1980s and the 1990s had risen just as the top income tax rates fell, then the statistical methods could decide whether or not "regressive taxation," which is a heavy burden on the poor and the middle class, enhances growth. But when a "91 percent tax rate" produces a much larger rise in the living standard, the answer should be crystal clear. *According to modern macroeconomics, the 1950s and the 1960s should have been decades of zero growth and poverty, because high income tax rates move the rich to withhold their labor and investments, generating widespread job losses and wage cuts. But nothing like this happened, as real wages then soared.*

While high taxes need not restrain growth, fairness demands that they should not be "confiscatory." However, that is a separate issue altogether. The point is that common sense backed by straightforward facts of history is a better guide than theory and possibly econometrics, especially if our goal is to raise the general standard of living. Then what about the Boskin–Feldstein idea, which is supposedly derived from credible empirical evidence? I am not sure what to make of such econometrics, when a confiscatory 91 percent tax rate of the 1950s coexists with much higher growth than a 28 percent rate during the 1980s.

This is just one example of a dogma masquerading as economics, and there are many others. This book explores such ideas whenever they underlie government policy. I believe that a basic textbook should only examine matters dealing with first principles and the essentials. It should not go into excessive details that end up confusing the student. There is no reason, for instance, to study all the major macroeconomic theories. The text should be limited only to those ideas that conform to logic, history and reality, and outdated but once popular views should be accorded minor treatment.

---

[2] Thomas Cooley and Stephen LeRoy, *The American Economic Review*, December 1981, p. 826.

A principles text that looks like a dictionary is very discouraging to students as well as instructors, who feel embarrassed if they do not come close to exploring all the chapters in one semester.

5. Dogmas are Dangerous

Why should we make a distinction between common sense and dogmas? History reveals time and again that dogmas can devastate an economy. Today, we believe that the Great Depression, which plagued much of the world for 10 long years in the 1930s, was mostly caused by faulty government policies. Taxes were raised in the middle of sinking demand for goods and services, turning an economic downturn into a depression. Similarly, the government failed to rescue depositors, while bank after bank failed, wiping out billions of dollars in people's retirement money and savings. These are some of the commonly cited reasons that are said to have transformed an ordinary recession of 1929 into the disaster of the 1930s.

But we forget that what encouraged these policies were the dogmas of contemporary economists. They were the ones who, obsessed with *laissez faire*, were ambivalent about government intervention in the banking system; they were the ones who feverishly recommended tax increases to balance the federal budget. It was the economic dogma of the day that catapulted a possibly routine recession into a catastrophic depression, causing mass unemployment and poverty.

During the 1970s the world suffered from what may be called the Great Inflation. Here again economic policy, supported by another dogma, turned a mild jump in prices into a persistent and enduring escalation. Obsessed with the so-called "Phillips curve," experts at the time recommended that money supply should be raised sharply to fight the recessions that had been triggered by huge increases in the price of oil. In hindsight, the Phillips curve viewpoint was a dogma pure and simple, with no common sense legs to support it. Not surprisingly, it has been long discarded, but for a while it spread misery in the world, with inflation and unemployment soaring simultaneously.

Many people describe the years 2000–2010 as "the lost decade," when the stock market crashed twice, employment and family income plunged, and the housing market collapsed. Clearly, popular economic theories hurt the people and continued to hurt them at that time.

You can now see why there is a need to distinguish between sensible hypotheses and irrational, sometimes self-serving, beliefs underlying the dogmas. We need to separate the wheat from the chaff, to identify what is useful and what is dangerous in macroeconomics. *The best microfoundation is our own common sense.*

6. Candidness

The text should be candid and truthful with students. Some economics writings are not. For example, it has been recently discovered that the real wages of a good number of Americans have been falling since 1972; yet few macro texts recognize the problem or deal satisfactorily with it. The wage meltdown is precisely why millions of families are in heavy debt today. Most texts either ignore this question or blame it on new technology without explaining why technology, constantly improving in the U.S. economy, did not hurt the living standard of Americans for nearly 200 years until the early 1970s.

During the 1950s and the 1960s trade theorists argued that when a country such as the United States imports labor-intensive products, it suffers a real wage loss from the growth in foreign trade. As this forecast came true during the 1970s and thereafter when foreign commerce grew manifold, the writers, instead of celebrating the accuracy of their forecasts, disowned their own theories, and blamed new technology for the real wage debacle. This is improper and brings discredit to economics.

Why cannot we just be candid enough to admit that globalization may be profitable for some countries and sections of society, but not for all? Let us be truthful in this regard and call a spade a spade. The approach adopted here is that *globalization, like most other things in the world, is a mixed blessing. It has costs as well as benefits.* It may raise the output and economic growth of an entire nation but still hurt a sizable section of the population, leading to high income and wealth inequalities.

7. Inequality and Wealth Concentration

Ever since the 1970s, income inequality and the concentration of wealth have been rising in the U.S. economy as well as in many other countries.

This trend accelerated in the 2000s and is bound to have serious economic and social consequences, yet few texts do justice to this subject. Today, more than 40 percent of American wealth is in the hands of just 1 percent of the families. Other nations such as India and China have also seen a sizable jump in inequality. The inequality is so bad that society is now said to be divided between the 1 percenters and the 99 percenters. The present book innovates in this regard by offering a thorough discussion of the economic consequences of mushrooming inequality in the world.

8. The Tax Structure

One of the biggest transformations of the American economy since 1950 has been in the area of taxation, which has become increasingly regressive. Taxes were extremely progressive from about 1935–1970, so that a large share of the tax revenue was paid by wealthy individuals and corporations. Since 1981 the tax system has become exceedingly regressive, not just in the United States but virtually all over the world, as the individual and corporate income tax rates have sunk, whereas the Social Security and sales taxes, which disproportionately burden the poor and the middle class, have soared. This trend is bound to have momentous consequences for the economy, but most textbooks ignore its effects. The present book innovates in this matter as well.

9. Regressive Interest Rates

In many nations today not only the tax structure but also the system of interest rates has become regressive. The poor and the middle class have to pay much larger interest rates on their loans than the rich. Actually, the rich as a class are lenders, not borrowers, but when the affluent do borrow money, the interest rates that they pay are much lower. For details on this anomaly, see the chapter on global poverty.

10. Too Many Models

Economists are notorious for inventing a new model for every new question. While this is an exaggeration, it also rings true. For instance, most texts use one model to explain the Great Depression, another to analyze long-run economic growth, still another to examine the great inflation of the 1970s and so on.

As another example, the central concept of macroeconomics is gross domestic product (GDP), which in turn is linked to social welfare, wages, employment, prices, interest rates and a variety of other financial concerns. But when it comes to the question of gains or losses from international trade, the standard texts switch to a different model where GDP is not directly involved. The student wonders why this is done, because the effects of trade, after all, deal with the entire society and are a macro issue.

This book mostly uses one central model to examine major macro questions, and one single model explains much of the macro history of the United States. This, I believe, is sorely needed. One single framework should suffice to analyze diverse periods and episodes in U.S. history.

One model explains why share markets periodically inflate like a vast bubble, why the Great Depression occurred, what caused the great inflation of the 1970s, what accounts for the growth slowdown of the 1980s, 1990s and the 2000s, why the real wage rose all through American history and then began to stagnate after the 1970s, and why growing inequality and wealth concentration are bad for society.

Similarly, what is the role of labor unions and Social Security taxes in the size of economic growth, what is globalization doing to the macroeconomy, what is the effect of transferring the tax burden from the affluent to the poor and so on.

It may be noted that even though this book mostly illustrates macroeconomic theories in terms of U.S. history, the policy implications of such theories apply to the whole world. This is because macroeconomic policy is virtually the same everywhere.

11. Unnecessary Complications

This text tries to simplify arguments and avoid unneeded complications, of which one example in terms of the concepts of supply and demand was presented earlier. As much as possible, the ideas offered here pertain to logic, common sense and the entire spectrum of U.S. history. No distinction is made between demand and quantity demanded.

In fact, Alfred Marshall, the British economist, who was among the first to originate the modern concept of demand, himself did no such thing. In his *Principles of Economics*, for instance, he wrote, "the amount demanded increases with a fall in price and diminishes with a rise in price. There will not be any uniform relation between the fall in price and the increase of demand."[3]

Thus, in describing the law of demand, Marshall used the words "amount demanded" and "demand" simultaneously. They meant the same thing to him.

We will also follow Marshall's tradition, and make no distinction between a change in quantity demanded and a change in demand. This way we avoid unnecessary complications throughout the text without altering the substance of the argument.

12. Ideological Neutrality

Some macro texts are biased in terms of a leftist or a rightist ideology. During the 1950s to the 1970s, the texts displayed what may be called the Keynesian slant or a leftist bias, although some of their prescriptions were irrational even to a layman. Today, and since the 1990s, the texts are biased toward classical macroeconomics and an ultra-rightist ideology, although government policy continues to be mostly Keynesian. This book tries to avoid any slant. It offers an evenhanded treatment of both theories, because it turns out that both may have logical flaws that dilute their effectiveness, and, in the long run, make them dangerous to society's well-being.

The classicists would have governments do nothing in a crisis, whereas the Keynesians inspire people, governments and corporations to frolic in debt.

Mountains of debt floating around the world today impede a lasting cure. Our finding is that "efficiency and ethics go together," so that the best economic policy is ethical, and does not put an undue tax burden on

---

[3] Alfred Marshall, *Principles of Economics*, 9th edition, London: Macmillan, 1961, p. 99.

the poor and the middle class. It fosters competition and generates free markets by preventing mergers among mega firms. It is the absence of such competition that caused the Great Depression and a bubble economy in the 1990s. Thus, economic policy aimed at creating a prosperous and debt-free citizenry is not only ethical but is also the most effective policy, promoting the welfare of all.

We adopt only one criterion for the validity of a theory: Is the theory supported by easily observed facts without resort to the complications of mathematics, statistical techniques and econometric models? If it is, then that theory is valid; if not, the theory is perhaps invalid and will not cure economic ills.

Chapter 2

The General Standard of Living

Macroeconomics is a study of the economic behavior of society rather than individuals, whose actions comprise what is known as microeconomics. Yet, the distinction between micro and macro should not be overblown, because the behavior of the economy in the aggregate has to be consistent with the behavior of its constituents.

The paramount macro question is the living standard of all, or at least the vast majority of people, whereas the paramount micro question is a person's own lifestyle. Yet, the two are interrelated. A nation's prosperity depends on how its components perform, whereas individual prosperity depends on the health of the economy at large. That is why macro and microeconomics should be studied together, as is done in the pages to come. Otherwise, we are bound to run into faulty logic and policies.

1. The Standard of Living

The most well-known measure for the standard of living in a country is the purchasing power of its gross domestic product (GDP), a concept that you first encountered in the previous chapter. The GDP is a monetary yardstick of a country's total output during a year. The United States, for instance, produced about $20 trillion worth of goods and services in 2019, so its GDP was that figure in dollars. Japan's GDP was some 50 trillion yen, whereas China's GDP was 100 trillion yuan. Each nation's GDP is measured in terms of its own currency. However, everyone is concerned with the purchasing power of their income. Therefore, a nation's living standard or output at a point in time is indicated by the purchasing power of its GDP, which is called real GDP. The name is appropriate, because everyone wants to know what their money is really going to buy.

Over time, population normally goes up, so that a better measure of the living standard is real GDP per person, which is also known as real per-capita GDP. Thus, real GDP and real per-capita GDP are the two most popular measures of a society's living standard — its prosperity as well as its poverty.

However, popular indexes can be deceptive if the distribution of GDP among individuals becomes more and more unequal over time. For the time being, let us assume that all output is distributed as income among individuals, and prices are constant so that the purchasing power of the dollar remains unchanged. These are just simplifying assumptions and not crucial to the ideas presented in the subsequent paragraphs.

As a simple example, suppose there are 10 individuals in a nation, and its GDP is $100. One person is very rich and earns $30 or 30 percent of GDP, six are in the middle class and together earn $60, and the other three live below the poverty line, taking home the remaining $10.

Suppose next year, the rich man earns $40, the six in the middle group make $60 and the poor earn only $6. The sum of their incomes or GDP has now climbed to $106 or grown by 6 percent, which is normally regarded as healthy growth.

Has the general living standard improved? No, it has actually declined, even though GDP has jumped. The rich man has indeed grown richer, but the middle-income group sees no change in lifestyle, whereas the poverty-stricken group has suffered an earnings drop of $4. One person, whose needs were already completely satisfied by his fabulous income, certainly enjoys an improvement, but three persons, barely making ends meet, experience a further erosion in their living. One has gained, but three have lost. Thus, the rise in GDP and per-capita GDP can be misleading measures of society's standard of living.

This example is not fictional, either. Believe it or not, something like this has been happening in America and many other nations ever since the

1980s, and possibly the 1970s. You will find this in straightforward figures in the annual economic report issued by the U.S. presidents and national accounts of other countries.

As another example, suppose Bill Gates, who according to Forbes had a net worth over $100 billion in 2019, walks into a destitute club that has 99 members. Including the guest, there are now 100 people present in the room. What is the average wealth of all these people? On average, everyone gathered there is a billionaire. Yet in reality, 99 are jobless and paupers. See how deceptive averages can be.

2. The Average Real Wage

For most people, consumption, housing and savings are directly related to their wages or earnings. However, a small minority earn the bulk of income from their assets that include savings, bonds (or loans), real estate and company shares. This way, they earn interest, rent, dividends and capital gains arising from the sale of assets at a profit. GDP includes all forms of incomes, but for the vast majority of people, wages are the principal source of living.

Wages may differ sharply among people, but they can be represented by an average. Adding up the salaries of all workers and dividing the sum by the number of employees yields the average wage. The purchasing power of this average may be called "the average real wage," which then is a superior index of individual as well as social well-being. This is a better measure than per-capita real GDP, because it portrays the lifestyle of the vast majority of people, virtually everyone in the society.

However, even the average wage is a highly aggregated concept and may not capture the reality about general living conditions. The few, who are well endowed with property or assets, generally control big companies and are in a position to command high salaries. Their sky-high wages may distort the economy-wide average enough to create a deceptive picture of society's standard of living. This is why we need to explore the average wage of the "asset-poor people," i.e., those who have few or no financial assets to assist them in getting good jobs.

3. The Production Wage

The U.S. Department of Labor has devised a category of what it calls a production worker, who, in any occupation, operates under the supervision of someone else. This is why such an employee is also known as a non-supervisory worker. The production or non-supervisory workers generally fit the portrait of the asset poor. Their compensation depends purely on merit, hard work and the state of the economy, rather than connections, luck and inheritance. The average real wage of production workers, to be called the "production wage," then offers by far the best measure of the general living standard not only because their salaries are independent of their meager assets but also because they constitute at least 75 percent of the labor force. According to some, "they are as much as 80 percent of the workforce." They and their families are the vast majority, practically the entire society.

Almost everyone is a non-supervisory worker. The supervisors are generally those in management or those who are self-employed. Thus, clerks, foremen, farm laborers, bus boys, truckers, secretaries, teachers, pilots, nurses, engineers and accountants are production workers. By contrast, anyone who has some say in setting their schedule and the work environment is a supervisory worker. This category generally includes doctors, managers, educational administrators, team leaders and the like. Towering atop the pyramid of all workers is a company's CEO, or the chief executive officer, who, of late, has been able to set his own salary that, at its extreme, may be thousands of times the production wage or even the economy-wide average wage. The CEO of Citigroup earned close to $290 million in 2000; that of Oracle earned over $700 million in 2002 alone.

According to *USA TODAY*, in 2019 a company called 24/7 Wall Street estimated CEO wages of the largest publicly traded American companies. Their salaries ranged from $8 million to $108 million, which do not include CEO perks and stock options (April 30, 2019). The newspaper reports that "there are even some major companies where the CEO makes over 1000 times what their employees make."

If wages and incomes related to assets rise, the GDP rises as well. However, if asset incomes soar, it is possible for GDP to climb even as the production wage sinks. Here then the living standard actually drops, because losers then vastly outnumber the gainers. For much of U.S. history, real per-capita GDP, the average real wage and the production worker's real wage conveyed the same message. They all went up every decade. Unfortunately, since 1972, the three have followed divergent paths. Per-capita GDP has continued its upward trend, but the average real wage has stagnated, while the production wage has sunk. *Thus, the vast majority of Americans, over three-fourths of the labor force, has seen a drop in their living standard ever since 1972.*

This is a startling and unnerving statement. Yet it is true, as shown by Figure 2.1, whose data source is none other than *The Economic Report of the President*, prepared annually by the government. Figure 2.1 displays the weekly real wage of production workers from 1950 to 1980 for every fifth year, except 1972, which turns out to be the peak year of the production wage.

The real wage is an inflation-adjusted quantity, which is an estimate of the purchasing power of your salary in terms of prices of some previous year, called the "base year." In the figure, the base year is 1982. If prices

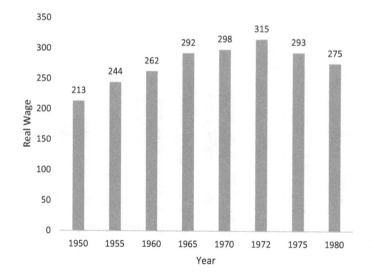

Figure 2.1:   Real Production Wage in the United States, 1950–1980: 1982 = 100

Source: The Economic Report of the President, various issues.

rise, as they now do year after year, your money buys less than before, so a higher salary may not amount to much if your raise lags behind the pace of inflation. Your salary has to be adjusted for inflation in order to obtain a true gauge of your living standard.

This is done by estimating the equivalent of what your salary buys today compared to its purchasing power in the base year. Figure 2.1 shows that real production wage went up from 1950 to 1972, almost in a straight line, reached a peak in 1972, and then started a slow but steady decline.

Let us examine the more recent data available from the 2019 *Economic Report of the President*. You may notice that here the 1972 value is $342, whereas in Figure 2.1 it is $315. This discrepancy, though hard to understand, is easy to explain. The data come from two different sources, and for our purposes, it is the trend that matters most. In both figures, 1972 represents the peak of the real production wage.

In Figure 2.2, the real production wage equals its peak value of $342, and then displays its slow decline until it hits a bottom at $268 in1995. Then it starts its upward crawl, but even in 2019, it was at $313, way below the 1972 value.

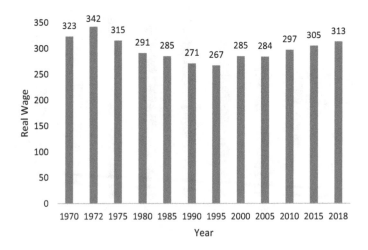

Figure 2.2:   Real Production Wage in the United States, 1970–2019: 1982–1984 = 100

Source: *The Economic Report of the President*, 2015 and 2019.

The real-wage drop is actually far worse than that depicted by the figure, because it does not include what are called "fringe benefits," such as health insurance and pensions. These benefits were steadily rising until 1972, but then started to decline, so much so that by 2019 pension and health benefits for production workers were the lowest in three decades.

The benefits rose steadily, even after 1972, but only for supervisory workers. Therefore, the real wage for all workers, supervisory as well as non-supervisory, does not reveal a drastic drop after 1972, because it also includes fringe benefits that have been growing fast for the affluent.

This is shown in Figure 2.3, where the economy-wide real wage rose sharply from 1960 to 1970, but grew slowly thereafter even when fringes are taken into account. In the first 10 years, the average real wage soared 30 percent, or at the respectable rate of 3 percent per year. However, over the next 20 years, its annual rise slowed to about 1 percent. Compare this with the behavior of real per-capita GDP, which, according to the World Bank figures, climbed at almost the same rate as the real wage between 1960 and 1970. Between 1970 and 1990, however, the real wage stagnated, rising at 1 percent a year, whereas per-capita GDP climbed almost twice as fast as the real wage. In the new millennium between 2000 and

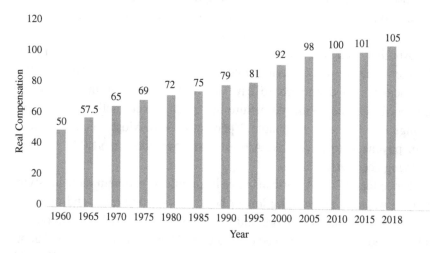

Figure 2.3: Real Compensation per Hour in Business Sector, 1960–2019

Source: The Economic Report of the President, 2019.

2015, the real wage growth crawled up by 10 percent compared to the per-capita GDP growth of 30 percent.

All this suggests that real GDP, and possibly the average real wage, are misleading measures of the living standard, because the real wage of production workers, who are at least 75 percent of the workforce, suffered a sharp drop after 1972. Real per-capita GDP in 2019 was almost twice its 1972 level, but the production wage, applying to over three-fourths of employees, was down by 9 percent. By 2019, production workers had seen some improvement in their wages, but it was illusory, because their taxes had sharply increased over time. The sales tax, the self-employment tax and the Social Security tax had all soared. For instance, the sales tax in most states was around 3.5 percent in the early 1970s, but it soared to about 8 percent by 2019.

4. Social Trends

The sinking living standard in America is confirmed by a variety of social trends, especially those reflected in bankruptcies and mushrooming debtors, the fastest growing group in the United States. It is now acceptable to be in hock, to consume more than you make, simply because the expenses of two-earner families outweigh the combined income of each partner. What a sole provider could do for the family in the 1950s and the 1960s cannot be done even by two earners today.

Another indicator of the shrinking living standard is the drastic decline in the household savings rate. During the 1950s, 1960s and 1970s, Americans earned enough to save about 8 percent of their after-tax income. But since 1980, the picture has changed substantially. The U.S. savings rate is now a laughable 3 percent or less. Most households live from paycheck to paycheck. Almost half have about a $1,000 in their checking accounts.

Since the 1970s, Americans have been able to maintain their lifestyle in three ways — by working longer hours, by sending more and more of their family members to work and by borrowing. In 2019, 65 percent of able-bodied Americans worked compared to 60 percent in 1972; total debt in the economy, excluding the government debt incurred during WWII, was more than twice the level of GDP in 2019 compared to that in 1972;

average working hours had jumped by 20 percent. *With real per-capita GDP soaring over the years, why should debt rise at all?* Instead, all major sections of the society, the government, the households and the corporations are now indebted as never before.

5. Mushrooming Inequality

Where did all the growth go? Much of it to CEOs. The CEOs have done exceptionally well, in times good or bad. If America goes into a recession, their incomes grow; when America booms, their wages grow even faster. The end result is what you see in the bar chart of Figure 2.4, which displays CEO compensation as a multiple of the production wage.

American CEOs, with all their perks, have always been the envy of the world. As early as 1965, they were paid 20 times the average production wage, and their pay went up as the economy boomed during the 1960s. Then came the inflation and stagnation of the 1970s when the economy repeatedly suffered recessions, but the CEO compensation

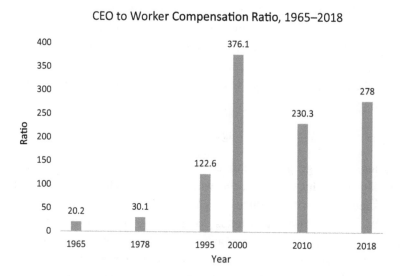

Figure 2.4:   CEO Wage as a Multiple of the Production Wage: 1965–2018

Source: Michel and Wolf, *EPI.org*, 2019.

inched up. After 1978, CEOs simply ran amuck as their pay began to soar and reached a peak by 2000. Even as late as 2016, their wages were more than 250 times the production wage.

The CEO Pay is now much larger than in 1960, at over 250 times the production wage.

6. The Real Wage and Labor Productivity

What is really puzzling to many is that the average wage has stagnated since 1972 in spite of rising productivity. National output per hour of work effort or per worker is known as the productivity of labor. Because of new investment and technology, productivity has increased every decade since the birth of the American republic in 1789, although its pace of increase has seen ups and downs. *The amount by which productivity rises from one year to the next is called the rate of productivity growth.* The rate has varied over time, but its direction has been generally positive.

Fairness and common sense demand that wages keep pace with productivity. Everyone expects to be compensated for their hard work and merit, and this rule held up well during the 1950s and the 1960s, when productivity growth was strong, as were labor's wage gains. In the 1970s and the 1980s, productivity growth fell but was still positive, while the average real wage barely budged. Merit was no longer rewarded, so a growing wage gap emerged. Let "A" be the average output of labor, and "w" be the average real wage. Then the concept of the "wage gap" may be defined by

$$\text{wage gap} = \frac{A}{w}$$

Thus, the wage gap is defined by productivity divided by the real wage. In a healthy economy, the wage gap is constant, so that the real wage keeps pace with productivity gains. When the real wage trails productivity, the gap rises, and tends to generate all sorts of unexpected events in society. For instance, as we will see in subsequent chapters, the stock market then goes into a frenzy, debt jumps, investment overflows and heavy trade deficits or surpluses follow. Eventually share prices crash, and a recession inevitably ensues.

The concept of the wage gap is a centerpiece of this book. It explains almost all the unexpected economic events of the 1980s, 1990s and the 2000s. It also applies to the roaring 1920s and the subsequent depression. The one central model developed here is built around the concept of the wage gap, which normally remains constant. But whenever it rises persistently, the macro economy turns topsy-turvy. Business activity zooms at first, inflates into a bubble, but then trouble follows.

Table 2.1 displays the behavior of the wage gap between 1970 and 2018 and during the 1920s. If we divide the index of output per hour in the business sector by the index of real employee compensation, both available from *The Economic Report of the President*, we obtain a measure of the wage gap in the United States. If real earnings rise in sync with productivity, which is the same thing as hourly output, then the figures in column 2 should be more or less constant. In 1970, the wage-gap index

Table 2.1: The Wage Gap in the United States for Selected Years: 1970–2018, and 1919–1929 (in percent)

Year	Prod/Wage*	Year**	Prod/Wage
1970	65	1919	111
1975	69	1921	128
1980	70	1923	130
1985	75	1925	148
1990	77	1927	154
1995	81	1929	156
2000	82	—	—
2010	99	—	—
2018	101	—	—

Notes: *Column 2 furnishes the wage-gap index, which is obtained by dividing two other indexes, one dealing with output per hour or labor productivity in the business sector, and the other with real employee compensation or national real wage.

**The wage-gap indexes in columns 2 and 4 are not comparable because of differences in the definition of wages.

Source: *The Economic Report of the President*, 2019, B-32; *Historical Statistics of the United States*, 1975.

stood at 65, and rose steadily thereafter, at first slowly, and then in a torrent to reach an all-time postwar high of 101 in 2018. *Clearly wages trailed productivity over time; in four decades the wage-gap index soared by almost 55 percent.*

However, from 1975 to 1980, the wage-gap index was more or less constant. *It is only after 1980, when tax policy changed drastically, that the index began a steady rise and has yet to reach a peak.* This is a remarkable feature of the post-1980 economy, and its importance will be clear in later chapters.

What is of interest here is that a similar wage gap had also arisen during the 1920s, when the stock market, as in the 1980s and the 1990s, went into a frenzy as well. This is just a surface demonstration of why bubble economies are born with a persistent rise in the wage gap. More about this will be said later, after we have developed our central model.

6.1. *Real Wage and Productivity: 1874–1972*

The rising gap between real wages and productivity is not normal for the U.S. economy. A century of data from 1874 to 1972 reveal that real wages in the United States went up every decade with growing productivity, and the wage gap index moved little except during recessions or depressions. Figure 2.5 displays the generally positive link between real wages and productivity between 1874 and 1950. Reliable productivity figures go as far back as 1874, and earnings figures are available from 1860 onward. However, for both entries our graph begins with 1874 to see if any association exists between them.

The lower part of the graph displays the index of the overall productivity with a base year of 1958, whereas the upper part depicts the index of real annual earnings of non-farm employees with the base year of 1914. These lines are almost parallel, indicating a one-to-one connection between real earnings and productivity. The productivity index rose from 16 in 1874 to 27 in 1900, and to 80 in 1950, whereas annual earnings jumped from $403 to $573 and then to $1,358. Thus, productivity and non-farm wages kept pace with each other between 1874 and 1950.

For comparisons over time, it matters little what base year or measure of productivity we use — output per hour, non-farm output per hour, or

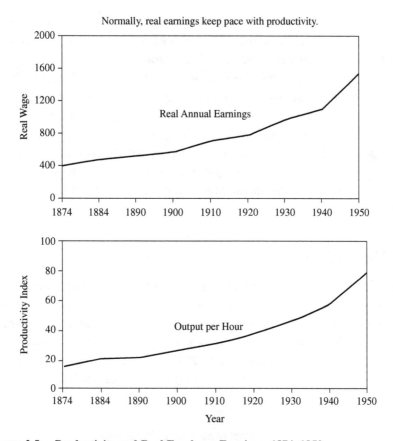

Figure 2.5: Productivity and Real Employee Earnings, 1874–1950

Source: Historical Statistics of the United States, Series D683, D726, and D736.

manufacturing output per hour. They all reveal the same trend. Similarly, it does not matter what measure of real wages we use; real wages of all workers, those of production workers, or those of non-farm workers, they all display hefty gains over time. *Real wages jumped even during the Great Depression*, as you will see in Chapter 10.

We have already seen that both the real wage and productivity growth were strong at all levels of work between 1950 and 1972. Therefore, we conclude that for almost 100 years, as far back as the data remain reliable, real wages generally moved in sync with hourly output. In fact, anecdotal evidence shows that real wages rose with productivity even prior to 1874.

It is only after 1972 that the positive historical link between the two was severed. Thus, something must have happened around that pivotal year that had never occurred in the American chronicle before.

What was that diabolical policy or event that completely transformed the U.S. economy, so much so that real wages in many occupations began to fall in spite of rising productivity? What happened that slowly but surely afflicted a vast multitude? Nothing like this has occurred in any other advanced economy, not even in Japan, which has been stagnating since 1990. We can only raise questions at this point, but will have to wait for answers until the development of our central model in Chapters 9 and 10.

7. Unemployment

Another indicator of a nation's living standard is the level of employment or its opposite, unemployment. For the time being, let us define the unemployment rate as the number of job seekers without a job as a percentage of the labor force. Take a look at Figure 2.6, which displays the rate of unemployment from 1930 to 2018 in selected years. It is evident that the jobless rate used to be much higher prior to 1945. It was at the

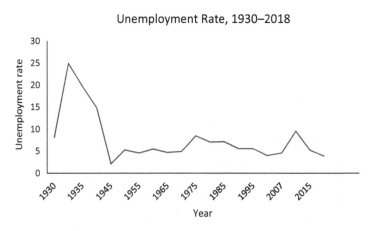

Figure 2.6:   The Unemployment Rate, 1930–2018

Source: Historical Statistics of the United States and *The Economic Report of the President,* 2019.

lowest level at the end of WWII and reached its zenith in 1933 at close to 25 percent. That was the worst year of the Great Depression and the whole world, including Europe, Asia and South America, was in agony at the time.

Even in the 1890s (not shown), unemployment reached intolerable levels of over 15 percent, a rate that has not been repeated in any recession since WWII. Here we discover a pleasant feature of our economy, namely that unemployment rates are way down below their pre-war levels. But this may also explain why the slowly sinking living standard since 1972 has not produced a social revolt in America. People have coped with this unprecedented phenomenon mainly through increased family participation in the workforce and through heavier borrowing. Still, our macro model should be able to explain the post-war stability in national employment and hence the real GDP.

8. Prices, Inflation and Deflation

Prices are also crucial to a country's living standard, because they enter into any formula determining the purchasing power of a person's salary. If your income rises by 10 percent, but prices go up by 15 percent, are you any richer? Of course not. You are poorer by 5 percent, because your higher salary buys that much less than before.

Here again, the pre-war and post-war trends are remarkably different, as in Figure 2.7, which examines the price behavior from 1820 to 2018 for every 10th year. The consumer price index (CPI) depicts the average price of goods and services generally entering into people's basket of consumption. This includes food products, clothing, shelter, medical care, transportation, education and so on.

A remarkable feature of this graph is that the CPI was exactly the same at 42 in 1820 as well as in 1940. In those olden days, prices would move up and down. When prices rise, inflation occurs; when they fall, deflation prevails. Thus, the price behavior before the end of WWII reflected both inflation and deflation, which was at its peak in the 1930s during the Great Depression. In fact, every burst of price increase in the past was followed by an almost equal burst of price decrease. But since 1940, the CPI has moved only in one direction, i.e., upward. Now there is

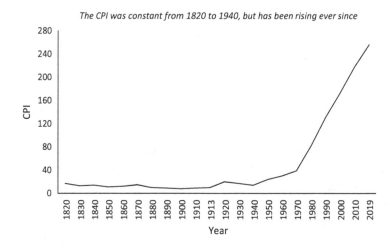

The CPI was constant from 1820 to 1940, but has been rising ever since

Figure 2.7:   The Consumer Price Index, 1820–2019

Source: The Economic Report of the President, various issues and *Historical Statistics*.

only inflation in the economy; deflation seems to have vanished forever. This is another macro puzzle that we need to solve.

9. The System of Taxation

Another crucial determinant of the general living standard is the country's tax system — its size and its structure. There is a well-known saying that death and taxes are here forever. People hate taxes, so much so that they equate them to loss of life. Yet, we all know that taxes are essential for a civilized life. They support the government, which is indispensable to law and order and hence to an organized and prosperous economy. As with almost everything else, the tax system today is drastically different from what prevailed in the United States until 1913, and as late as 1935.

Until 1913, the United States was in the midst of what may be called the era of small government. Government spending at federal, state and local levels was miniscule, and revenue needs were meager. The main source of revenue were taxes on imports that came mostly from Europe. Such taxes are called tariffs or customs duties. If you take a trip to a foreign land, then upon your return you have to fill a customs form detailing your purchases abroad, and if they exceed $800 you are supposed to pay levies approximating 10 percent of the value. These are the tariffs. They date back to the birth of the nation.

During the 19th century, as much as 80 percent of federal tax revenue came from tariffs. Unlike today there was no income tax, no Social Security tax and no Medicare tax. There were indeed sales or excise taxes, but they tended to be very small. The United States was essentially a "tax haven," offering nirvana to tax avoiders. But then the government also provided few services, which were mainly police protection and national defense. Absent were state pensions, Medicaid and Medicare, unemployment compensation, food stamps and a host of other state-provided amenities to which Americans have become accustomed in the post-war period.

9.1. *Free Trade and the Income Tax*

America's tax-haven status lasted till 1913, when the 16th amendment was added to the constitution to pave the way for an income tax on individuals and corporations. The tax had become necessary because the government, especially President Woodrow Wilson, wanted to introduce free trade and trim tariffs. Thus tariff cuts, and the income tax to make up for lost revenue, were enacted at the same time. *So it was that under the prodding of free traders a monumental shift occurred in the tax structure, beginning with 1913.* The U.S. revenue system would never again be the same.

Wilson had promised to keep income tax rates low, and, like most politicians, he indeed kept his promise — in the first year. The initial rate ranged from 1 percent to 6 percent in 1914. But as tariffs were cut in half from 40 percent to 20 percent, revenues plummeted, while government spending needs soared because of the onset of WWI. Therefore, the top-bracket income tax rates paid by the wealthy rocketed all the way to 70 percent by 1918. Thus, was born the adage: never trust a politician with your money.

Republicans, who at the time were protectionists and anti-free trade, won the presidency during the 1920s; income taxes fell, but tariffs soared. When Franklin D. Roosevelt (FDR) took over in 1932, the tax policy was

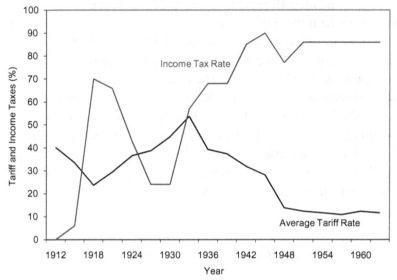

Whenever the tariff rate fell, the income tax rate went up from 1913 to 1963. Thus the income tax is the lasting gift of free traders to Americans.

Figure 2.8:   Average Tariffs and the Top-Bracket Income Tax Rate
Source: Historical Statistics of the United States.

reversed: this time income taxes soared, but tariffs fell. As Figure 2.8 shows, the tug of war between tariffs and income taxes continued until the rise of FDR, that is, whenever tariffs fell, income taxes soared, and *vice versa*. But after 1932, free or freer trade came into being, so tariffs declined virtually in a straight line, while income taxes on the wealthiest people climbed all the way to 90 percent, to levels unheard of even under Wilson.

1913 was thus a monumental year that marked the beginning of the nation's switch away from tariffs and toward income taxes, which were first enacted at the federal level. Later, from the 1960s on, income taxes were also introduced at state and city levels.

Another landmark year was 1935, when the Social Security tax was enacted. As usual, it started out small, but gradually grew tall, taller and the tallest until it really began to bite the poor and the middle class. Initially, it was set at 2 percent, on the first $3,000 of wages, to be shared equally by the employer and the employee. It increased to 4 percent in the 1950s, to 9.6 percent in the 1970s, and finally peaked at 13 percent in the 1990s. The taxable wage base also soared — to over $125,000 by 2019.

The U.S. tax system thus has had a volatile career. It started out as a "regressive system," where the burden falls mostly on the poor, in the sense that they pay a larger percentage of their income in taxes than the affluent. When tariffs prevailed, the poor felt its maximum weight, because the levies raised consumer prices equally for everyone. As a result, taxes as a percentage of income were much larger for the poor simply because their incomes were much smaller.

When income taxes began replacing the tariff, the revenue system became progressive, especially under those giant rates prevailing from 1932 to 1963. Throughout this period, Social Security levies remained low. Social Security taxes hit the poorest the hardest, because they cannot be avoided and offer no exemptions. Even those earning the minimum wage have to pay them, although the poor can mostly escape the bite of the income tax that exempts those subsisting at the bottom. "1963" is another landmark year, because the income tax rate began to fall thereafter, although the revenue system still remained very progressive. The system became less progressive in the early 1970s, and then actually became regressive from the early 1980s, when income tax rates started a steady fall, but the Social Security tax kept climbing.

By 1990, the top-bracket income tax rate had sunk to 28 percent, but the Social Security rate had jumped to 13 percent. This was an ugly combination.

Never before in the history of the American republic had taxes been transferred from the affluent to the poor. The tax system had become "ultra-regressive." The macroeconomic effects of such a system will be explored later in Chapter 12.

Income tax rates were raised in 1993 and then lowered slightly in 2001, with the top rate at 35 percent. But the wage base for the Social Security tax continues to rise, so the tax structure remains ultra-regressive. In fact, at present people at all income levels also have to pay another levy called the Medicare tax that is 2.3 percent of the wage. Thus, the total, unavoidable tax bite on the wage is now 15.3 percent, half paid by the employer and half by the employee. For the poor and for small businesses, this is a crippling burden.

10. Globalization of the Economy

Current thinking supports the idea that globalization of the economy resulting from the replacement of tariffs by income taxes is the best way to raise society's living standard. As customs levies decline around the world, imports go up in all trading countries, so that exports also rise from each nation. Some economists question the beneficence of free trade, because first, it introduced the income tax, and second, the United States became the world's industrial giant and economic leader at the end of the 19th century, in the midst of a century of exorbitant tariffs.

What is perhaps incontrovertible is that industrialization is the key to prosperity. Nevertheless, international trade has major consequences for an economy, and some countries definitely gain from expanding trade. With the transformation of the tax system after 1913, and especially after WWII, the American economy was not the same as before. Foreign trade gradually came to have an important role in the U.S. living standard.

As you will see in Chapter 14, from 1950 to 1970 total trade as a fraction of the GDP hovered around 10 percent, divided roughly between exports and imports. Then the trade/GDP ratio began to rise as tariffs continued their fall, exceeding 15 percent by 1975, and then all the way to a quarter of the GDP by 2019. Historically, international commerce played a minor role in the evolution of the U.S. economy, because average tariffs on imports were as high as 65 percent. With foreign goods taxed heavily at the port of entry, little came into America from abroad, and little went out in return. Such a system is basically closed to the goods of the world. That is why it may be called a "closed economy." Another word for a closed economy is "autarky," or self-sufficiency.

For much of history, America was a closed economy, with exports and imports each hovering around a lowly 5 percent of GDP. After 1970, however, the nation became an "open economy," as both imports and exports grew swiftly in an atmosphere of sinking tariffs. At first, during the 1970s, rising American purchases from abroad (i.e., imports) matched American sales to the world (i.e., exports), so that trade was roughly in balance. But after 1980, imports began to outgrow exports, and a trade deficit emerged. America then began to borrow money from the rest of world to finance this deficit. As the deficit grew, so did U.S. borrowing. By 2019, the deficit had mushroomed, with the United States earning the dubious distinction of being the largest debtor in the world.

In fact, as the new millennium began, America borrowed close to $400 billion per year to maintain its living standard. Recall that a rising per-capita GDP does not ensure an improving lifestyle for the majority of people, as 80 percent of the U.S. labor force has lost out to the remaining 20 percent since 1972. *America's foreign borrowing, at $1 trillion in the 2000s alone, simply finances the soaring living standard of CEOs and other supervisory workers, while the nation as a whole is stuck with a giant bill.*

The soaring trade deficit has transformed the United States into the biggest debtor the planet has ever seen.

11. Manufacturing, Farming and Services

Another important factor that affects the living standard is the allocation of resources among the major sectors of an economy. At its birth, the United States was predominantly an agricultural nation with about 70 percent of the labor force employed in farming, 20 percent in a variety of services such as retailing and transportation, a meager 5 percent in manufacturing industries and the rest scattered among other activities. The country exported farm products such as cotton, wheat and tobacco, and imported industrial goods such as textiles and machinery. When tariffs rose after 1816, local manufacturers faced little competition from European firms, and domestic manufacturing began to prosper. Labor, lured by higher wages, moved out of agriculture and into industries.

Tariffs also encouraged foreign investment into the rapidly growing industries. Thus, productive resources, capital and labor were allocated in a way that sharply raised manufacturing, which by the end of the 19th century employed a quarter of the workforce. Farming then claimed only 40 percent of labor, with the rest employed mostly in services. After 1900, agriculture expanded because of increased efficiency from improved technology, and labor continued to move out of farming, but this time into services. By 1965, services had a 60 percent share of employment, manufacturing 28 percent and farming only 9 percent.

Then came the aftershocks of falling tariffs. Domestic producers faced ever-increasing competition from low-wage manufactures from Japan, China and the Asian Tigers such as Taiwan, South Korea, Singapore, Malaysia and Hong Kong. So American companies lost their lead in one industry after another. One by one, textiles, electronics, shoes, autos, motorcycles among many others were trimmed or reduced to skeletons. As a result, the real wages of production workers first fell in manufacturing. Another reason for the layoffs in manufacturing was new technology, especially computers, which raised worker productivity so much that fewer workers were needed even to produce rising levels of output. Those who were discarded by manufacturers, either because of increased import competition or because of new technology, mostly moved into services that pay lower wages.

Employment swelled in retailing, restaurants, transportation, hotels and the like. Workers in such industries faced increasing competition from manufacturing layoffs, so that real wages also fell in most services. The end result was a massive jump in service employment coupled with a major fall in production wages in services as well.

It may be noted that in the past, new technology had not been associated with declining real wages in any industry. But following 1972, some economic transformations made it inevitable for the production wages to fall. We will study these new transformations in detail in subsequent chapters.

Now farming employs about 3 percent of the workforce, manufacturing about 9 percent and the services a gargantuan 75 percent, of which about 60 percent have seen a decline in their real earnings. The farm sector has continued to make impressive gains in productivity, so that only 3 percent of American labor today feeds nearly a quarter of the world.

Figure 2.9 displays the shifting pattern of resource allocation in the U.S. economy, starting from 1800, and confirms the trends that have been just described. Macroeconomic effects of the tariff versus income-related levies, such as the income tax and the Social Security tax, have been rarely studied before, even though our living standard was and is tied intimately to them. This is another challenge facing our macro model.

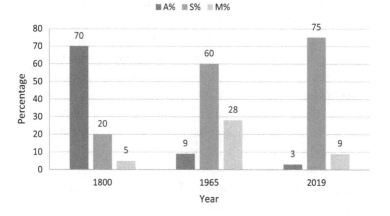

Figure 2.9: **Employment Shares in Agriculture (A), Manufacturing (M) and Services (S)**

Source: Fite and Reese, *An Economic History of the United States,* and *The Economic Report 2003, 2019.*

12. Summary

(1) "Real GDP" and "real per-capita GDP," though most well known, are not the best measures of a country's standard of living. A better measure is the economy-wide real wage, but the best measure is the production wage, which is the average wage of production workers, who operate under the supervision of others.

(2) Production workers constitute as much as 80 percent of the American workforce.

(3) For over 150 years of U.S. history, real per-capita GDP, the economy-wide wage and the production wage went up with growing labor productivity. However, since 1972 the per-capita GDP has continued to rise with rising productivity, but the economy-wide wage has been stagnant, whereas the production wage has slowly declined. Thus, since the 1970s the living standard in the United States has decreased for the vast majority of the population, jumped for supervisory workers, and skyrocketed for the CEOs.

(4) The general standard of living is also determined by the unemployment rate, which has generally declined after WWII.

(5) Prices of goods and services play a crucial role in the living standard. Until 1940 they went up as well as down in the United States, but have been on an upward march ever since.

(6) Another important factor is the structure and size of taxation. Until 1913 the primary source of government revenue were tariffs, which were gradually replaced by the individual income tax to pave the way for free trade. Another levy, the Social Security tax, was introduced in 1935, and by now is the second largest source of revenue.

(7) With the fall in tariffs has come the globalization of the American economy, where the service sector reigns supreme, employing as much as 75 percent of the labor force. Manufacturing, another important sector, grew sharply in the 19th and the early part of the 20th century, but now employs only 9 percent of labor.

(8) Since 1980 the trade deficit has zoomed, turning the United States into the largest debtor in the world.

Chapter 3

GDP Accounting

Macroeconomics is a relatively young discipline. According to some it was invented by a British economist named John Maynard Keynes, who wrote his masterpiece, *The General Theory of Employment, Interest and Money*, in 1936, at a time when the world languished in a catastrophic depression. Until then words like "GDP" (gross domestic product), "national income," etc., were not in general use. Economic data were not readily available, and policymakers were severely handicapped because they had no idea of the gravity of the problem. There was no accounting system that offered definitions and estimates of economic aggregates. It was economist Simon Kuznets who first developed such a system soon after WWII. For this stellar contribution to macroeconomics, he was later awarded the Nobel Prize.

1. GDP

Gross domestic product (GDP) is the retail value of all final goods and services produced in a country during a year. Several questions immediately arise. First of all, what is a retail value? There are two types of market prices, wholesale and retail. The prices that consumers like you and I pay in the purchase of any good are called retail prices, whereas those that a retail store pays to its suppliers for stocking products are known as wholesale prices. GDP thus uses retail, not wholesale, prices in its calculations.

Second, what are final goods and services? Goods that are used up in the production of other goods within a year are called *intermediate goods.* Steel, cotton, aluminum, plastics, etc., are prime examples of such goods, as they are used to make a lot of our everyday items. All goods that are not intermediate products are then final goods, which are of two types — "consumption goods and capital goods." *All goods lasting more than a year but used up in the production of other goods and services over time are called capital goods.*

Machines, roads, bridges, parks, office buildings, etc., are thus capital or "investment goods." All other final goods are consumption goods. From now on, "the term 'goods' will represent both goods and services."

The end use of a product primarily determines its nature. Potatoes purchased as baked potatoes are consumption goods, but, when used in the production of chips, they become an intermediate good. Cotton used at home for nursing wounds is a consumption good, but, when used by a business in producing shirts, it becomes an intermediate good. Similarly, cotton used for treating wounds in a hospital is an intermediate good, because then it produces another service called healthcare, which is a final good.

The amount of gasoline that your car burns to bring you to class is a final good, but when used in a taxi it becomes an intermediate good. Your car is a final consumption good, but for a taxicab company it is a capital good, because it lasts more than a year. If the cars were to break down within a year, then taxis would also be intermediate goods. Thus, the durability and the end use of a product define whether or not it is an intermediate or a capital good, or whether it is a consumption or capital good.

GDP includes only the market value of final goods, because prices cover the cost of intermediate goods as well. If General Motors (GM) sells a car to its dealer for $10,000, the price includes the cost of steel, wood, plastics and other parts in producing the car. GM's revenue then includes the contributions made by the producers of intermediate products, so do the revenues of all firms that produce final goods. If we were to include the output of intermediate goods separately in GDP, there will be double counting of such goods, leading to an overestimate of aggregate output. *Therefore, GDP excludes intermediate goods from its definition.*

GDP includes only new products, because goods produced in previous years were included in GDPs of the past. A house produced on December 31, 2019 but sold a day later on January 1, 2020 is included in the GDP of 2019. GDP is concerned with production, not sales.

Goods remaining unsold at the end of a year are counted as final goods as well, even if by nature they may be intermediate goods. If a steel firm cannot sell all its output within the year then its unsold stock is treated as a final product and included in the firm's investment for the year. In fact, any increase in a firm's inventory at year-end is included in the economy's inventory investment, which may also be negative. In the latter case, goods sold in a year exceed that year's output, so that companies draw down their inventories of previous years.

2. Other Measures of Economic Activity

GDP is the most well-known measure of a country's economic activity, but some people do not like it. Perhaps they find it too gross for their taste. They may indeed be right, because it is certainly not the best measure. For a better yardstick, we must deduct the wear and tear that capital goods undergo every year in the production process. In fact, a large part of the production of capital goods is used just to replace the worn out or obsolete machines and factories. The breakdown and replacement of capital goods is a cost to the economy and must be excluded from the year's level of output. When this is done, we get "net domestic product" (NDP). Thus,

$$NDP = GDP - capital\ consumption$$

Capital consumption is also called depreciation, which normally turns out to be 10 percent of GDP. In other words, for the United States, NDP is usually 90 percent of GDP.

However, NDP is not the best measure of a country's productive activity. Even better is "national income." Recall that GDP is production valued at retail market prices, which include taxes on business sales. Such levies are called "indirect business taxes" that include sales and excise taxes. When you buy a hamburger from Burger King your price includes a tax; when you buy gasoline from Shell, you pay another tax. These are indirect taxes and are included in retail prices. They must be excluded from NDP to obtain a true gauge of economic activity; otherwise, just by raising indirect taxes, a country could claim a rise in GDP and NDP, but that would be a misleading increase in economic activity. When these taxes are deducted, we get what may be called "domestic income." Thus,

$$\text{domestic income} = \text{NDP} - \text{indirect business taxes}$$

This then is the best measure of economic activity within a country's borders.

Domestic income, however, is not a nation's total income, especially in these days of globalization, when people routinely invest money abroad. They earn dividends and interest from their foreign holdings of company shares and bonds. Similarly, a nation pays dividends and interest to foreign investors. The difference between earnings received from abroad and those paid to foreign nationals is called "net factor payments from abroad" (or NFP), which when added to domestic income yields national income. Thus,

$$\text{national income} = \text{domestic income} + \text{NFP}$$

National income is the total income of a country's nationals regardless of where they reside. If Michael Jordan runs a commercial for Mercedes Benz, a German firm, his fees so earned will be included in American national income. On the other hand, Queen Elizabeth's interest income originating in the United States is a part of British income. For those countries, where NFP is small, national income is the true measure of domestic economic activity. Otherwise, it is domestic income.

This takes us to the concept of what is known as "gross national product" (GNP), which measures the economic activity of a country's nationals. GNP is the market value of final goods and services produced by a country's citizens and immigrants during a year regardless of where they reside. If Toyota builds a factory in the United States, its output is a part of U.S. GDP, but its profit income comprises Japan's GNP. Whenever Roger Federer, an all-time tennis great and a Swiss national, won the Wimbledon tennis championship, his prize money constituted Swiss GNP but British GDP. His award comprised British GDP, but not British GNP, because the tournament generated economic activity in the United Kingdom. Thus,

$$GNP = GDP + NFP$$

For a large economy such as the United States, GDP and GNP are close to each other, because NFP is a tiny fraction of its GDP, but for smaller economies such as Canada and Australia, where foreign investment looms large and NFP is substantial, there is a big difference between the two measures. Both measures are thus important.

GDP usually determines a country's employment, whereas GNP generates its living standard. Brazil and Argentina have substantial levels of GDP, but because of their huge payments to foreign investors, their GNP is smaller and produces a lower living standard than indicated by their employment and production activity.

3. Measurement of GDP

There are three ways to measure and estimate GDP, each serving as a check on the other. These are as follows:

(1) The expenditure approach
(2) The income approach
(3) The value-added approach

By definition GDP is the revenue or value of output of final goods produced by firms inside a country; but output is either sold or unsold, and the value of unsold goods is the change in the inventory investment of all firms. Therefore,

$$GDP = \text{sales of final goods} + \text{changes in inventory investment}$$

Both the sales as well as inventory investment are money spent inside a country. Firms stuck with unsold goods spend money in either stocking or producing such goods. This type of spending is included in what is known as "gross investment" (I), whereas sales come obviously from spending by domestic consumers, businesses, government and foreigners.

Households buy consumption goods as well as new residences, which are included in the category of capital goods. Businesses buy capital goods as well as inventories, whereas the government buys both types of goods. Let C be spending on consumption goods, I be spending on capital goods and inventories, and G be government spending on final goods. Then,

$$\text{aggregate spending on final goods} = C + I + G$$

In order to see how much of this expenditure is on domestic or American goods, we have to add foreign spending on American goods, i.e., exports (X), and subtract American spending on foreign goods, i.e., imports (M). Therefore, from the "expenditure approach,"

$$\begin{aligned} \text{GDP} &= \text{spending on domestic goods} \\ &= C + I + G + X - M \\ &= C + I + G + \text{NX} \end{aligned}$$

where $\text{NX} = X - M$ is net exports, which can be positive, negative or zero.

Consumption spending includes people's purchases for personal use such as food, cars, appliances, consumer electronics, cigarettes, gasoline, cotton and the like; gross investment, as stated earlier, includes household spending on new residences, plus business spending on plant and equipment and on unsold stocks of all types of goods; and G represents spending by federal, state and local governments on the purchase of final goods.

The government spends money for national defense, to maintain law and order, to construct roads and bridges, to provide education and so on. All these are a part of G. Government spending for any other purpose is not included. For instance, government pensions and interest payments for debt are excluded from G. They enhance people's incomes and hence consumption spending, and if they were included in G there would be double counting.

In addition to buying domestically produced goods, Americans buy goods imported from abroad. Almost everything you purchase nowadays seems to be made in China, Japan, Taiwan, Europe or South Korea — TVs, cars, cameras, tennis rackets, the *American flag*, footballs, washers, dryers, air conditioners and the like. All these are U.S. imports.

Table 3.1: **Expenditure Estimate of GDP in the United States, 2018**

	Billions of Dollars
Personal Consumption Expenditure	13,952
Gross Private Domestic Investment	3,596
Government Purchase of Goods and Services	3,522
Net Exports	−626
Change in Inventories	56
Total (equals GDP)	20,500

Source: *The Economic Report of the President, 2019, B-3.*

Foreigners also buy goods made inside the United States, such as Boeing airplanes, some autos, Dell computers, Microsoft Windows and software, rice, wheat, beef, timber and weapons. These are American exports. The difference between exports and imports is net exports, which may be negative or positive.

A positive value of net exports, also called a "trade surplus," raises total spending on domestic products and thus GDP, whereas negative net exports, also called a "trade deficit," lowers them. Table 3.1 offers a bird's eye view of how GDP is calculated by adding the five items contained in the expenditure estimate. It may be noted that the symbol *I* of our equation for GDP includes gross private domestic investment and changes in inventories.

Once you obtain GDP, you can get NDP by subtracting depreciation from the GDP estimate. When depreciation is deducted from gross investment, we get net investment (*NI*). Therefore,

$$NDP = C + NI + G + (X - M)$$

4. The Income Approach

Spending springs from income, so that GDP can also be estimated by adding a variety of incomes in the economy, including net factor payments from abroad (NFP). Thus, in this approach, national income is estimated first, and then GDP.

Every firm's revenue is divided into someone's income. Suppose you own a restaurant chain, say, Hentucky Fried Chicken, with franchises at home and abroad. Obviously, your enterprise has something to do with hens and their offspring — the chickens. Your intermediate goods are oil, electricity, spices and above all chickens. You hire chefs, waiters, waitresses and managers. You borrow money to finance the purchase of your equipment, and you sign leases for the premises.

How is your revenue or sales utilized? First and foremost, you have to pay your suppliers of intermediate goods or raw materials. From what is left, which may be called net revenue, you pay wages to your employees and a salary to yourself, rent on your leases and interest on your loans. You also have to set aside money for the depreciation of your capital, and for payroll and indirect taxes that you have collected for the government. Whatever remains is your profit. If you are incorporated, your profit is called corporate profit. If not, your profit plus your salary is known as proprietor's income. Thus, the net revenue of all firms is distributed as some type of income, depreciation and indirect taxes. It may be noted that interest and profit incomes also include NFP. From all this,

$$\text{national income} = \text{wages} + \text{rent} + \text{interest} + \text{corporate profit} + \text{proprietor's income}$$

In addition,

$$\text{national income} - \text{NFP} = \text{domestic income}$$
$$\text{domestic income} + \text{indirect taxes} = \text{net domestic product}$$
$$\text{net domestic product} + \text{depreciation} = \text{GDP}$$

5. The Value-Added Approach

Net revenue defined previously is also called value added, because each firm buys raw materials from other firms, transforms them into its own product and in the process adds some value to the economy's output. *The firm's own contribution is its value added.* Specifically, value added of an industry is its total revenue minus payments made to other industries for raw materials. It also equals the contributions of labor, capital and land utilized in the production process. If we add the distributions of all net revenues to a country's nationals in the form of incomes, depreciation and indirect taxes, we get GDP. This means that if we simply add the net revenues themselves, we should again get GDP. This is the value-added approach.

There are then three ways to estimate GDP, and, in theory, all lead to the same answer, because of their very definitions. The retail value of goods must be equal to money spent to buy them. It also must equal the net revenue of all firms, as in the value-added approach. It is also the same as the sum total of all types of incomes, depreciation and indirect taxes, as in the income approach. Therefore, in theory the three approaches yield the same answer. They serve as a check on each other. Thus,

$$income = output = expenditure$$

In reality, there are minor statistical differences in actual computations, but the estimates are very close to each other. In most advanced economies such as the United States, Canada, Japan and Germany among others, all three methods are used to compute GDP; but in developing and medium-sized economies, where governments lack resources and adequate personnel, the expenditure method, the simplest of the three, is mainly used.

6. Personal Disposal Income

National income does not truly measure what people or households have at their disposal for spending or saving, because it includes some other forms of taxes that they have to pay on their incomes and excludes various types of incomes received from the government. It also includes corporate earnings, which are only partly distributed to households or shareholders in the form of "dividends." For these reasons, we first obtain "personal income," which is

$$personal\ income = national\ income + transfer\ payments$$
$$+ government\ interest - corporate\ retention$$

where

$$corporate\ retention = corporate\ taxes + payroll\ taxes + retained\ earnings$$

Transfer payments include checks written by the government for Social Security pensions, unemployment compensation, Medicare and welfare such as food stamps, income supplements, etc. Government interest, which is in addition to people's interest income from private firms, is the interest payment by the government on its debt.

Corporate retention is essentially money that firms have set aside for a variety of purposes such as their own payment of corporate and payroll taxes. It also includes Social Security taxes that employees pay from their wages, and retained earnings left after dividends have been paid to shareholders. Corporate retention is excluded from national income while transfers and government interest are added to obtain personal income. When personal taxes such as the individual income tax and property tax are deducted, we obtain, "personal disposable income":

personal disposable income = personal income – personal taxes

This is what is left at the disposal of households after all taxes have been taken into account. This is what people use for their spending and saving. Therefore,

personal disposal income = consumption + household saving

7. Real and Nominal Values

We already know from previous chapters what real GDP and real wages are. They represent the purchasing power of GDP and salaries. This suggests that there are real values and money values, real variables and nominal variables. A *variable*, as opposed to a constant, is simply anything that varies in the economy. A "constant," by contrast, does not vary in the short run but may do so in the long run.

Money value, also called nominal value, of anything is its value in terms of current prices or, in the case of the United States, current dollars. It is something that everyone actually deals with. Every worker receives a salary in terms of the national currency, which is the nominal value of their wage. Most of us are normally paid in nominal terms, i.e., in terms of our currency, not in terms of commodities. By contrast, the purchasing power of a nominal variable in terms of a base year's prices is called its real variable, which is expressed in terms of constant prices or constant dollars.

Both concepts are important in our everyday lives. *We all have to deal with nominal values but are subconsciously aware of their purchasing power or real values.* Suppose you receive a 3-percent pay raise; chances are you will be dissatisfied, because you would immediately wonder, "Did my raise beat the rate of inflation? Can I still afford to buy the same things that I could last year, and so on?" Your raise is in nominal terms, but your thinking is in real terms.

When nominal values are adjusted for changes in prices, we obtain real values. Thus,

$$\text{real GDP} = \text{nominal GDP/price level and}$$
$$\text{price level} = \text{a price index}/100$$

Real variables are especially useful if we want to compare "physical quantities" over time. If you seek to find out how national output has behaved over two periods, nominal GDP will give a misleading answer, because it is a combination of retail prices and outputs of various goods. Therefore, nominal GDP may rise because of an increase in prices, outputs or both. Thus, *if the price level jumps, real GDP may decline even if nominal GDP increases.*

That is where the price index comes in. It is used to eliminate the effect of changing prices from any variable. A real variable is one that is obtained not by using current prices but the prices of a base year. The idea is to keep prices fixed at the level of some year selected from the past, so that any changes in the variable will be purely from changes in its physical quantities.

A price index represents an average of all relevant prices. A variety of price indexes have been devised by economists. They include the consumer price index (CPI), the GDP deflator and the producer price index (PPI), which is close to the wholesale price index (WPI).

8. Real and Nominal GDP

The price index used to obtain real GDP from its nominal value is called the "GDP deflator," or simply the deflator. The deflator and real GDP depend on each other. Real GDP in a year is the value of the economy's production of all final goods using the prices of a base year, currently selected to be 2012 in the United States, whereas nominal GDP uses current prices. Therefore, the

$$
\begin{aligned}
\text{GDP deflator} &= \left(\frac{\text{nominal GDP}}{\text{real GDP}} \right) \times 100 \\
&= \frac{[\text{value of current output at current prices}]}{\text{value of current output at base year prices}} \times 100
\end{aligned}
$$

The deflator is thus nominal GDP expressed as a percentage of real GDP. By convention, a price index is set in multiples of 100. For the base year itself, the deflator equals 100.

From the formula for the deflator, you can see clearly, through cross multiplication, that

$$
\text{Real GDP} = \left(\frac{\text{nominal GDP}}{\text{the deflator}} \right) \times 100
$$

Real GDP is thus nominal GDP expressed as a percentage of the deflator. Table 3.2 illustrates how real GDP and the deflator can be computed, using the example of a simple economy that produces only food, houses, machines and steel. The table has three columns, listing output, unit price in 2020 and in the currently used base year of 2012.

Nominal GDP in the current year, say 2020, is the sum total of the value of output in that year at current prices. In 2020, $700 of food, $5,500 worth of homes, $1,800 worth of machines and $300 worth of steel are produced. These figures add up to $8,300. Is this nominal GDP? No, because it includes $300 worth of steel, which, being an intermediate good, is excluded by definition. Nominal GDP then, using current prices, is not $8,300 but $8,000.

However, real GDP equals the value of output in 2020 using 2012 prices, or $6,400, and the GDP deflator is 125. We can also obtain real GDP by dividing nominal GDP of $8,000 with the deflator of 125 and multiplying the result with 100.

Table 3.2: **Computing Real GDP and the GDP Deflator**

Output in 2020	Unit Price in 2020	Unit Price in the Base Year (2012)
10 tons of food	$70	$40
50 houses	110	60
60 machines	30	50
20 tons of steel	15	20

Notes: Nominal GDP = value of production in 2020 using current prices
$$= \$700\,(\text{food}) + \$5,500\,(\text{houses}) + \$1,800\,(\text{machines})$$
$$= \$8,000$$
Real GDP = value of production in 2020 using base year prices
$$= \$400\,(\text{food}) + \$3,000\,(\text{houses}) + \$3,000\,(\text{machines})$$
$$= \$6,400$$
GDP Deflator $= (8,000\,/\,6,400) \times 100 = 125$
Real GDP $= (8,000\,/\,125) \times 100 = \$6,400$

At present, 2012 is being used as the base year for the deflator. However, because of the constant development of new products, the base year itself has been changed time and again. Updating the base year then brings its mix of output closer to goods and services produced in recent years. However, frequent updating is also undesirable, because with each new base year, the value of the deflator changes so that the history of real GDP has to be rewritten. For this reason, a new type of deflator called the "chained price index" has been devised.

The chained index is a complicated method for price adjustments, but it is considered to be more satisfactory than the unchained method used until 1995. Therefore, the real GDP series currently offered by the U.S. Department of Commerce is a chained version, using a price index of chained 2012 dollars.

The chained method uses average unit prices for any two consecutive years. For instance, with 2012 and 2011, the unit price for all final goods and services in 2012 will be an average of the prices prevailing in the two years. Similarly, with 2011 and 2010 the unit price for 2011 is the average of prices prevailing in these two years, and so on. Thus, the chained deflator is more complicated than the unchained one. Let us hope its end product is worth the complication.

9. The Consumer Price Index (CPI)

The GDP deflator can be used not just to obtain real GDP but also real values of many other variables such as consumption, investment, government spending, transfer payments, exports and imports. It can also be used to obtain the real wage but that is rarely done, because some final goods, such as capital goods, do not enter into people's consumption basket.

In order to obtain the real wage, a price index of goods and services commonly consumed by the populace is required, and that is where the consumer price index or the CPI comes in. The CPI is computed by using the same method as the deflator, except that the market basket is fixed and includes only items commonly entering into people's consumption in the base year. Items like bread, beef, housing, education, transportation and movies are included in that basket, whereas items such as helicopters and cannons that would enter into GDP calculations are not included in the CPI, because they are not commonly used. As stated earlier, the CPI is mostly used to calculate the real wage.

Normally, the deflator and the CPI move closely together, but at times they have diverged. This may occur when prices rise rapidly, as during the 1970s, when the CPI rose faster than the deflator.

10. Inflation

Price indexes are useful in yet another way. They can be used to estimate rates of inflation or deflation. Recall that the United States has generally experienced nothing but inflation since 1940, although prior to that year each burst of inflation was followed by deflation. Inflation may be defined in terms of the GDP deflator or the CPI. In each case, it is the percentage change in the price index. Suppose the deflator in 2013 was 105; then the rate of inflation that year was 5 percent, because the deflator for the base year of 2012 was 100.

If the deflator in, say, 2003 is 121 and that in 2002 is 110, then the annual rate of inflation in 2003 is 10 percent, i.e.,

$$\text{inflation rate} = \left(\frac{\text{change in the deflator}}{\text{the previous year's deflator}} \right) \times 100$$

$$= \left(\frac{11}{110} \right) \times 100 = 10 \text{ percent}$$

Thus, the inflation rate is the change in a price index expressed as a percentage of the previous year's price index. *The CPI is used to calculate real wages or the annual adjustment for Social Security checks* paid by the government to retirees, but the inflation formula is the same as presented earlier.

As regards deflation, it is simply negative inflation. Since 1940, prices have generally risen continuously, although the rates of inflation have fluctuated, that is, prices have risen at different rates. Therefore, inflation rates have moved up or down, but there has been no general deflation.

11. Growth and Business Cycles

It is well known that over time nothing moves in a straight line. Everything evolves in terms of an up-and-down path, or cyclically. The same applies to national output and its growth. As population grows year after year, new mouths have to be fed, new bodies have to be clothed and educated, and for all this to be accomplished output must rise. This requires a rise in investment and often new technology. The result is that real GDP normally grows every year. The rate of economic growth, say, in 2020 may be defined by

$$\text{growth rate} = \left(\frac{\text{increase in real GDP in 2020}}{\text{real GDP in 2019}} \right) \times 100$$

For a variety of reasons to be explored in subsequent chapters, economic growth is not the same every year. It may be 3 percent in one year, 6 percent in another and might even be negative in yet another. Thus, economic growth follows a cyclical path, as displayed in Figure 3.1, which examines the growth experience of the U.S. economy from 1968 to 2018. The average growth rate is 2.5 percent per year, but the actual rates of growth oscillate around the average line.

A special case of the growth cycle is called the "business cycle," in which GDP growth is positive as well as negative. Traditionally, a business cycle is supposed to deal with short-run fluctuations, lasting on average from one to five years, whereas economic growth is concerned with long-term trends. But as you can see annual growth rates are rarely

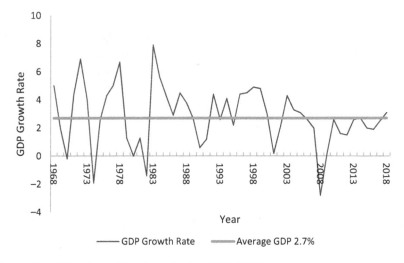

Figure 3.1:   Growth and Business Cycles: 1982–2018

Source: *The Economic Report of the President*, 2019.

negative. From 1968 to 2018, for instance, only in 1973, 1982, 1991 and 2001 was output growth below or close to the zero line. In most years, U.S. growth rates were positive. More recently, growth was negative in 2008 and 2009 in much of the world.

Thus, business cycles are no longer as frequent as they were in the past, whereas growth fluctuations have become far more common. It turns out that growth moves up and down annually and over long periods. A major task before macroeconomics is to explain why economic growth varies in the short run as well the long run.

The bulk of conventional macroeconomics explains the business cycle and the non-fluctuating average growth rate over the long run. The present text, however, deals with both the growth and the business cycles. *It will be shown that economic policy may be useful not only to bring an economy out of a recession but also to stimulate GDP growth as well.*

A business cycle normally has five phases that include a recession, trough, expansion, boom and peak. There is actually an intimate link between the business cycle and the growth cycle. The five phases of the business cycle coincide with various stages of the growth cycle.

A "recession" is said to occur when real GDP declines consecutively over two quarters, and normally produces negative or zero growth for the year. The bottom point of a recession is called a "trough," the point where the recession actually ends. This is followed by a period of "expansion," or positive growth.

A "Boom" arises when the growth rate rises above the average rate, or the average line. When the expansion phase hits a ceiling, the business cycle is at its "peak," which also coincides with the peak rate of growth. The peak is followed by a period of business contraction during which growth is normally positive but below the average line, and when the contraction is severe enough to take the growth path below the zero line, another recession ensues.

Thus, the business cycle is an integral part of the growth cycle, and both need to be explained by macroeconomics. In fact, in the post-WWII period, which has not witnessed a depression, the growth cycle deserves more attention than the business cycle.

12. The Cycle of Inflation

As with economic growth and business activity, there is also a cycle of inflation in the United States. However, this is not an ordinary cycle, but almost an exact cycle. Among various price indexes, the PPI as well as the WPI are the most volatile and subject to wide swings. The data on WPI go as far back as the mid-18th century. When studying an economy over such a long period, it is customary to divide the time period into decades. The next step is to obtain the average WPI per decade, and then obtain the decennial rate of inflation, or the inflation rate occurring over a 10-year period. When you plot these data, you obtain a graph such as that displayed in Figures 3.2 and 3.3.

In Chapter 2, we tracked the behavior of the CPI in the United States in Figure 2.7 and discovered that every burst of price increase in the past was followed by an almost equal burst of price decrease. But following 1940, the CPI generally moved in only one direction — upward.

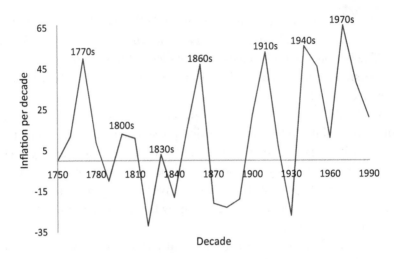

Figure 3.2:   The Cycle of WPI Inflation in the United States: 1750s–1990s

Source: Ravi Batra, *The New Golden Age*, Palgrave Macmillan, and *Historical Statistics of the United States*, 1800–1975.

This was a drastic change. The CPI behavior in the 19th century was very different from that in the 20th century. However, with the cycle of inflation, starting as early as the 1750s, there is no such discontinuity.

The cycle of inflation, which is described by price growth per decade, not just the average price like the CPI or the WPI, follows an oscillating path throughout American history. Furthermore, it reveals an amazing phenomenon. Except for the post-Civil War period, Figure 3.2 displays an incredible track, namely that over the past 250 years the decennial rate of inflation reached a peak every third decade and then usually declined over the next two. As far as inflation is concerned there is no discontinuity between the 18th and 19th centuries on one side and the 20th century on the other. Thus, the long-run cycle of inflation displays great resilience. It is elegantly displayed by the lines moving rhythmically up and down through 25 decades, beginning with the 1750s and ending in 2003.

Inflation first peaks in the 1770s, then declines over the next two decades and peaks again in the 1800s. It falls over the two subsequent decades, rising to its zenith in the 1830s. This time the inflation rate falls for only one decade, but still the next peak appears 30 years later in the 1860s.

At this point, the cycle hits an impasse, but begins anew with the 1880s, because within two decades another peak appears in the 1910s, which is the first inflationary peak of the 20th century. Three decades later the cycle crests in the 1940s, and then again in the 1970s. In the 1980s and the 1990s, the rates of inflation plunge, just as the cycle prophecies.

The inflation peak of the 1830s is somewhat curious, for it clings to the zero line. But deflation reigns in the decades immediately preceding and following the 1830s. Hence, compared to these years, the zero rate of inflation represents at least relative inflation. Therefore, the cycle remains intact. Thus, we may regard the 1830s as one of the peak points of the cycle.

Figure 3.3 examines the behavior of the PPI, which is a broader concept than the WPI in that the PPI also includes the prices received by service producers. These data start from 1913, so that for the 1900s, this graph uses the WPI inflation rate. The PPI cycle is valid all the way

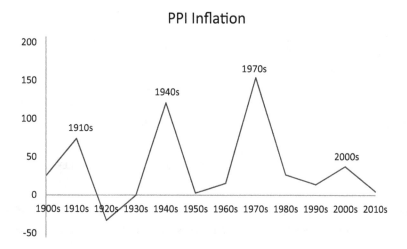

Figure 3.3:   The Cycle of PPI Inflation in the United States: 1900s–2010s

Source: Bureau of Labor Statistics, or FRED.

until 2019. Every third decade since the 1900s is the peak decade of inflation.

13. The Cycle of Money Growth

Parallel to the cycles of inflation exists another neat arrangement of history, namely the long-run cycle of money growth. Specifically, ever since the 1770s, as far back as the data go, every third decade in the United States has also been a peak decade of money growth, with the one exception after the 1860s, owing to the Civil War. This is not surprising. Inflation cannot be sustained unless the State prints large amounts of money over many years. There may be other reasons for sizzling prices, but they are all temporary, and cannot maintain the spiral of inflation. There have to be too many dollars chasing too few goods for an enduring rise in the cost of living. It is as simple as that.

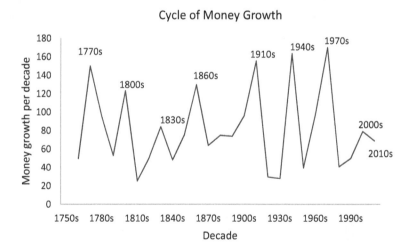

Figure 3.4:   The Long-Run Cycle of Money Growth in the United States: 1750s–2010s

Note: Except for the aftermath of the Civil War, money growth peaked every third decade in the United States.

Source: Historical Statistics of the United States, 1975; The Economic Report of the President, 2019.

The link between money and inflation is so strong that if there is a cycle of inflation, then there must be an almost parallel cycle of money growth as well. This is precisely what Figure 3.4 displays.

Why do we examine money growth instead of money supply? The reason is that real GDP tends to rise every year because of new investment and growing population. To buy this extra output, people need more cash, in hand or in their checking accounts; otherwise, product prices will fall and the economy will malfunction, as no business can plan properly without the certainty of prices. Therefore, just to keep prices stable, money supply has to rise in proportion to the increase in production.

In other words, as long as money growth is close to GDP growth, prices remain stable. Thus, if output increases by 5 percent, then money supply must also increase by 5 percent to avoid a prolonged price decline or deflation. For prices to rise, money growth has to outpace production, and exceed the level of 5 percent. That is why inflation is fed more by money growth than just by the supply of money.

The cycle of money growth is easier to obtain than the cycle of inflation. Consistent estimates of money supply can be obtained from Friedman and Schwarz, going as far back as the birth of the American nation in 1776. The data used are for every 10th year. A simple transformation of these observations into rates of change per decade yields a vivid cycle, presented in Figure 3.4.

The first peak of the cycle starts with the 1770s, which saw the birth of the American Revolution and an extraordinary use of the money pump to finance it. Historians argue that money growth at the time dwarfed any that preceded it in colonial times with the exception of the two decades following the Civil War.

The Civil War also disrupted the money growth cycle, just as it did the inflation cycle. The nation took about 20 years to recuperate, but once the economy's recovery was complete by the early 1880s, the cycle resumed its rhythmical course. Within two decades money growth crested in the 1910s, which is the first inflationary peak of the 20th century. Thirty years later, the peak recurred in the 1940s, and then again in the 1970s. Not surprisingly, in the 1980s and 1990s, money growth fell, and then surged again in the 2000s.

Thus, Figure 3.4 shows that, except for the post-Civil War period, money growth crested every third decade over two centuries. This is another remarkable trait of the American economy.

14. Inflation and Money Growth

What sparks inflation? On this question there is now a rare agreement among economists, who believe that inflation springs primarily from prolonged monetary expansion. There may be other factors, but they cannot sustain the spiral of escalating prices in the absence of high money growth. Thus, a sustained rise in the growth of dollars is a prerequisite for sustained inflation.

Figures 3.2 and 3.4 present the paths of money growth and inflation and show that the two cycles run almost parallel to each other. Not only do their peaks match but the Civil War also disturbed them both. The figures thus clearly reveal that brisk money growth breeds inflation. Inflation crests just as money growth crests.

Money and inflation cycles are remarkable traits of the U.S. economy. Clearly money is the main spark behind sizzling prices. Apparently, only one of the two cycles is independent, because one guides the other. Given that the supply of money depends upon several unrelated factors such as behavior of banks and policies of the Federal Reserve, the observed pattern of money growth is simply astounding.

15. Cycles as Forecasting Devices

It is very difficult, if not impossible, to offer a rational explanation for the rhythmical cycles of money growth and inflation crisscrossing the historical landscape in the United States. They appear to be surreal and unfathomable. I have explored them elsewhere but with reluctance. How can you possibly explain data that move with exact peaks and valleys?

While the cycles are beyond the realm of rationality, they are impeccable as forecasting devices. To paraphrase Mark Twain, it is very difficult to make predictions, especially about the future. But the cycles of money growth and inflation make the job somewhat easy. As predictive tools, they are peerless. I first discovered them in 1983, and, contrary to everyone's belief at the time, predicted that inflation would generally decline over the next two decades. With declining inflation comes a fall in nominal interest rates and a rise in stock and bond prices. Real estate values also soar, and so on. All this came to pass during the 1980s and the 1990s.

The two cycles also explain why inflation eased during the 2010s, and will remain low in the 2020s. Both cycles were disturbed by the aftermath of the Civil War, but nothing else could disrupt them. Given that another calamity like the Civil War is unlikely, the cycles will hold as long as capitalism does, because they are the cycles of the American capitalist system.

16. The Cost of Inflation

Inflation is a state of persistent increase in average prices. A one-shot upswing is not enough for the situation to be called inflationary. Moreover, it is not necessary that all products become expensive over time. So long as the average price level, measured by the CPI or the deflator, increases persistently, there is inflation.

People instinctively fear inflation, and rightly so. For even though a persistent but slow increase in prices need not reduce the living standard of the nation as a whole, it does hurt the weakest sections of society. For everyone who pays a price to buy something, there is a recipient. For instance, if your telephone bill goes up, you feel the pinch, but the phone company and its employees prosper. Most of us are buyers and sellers. We buy goods but sell our labor. When goods become expensive, wages also go up, so that rising prices need not crimp our living standard. *For the nation as a whole, price appreciation may not result in lifestyle depreciation.*

However, for the weakest sections of society, especially the poor, inflation can be slow torture. Take for instance the case of those who subsist on the "minimum wage." There are 10 million workers in America who earn the minimum; another 20 million, such as those in retailing and temp jobs, have their salaries tied to the minimum. These people are all victims of inflation, for their incomes are fixed year after year, while prices advance relentlessly, until congressmen, out of the goodness of their hearts, swing into action and, instead of giving themselves a raise, legislate an increase in the minimum wage.

At this point the minimum wage is $7.25 per hour, which, in terms of purchasing power, is way below the 1968 peak of $11. Typically, a minimum wage earner is an unskilled worker, with very little bargaining power. Such workers are among the weakest sections of society; few lobby for them in Washington.

The elderly or retirees are another weak section that may suffer from inflation. No doubt, their Social Security paychecks are indexed to the CPI so that their overall purchasing is preserved with the rise in the price index. But the cost of medicines and healthcare has escalated sharply since the 1980s. These prices have jumped faster than the overall rate of inflation, and since the elderly are most in need of healthcare, the increase in their Social Security income falls short of their soaring medical bills. The elderly too are among the weakest sections. They do have a strong lobby and voice in Washington; yet their incomes have not matched the true rise in their cost of living.

People can avoid the bite of inflation only if their wages keep pace with price escalation. Some such as skilled or unionized workers are able to do so, because they seem to have strong bargaining power in their relations with companies. But others such as older and less-skilled workers are not so fortunate. Their salaries usually trail inflation. This lack of bargaining power is the main reason for the slow but steady erosion of the real wage that the production worker has suffered in the United States since 1972.

While the weakest sections of society are hurt by inflation, those entrenched in the corridors of power usually benefit from it. The CEOs of America and elsewhere have been in the driver's seat, and their salaries, as you discovered in the previous chapter, have skyrocketed. Others with strong bargaining power are labor unions, skilled workers and professionals such as doctors, lawyers, accountants and engineers. Their incomes have generally outpaced the cost of living.

17. The Lenders

Another group that normally suffers comprises "lenders," especially those that lend money at fixed rates over a long period. Mortgage loan companies, for instance, lend out money for as many as 30 years, charging a fixed interest rate. If inflation heats up in the meanwhile, the interest rate goes up but the borrower still pays the lower rate until the loan matures, or the house is sold, requiring a new loan. The lender's loss is of course the borrower's gain.

Some economists suggest that if inflation is properly anticipated, the lender need not be hurt by loan activity. In theory they are right. Anticipating a higher rate of inflation, the lender automatically raises the interest fee on the mortgage. But anticipating inflation is by no means easy. By the time prices start escalating, it is usually too late. At least that has been the experience of lenders in the United States.

The cycle of inflation reveals that inflation usually soars over a decade, and then declines over the next two decades. When something remains dormant for as long as 20 years, how can you possibly anticipate its return? That is why mortgage lenders have been devastated again and again in U.S. history.

During the 1970s, many Savings and Loan associations as well as some banks made housing loans at an interest rate around 8 percent. Then inflation heated up and sharply raised the mortgage rates. Later, in the early 1980s, the government's attempts to control inflation raised the interest cost even more. But the mortgage lending industry was stuck with low interest fees that were fixed in the 1970s. In order to attract savings deposits in the 1980s, the industry had to pay interest rates as high as 15 percent to its depositors, thus suffering huge losses on prior loans. The result was an unprecedented crisis in 1986 in which many lenders went bankrupt, and the government, which insured the deposits held by the saving associations, bailed out the industry at a taxpayer cost of nearly $250 billion.

Do borrowers get hurt when they borrow in the midst of roaring inflation? Sometimes, but not always. Nowadays, the borrower retains the right to refinance a mortgage at any time. Therefore, when the interest rate declines, the borrower can simply switch to another lender and avoid the high cost of the previous loan. In some other countries such as England the mortgage rate is linked to the rate of inflation. There, lenders and borrowers are not affected by inflation.

18. Summary

(1) "GDP" is defined as the retail value of all final goods and services produced during a year inside a country, whereas GNP is the yearly value of all final goods and services produced by a country's nationals around the world.

(2) GDP and GNP are the most well-known yardsticks of economic activity, but they are not the best measures. The best yardstick is "national or domestic income," which equals the sum of all types of incomes, and excludes indirect business taxes and depreciation of capital from GDP.

(3) Personal disposal income is after-tax income available to households after all funds retained by corporations are excluded from national income, and all funds transferred from the government to families are added.

(4) There are three ways to estimate GDP, each serving as a check on the other. These are the expenditure approach, the income approach and the value-added approach. The first method obtains GDP by adding total spending on domestically produced goods and services in the economy; the second does it by adding up all types of incomes, the depreciation expense and indirect taxes; and the third does it by adding the net revenue of all firms after their payments to other firms for raw materials are deducted from their total revenue.

(5) The purchasing power of any monetary variable relative to the prices of a base year is called its real value. A monetary measure is called a nominal variable, one that is obtained by using current prices. If prices are constant then real and nominal values are the same.

(6) When nominal values are adjusted for changes in prices, we get real values. "Real GDP" is current output valued at some base year's prices. A price index called the "GDP deflator" is nominal GDP

expressed as a percentage of real GDP. In fact, all real values can be obtained from their nominal values, when the latter are expressed as a percentage of the deflator.

(7) Real wage is nominal wage as a percentage of the CPI, which is the nominal value of a market basket of commonly used goods and services expressed as a percentage of their real value.

(8) The rate of inflation is the change in a price index expressed as a percentage of the previous year's price. Negative inflation is deflation.

(9) U.S. history reveals that in normal circumstances inflation has peaked every third decade.

(10) So has money growth. Thus, the cycle of inflation runs parallel to the cycle of money growth, indicating that high money growth breeds inflation. Both the cycles have an impeccable forecasting record. They now suggest that the 2020s are likely to be disinflationary.

Chapter 4

The Classical Micro Model

The body of writings originating in 1776 from Adam Smith, anointed as the father of modern economics, and subsequently appearing in the works of David Ricardo, J.B. Say, Alfred Marshall, Irving Fisher and A.C. Pigou, is known as classical economics. The term was coined by Karl Marx, the founder of communism, and later popularized by Keynes. Classical microeconomics is the starting point of the orthodox macro model. We shall examine this system in detail in order to set the stage for ideas that evolved later.

To be sure few classical economists were directly concerned with issues of national importance, such as total employment, business cycles, GDP and economic growth. Their focus was on individuals, not society. They explored the behavior of demand and supply in various industries but paid scant attention to demand and supply at the national level. Yet from their explorations of microeconomic behavior, we can gain enough insight about their views on macro issues and about their attitudes toward government's economic policy. Thus, classical microeconomics is the foundation of classical macroeconomic theory.

1. Assumptions

Classical economists usually began with a common set of assumptions regarding the behavior of consumers, businesses and employees. Their principal assumptions were as follows:

(1) Consumers are rational in the sense that they want to maximize pleasure or utility from their consumption of goods.
(2) Producers want to maximize profit.
(3) Workers want to maximize the fruit of their work that generates incomes and minimize the discomfort or disutility of work.
(4) Each industry has numerous firms, which face intense competition from each other, so that no single company has any impact on product prices or the wage rate paid to its workers.
(5) The intense competition among firms and workers ensures that prices and wages are fully flexible upward and downward.

For the most part, these assumptions explain themselves, and you can see that some of them reflect your own behavior and nature. Whenever needed, we will elaborate them further. All of them seem to be reasonable, except number 4, which ceased to be relevant at the turn of the 20th century, and no longer describes the modern world in which mega firms control their industries.

2. The Invisible Hand

The idea that made Adam Smith a celebrity is called the invisible hand, which appeared in his masterpiece, *The Wealth of Nations*. The book offered an elegant defense for what is today called the free-market system. Although an industrial revolution had begun 200 years before his birth, capitalism was still in its infancy. Under the pervasive influence of religion at the time, the public generally distrusted the profit motive and the ideas of individualism, which was feared for its potential for anarchy. Smith's peers generally championed the interest of the State, not of the people.

Smith offered a new idea that admired self-interest as well as the human quest for money and profit. He argued that self-preservation comes naturally to everyone, so that the pursuit of self-interest and ambition is virtue not vice, and leads to prosperity not anarchy. This is what motivates employers and employees to put capital and labor to uses that are the most productive. A firm seeks maximum return from its investment, whereas a worker chases the highest salary for his or her effort. Facing keen competition from others, a producer has to offer high-quality goods at a low price, whereas to compete with their colleagues, everyone has to work to their best potential. This is how self-preservation works.

The mechanism that brings the best out of producers and workers is Smith's invisible hand of a free market. The invisible hand brings consumers and producers to interact with each other. Each party pursues its self-interest, and in the process helps itself and the other attain its goal. Businesses know that people want quality products, so they produce goods and services in demand, using technology and resources in an efficient way to minimize costs and thus prices. Everyone is happy in a free-market economy characterized by intense competition among firms, consumers and workers. Consumers enjoy superb quality from their low-cost purchases, producers earn adequate profits because they produce goods at minimum cost and workers enjoy high salaries arising from their hard work.

The pursuit of self-interest by everyone thus ensures that society's resources are put to their best use, generating the highest living standard from available technology. Smith's analysis of a market offered a variety of new prescriptions. How may society maximize its living standard? Smith provided a simple answer. *Create keen competition at all levels of economic activity. Make sure there are no monopolies at the level of production or workers. Keep the markets free by discouraging mergers among profitable firms.*

Smith assailed various government regulations that generate monopolies and constrict business competition. In his view, small-scale enterprises were a constant source of new competitors. This point is very important, because the CEOs of modern-day giant firms have generally invoked Smith's free enterprise to justify their unseemly incomes. Adam Smith did not denounce avarice, which is inherent in most of us, but the State institutions that tolerate mega mergers, restrict competition and in the process enable some to be enormously wealthy, while forcing others into destitution. He justified the profit motive, not "profiteering."

3. The American Republic

It is an irony of history that a pioneer is acclaimed everywhere except at home. Britain, where Smith was born, paid lip service to its brilliant writer, and continued to protect the State trading monopolies. However, a feisty new republic, the United States of America, that had declared independence in the same year that saw the arrival of *The Wealth of Nations*, heartily followed his prescriptions. Individualism permeated America's freedom fighters, who generally disliked state intervention in private matters such as the hunt for profit in a business venture.

Leaders of the new republic turned out to be worthy disciples of the revolutionary economist, except in his admiration of free trade. Smith was in principle against tariffs, except when it came to self-defense and retaliation against excessive foreign tariffs. However, American presidents, from George Washington to Thomas Jefferson to Abraham Lincoln, generally adopted high import duties and protected the home market for manufactured goods. American firms thus faced little competition from foreign producers, but they had more than enough at home. The birth of hundreds of new and small companies generated intense rivalry among businesses even though foreign goods were expensive. Smith's idea of free enterprise had found a fertile field to prove itself. All the preconditions for the triumph of the invisible hand then existed in the United States.

Early ventures by US entrepreneurs were small, unable to dominate any market. *Keen competition is a dynamic force that lubricates industrialization and prosperity*. Americans, just like modern Japan, China and South Korea, imported technology and capital, and combined them with domestically available resources. But unlike the Asian nations, they sold their goods mostly to domestic customers. The rest is history.

By the turn of the 20th century, the young republic had come of age. Starting practically from nothing, it had bested the well-established economies of England, Germany and France. America emerged as the global leader in technology, industry, per-capita GDP and, above all, the real wage. *The invisible hand of Adam Smith had built a most visible industrial empire in the world. Henceforth, free enterprise would become a gospel for economists, politicians and the people.*

4. Supply and Demand

Today, the workings of the invisible hand are described by the concepts of supply and demand in any industry, with supply coming from the handiwork of workers and producers, and demand from consumers. Supply and demand together are the foundation stone of economics and will remain so forever. Like the two blades of a pair of scissors, both have to be equally strong and developed for smooth functioning of any market. *Every economic puzzle in the world can be solved if you properly understand the operation of these two forces.*

People buy a variety of goods and services, and in the process create demand. Their buying behavior can be represented by a line or a curve in a two-dimensional graph such as Figure 4.1. The graph depicts the typical behavior of a consumer regarding the purchase of any product, say, a T-shirt. The price of a shirt is displayed along the vertical axis, and the number of shirts in demand along the horizontal axis. A line such as AB is a line with a negative slope, and it indicates a negative relationship between the shirt price and the number of shirts bought.

The line AB may be called a demand curve because it portrays a link between what is displayed along the two axes. In economics, the distinction between a line and a curve is generally ignored. AB is a demand line or a demand curve. The negative slope of the line, as mentioned earlier, captures the negative relationship between consumer purchases and the product price.

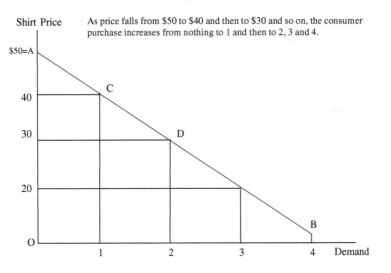

Figure 4.1:   A Demand Curve

Suppose you are thinking of buying some T-shirts, especially the Polo brand that you have used before. You visit a shopping mall and find that the shirt sells for the price of OA or $50 apiece; this price is so high that you do not care much for the apparel, no matter how nicely it fits and impresses your friends. You then buy zero shirts, so that point A becomes the starting point of your demand curve for T-shirts.

As you are about to depart in dismay the storeowner comes, greets you with a smile and is ready to make a deal with you. "How many shirts will you buy if I were to drop the price?" she asks you in earnest. Sensing that she is serious about her offer, you reply with a grin, "At $50 apiece the price is too high for my budget. At 40, I would consider taking one, at 30, I would take 2, at 20, I might even buy three, and if you were to drop the price all the way to $10 apiece, I would take as many as four, but no more than four, because that's all I need right now."

In terms of the lingo of economics, you have just described your demand curve or demand schedule to the owner. Take another look at Figure 4.1. The combination of one shirt and its price of $40 generates a point such as C that lies on the demand curve AB. If the price falls further to $30, you are willing to buy 2 shirts; their combination generates a point such as D that also lies on AB. In the extreme case, at a price of $10, you are willing to buy 4 shirts, but no more. This price–quantity combination yields a point such as B. Joining all the points such as A, C, D and B yields AB, which is your demand curve for shirts.

The curve displays what is regarded as universal consumer behavior. *Other influences remaining the same, you purchase more of a product, as its price declines.* Similarly, you buy less of a product, if its price rises, other influences or things, of course, remaining constant. This is called "the law of demand." It is portrayed by the negatively sloped line such as AB that reflects a negative relationship between price and quantity demanded. In general, a demand curve displays a consumer's potential purchases of a product at various prices.

4.1. *Other Things Remaining Constant*

Graphs are commonly used in economics, because they enable us to understand complex phenomena in a simple way. But every curve or line is subject to the phrase "other things remaining constant, equal or the same." Your demand for Polo T-shirts, for instance, not only depends on their own price but also on your income, your tastes and on the prices of other competing brands. Suppose Nike shirts become much cheaper than the Polo brand, then even if the Polo price falls, you may not buy more Polos, because you would rather have the inexpensive Nikes. Does this negate the law of demand concerning Polo shirts?

No, because in this case those "other influences" did not remain constant. Two things changed at the same time. The Polo shirt price declined but the Nike price fell even faster, so the Polo shirt demand did not rise.

An economic variable may be subject to a variety of influences. In order to make any sense, we study these influences one at a time, and then combine them to obtain an overall picture. This is why every law or relationship in economics is defined in terms of "other things remaining constant," so that we can tackle one question at a time. In technical terminology, the phrase "other things remaining equal" is known as the *ceteris paribus* clause.

5. Movement along a Curve and of a Curve

In order to explore all the influences on a variable in terms of a diagram, we make a distinction between moving along a curve, and the movement of a curve. In Figure 4.2, there are two lines, AB and ab. When your Polo shirt's demand changes because of a change in its "own price," you are, in effect, moving along the curve AB. When the price falls from $50 to $40, you move from point A to C; when it falls further to $30, then you move from C to D and so on. But suppose the Polo price is constant and your Polo purchase changes for some other reason, then your behavior will be represented by a shift in the curve itself. In this case, with the shirt price unchanged, there is no possibility of moving along AB. The only way then to display your behavior is through a shift in the entire curve.

In general, a simultaneous change in both variables represented by the two axes is displayed by a movement along the curve, whereas a change in only one of the two variables is represented by a shift of the entire curve, up or down. The focus on what is listed on the axes is very important, because those other influences are not mentioned on

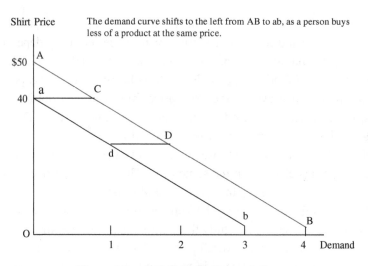

Figure 4.2:   A Shift in the Demand Curve

these axes. Remember these rules apply to all two-dimensional graphs, not just the demand curves presented in Figures 4.1 and 4.2.

In the figures, if all other influences on your Polo demand are unchanged, then your behavior regarding shirt purchases is represented by the curve AB. But suppose the Nike price falls, then you are likely to buy fewer Polos than before even if the Polo price is unchanged. Since your shirt spending has some limits, if Nikes become cheaper you will buy fewer Polos, and if Polos become cheaper you will buy fewer Nikes. How do we depict this behavior in Figure 4.2? The only way to do so is through a shift in the curve AB, because AB depicts the effects of a change in the price of Polos, not Nikes.

Point D on the AB curve shows that you would like to buy two Polo shirts at a Polo price of $30 apiece. Now suppose Nikes become inexpensive, but the Polo price is unchanged, and you buy one Polo shirt and one Nike shirt. Your Polo demand goes down even though the Polo price is constant, because now you have bought a Nike shirt as well. Since you buy only one Polo, when Nikes become inexpensive, point D shifts horizontally to point d, which now represents the right price–quantity combination of one Polo shirt and its price of $30. If originally you had bought only one Polo shirt at a price of $40, with cheaper Nikes, you may not buy any at all. Here your demand point moves from C to a. This way you now have a new demand curve given by the line ab.

This is the downward movement of the demand curve, which occurs even as the Polo price is unchanged, but the Nike price sinks. The effect of a fall in the price of Nikes on your demand for Polo shirts can only be depicted by a shift of various points on the curve AB to their left, because the Polo price is constant.

You, of course, end up buying more Nikes, but that behavior is represented by your demand curve for Nike T-shirts. Thus, you see that when the "own price" of a Polo shirt changes, you move along the Polo demand curve, but if the price of a competing good, such as Nike shirts, changes, your Polo demand curve shifts entirely. It shifts to the left if your Polo demand declines, and to the right if your Polo demand rises.

Suppose your income goes up. Then your demand for all goods is likely to rise, provided their prices remain constant. This change will then shift the shirt demand curve to the right. This way, just in a two-dimensional graph, we are able to examine all influences that impact a variable. *As a simple rule, when changes occur simultaneously in both variables mentioned explicitly at the end of the two axes, you move along the same curve, but if only one of the two variables changes because of some other factor, then the entire curve shifts up or down.* You should memorize this rule, if you want to learn economics without tears.

6. Market Demand

Figure 4.1 describes the demand curve for one individual for one brand of T-shirts. If we add up the demand curves of all individuals with a taste for Polo shirts, we obtain the demand curve for this product in the entire nation. Suppose there are 100 people living in your town, and for simplicity suppose they all behave like you. Then all we have to do is to multiply each number on the horizontal axis of Figure 4.1 by 100 to obtain the Polo shirt demand curve in your area. Thus, at a price of $50, the market demand for Polo shirts is zero; it is 100, if the price falls to $40, 200 if it falls further to $30 and so on.

Thus, the market demand curve for a product in any area can be obtained by adding potential purchases of the product by individuals at different prices. Similarly, the national demand curve for a particular product can be obtained by adding up potential purchases of all areas in a nation, at different prices. For the T-shirt industry as a whole we will have to add the potential purchases of all brands in a nation at various prices.

7. Market Supply

Supply, in general, represents the behavior of producers and workers engaged in the production of goods. Graphically, in a competitive industry, it is depicted by a positively sloped line such as MN in Figure 4.3. The vertical axis still measures the price of Polo T-shirts, but the horizontal axis now represents the supply of such shirts. MN is a supply curve, and its "positive slope" suggests that the link between shirt supply and its "own price" is positive. If shirts become expensive, shirt-making firms increase their hiring to produce more of the product, and if shirts become cheaper, the firms lay off workers and produce less of the product.

This type of firm behavior occurs mainly in a competitive environment, where intense rivalry among companies forces the price to be flexible, both up and down. In the absence of keen competition, the product price becomes sticky and usually moves only in one direction — upward — because the

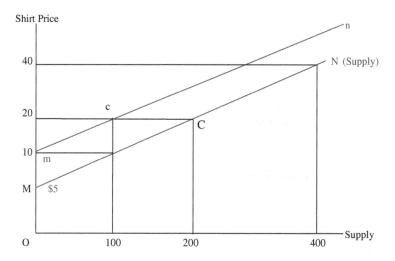

Figure 4.3:   A Supply Curve and Its Shift

firms are then able to control their prices. Intense competition means that businesses are unable to fix their prices and are subject to the vagaries of their markets. Now if the product price is inflexible, we cannot even define a supply curve, let alone describe its properties. This is why the assumption of perfect or keen competition is crucial to the existence of a supply curve such as MN in Figure 4.3.

7.1. *Why Is the Supply Curve Positively Sloped?*

Why does a competitive firm need a price increase to raise its output? This is needed especially in the short run, where the firm is unable to expand its factory and capital equipment. It takes time to build new factories and install new machines, so that in the short run capital stock is constant. An output rise generally requires increased hiring, and new workers usually need on-the-job training and, in the short run, have to work with a fixed amount of capital. For these reasons they are less productive than the old, experienced workers.

Raising output then means that new production costs more than the old level of output. The price must then rise to compensate the producer.

On the other hand, if the product price falls, some workers, especially the least productive ones, are laid off, so that those left behind are more productive than those fired, and the cost of output per worker declines. With layoffs, production must fall. Some firms will go out of business, but some will remain solvent, because output now requires lower cost to produce. Price has fallen, but so have costs, so that the industry's output will fall but will not cease completely, unless the price declines so much that costs cannot be covered at all by the revenue.

In Figure 4.3, if the shirt price is $5, supply equals zero. This is the starting point of the supply curve at point M. Here the price is so low that firms prefer not to stay in business; at this minimum price, companies would rather shut down and minimize their losses. In economics lingo, it means that a firm's revenue from production must cover the cost of using the variable inputs, such as labor and raw materials. Otherwise, it pays the firm to cease operations altogether, because its losses are then limited to its overhead costs, which are the costs of its fixed inputs, such as machinery and office lease, and so on.

In Figure 4.3, when the price rises to $10, supply equals 100 T-shirts; when it rises to $40, supply increases further to 400 shirts and so on. The curve MN is the supply curve of one firm that produces Polo T-shirts. In order to obtain an industry-wide supply curve for T-shirts of all brands, we have to add the potential offers of all relevant firms at various prices. It is derived by adding up the supplies of all firms operating in that industry.

However, the basic makeup of the supply graph changes little. In the case of the industry-wide supply curve, only the unit of measurement along the horizontal axis alters. Thus, at a price of $20, the industry may offer 20,000 shirts, while a single firm supplies only 200. Hence, each firm may offer only a small fraction of the total industrial output. This is how high competition operates; each firm is too small to impact the industry-wide output.

8. The Shift of the Supply Curve

Just like the market demand curve, the market supply curve also shifts if other forces affecting the output change. A supply curve at any level — the firm, area or national industry — is drawn under the assumption that other relevant influences are unchanged. Anything that affects a firm's cost of production will generally cause a shift in the supply curve. In order to understand this, let us raise a question: What happens to T-shirt production if its own price is constant but some other related prices have changed? The curve shift rule applies here as well: if only one of the two variables mentioned on the axes changes then the entire supply curve shifts.

Suppose the prices of raw materials, such as cotton, energy, etc., used in shirt production climb. Then the current price of one shirt will be unable to cover the cost producing that shirt. The firm must cut production or raise its price to the level of the new cost. Either way, the supply curve must shift to the left. This means that at the same old price, output must fall, or at the same old level of production, price must rise.

For instance, suppose the market price is $20, and a producer supplies 200 shirts at that price. With a rise in raw material costs, the firms may offer only 100 shirts at the same old price. Then the price–output combination in Figure 4.3 shifts horizontally from point C to c. Such a leftward movement will occur at all prices, because at all output levels the shirt price barely covers unit cost if the industry is highly competitive. Thus, at every price level, output falls, which is then displayed by the leftward shift of the supply curve. You can also confirm from this curve shift that to produce the same output level the firm now requires a higher price.

Whatever raises the firm's cost of production per unit of output will move the supply curve to the left. Poor climate and rising wages, in addition to the rising cost of raw materials and energy, also tend to raise unit cost. Therefore, they too shift the supply curve to left. On the other hand, shrinking wages, good weather, sinking raw material prices and new technology tend to trim unit cost. Then the supply curve shifts to the right.

9. Equilibrium Price

One of the most fundamental ideas in economics is the notion of equilibrium. The notion does not mean some kind of peace of mind, but rather a state of the world, a market or the participants in a market. *Economic equilibrium implies a state of rest, in which there is no pressure for change because the parties in question, given their constraints, feel satisfied with the outcome. By contrast, in disequilibrium there is enormous pressure to move away from the existing environment.*

Returning to the case of your purchase of Polo T-shirts, recall that you had described your demand curve to a storeowner. You were willing to purchase one shirt at a price of $40 apiece, two at 30, three at 20 and a maximum of 4 at a shirt price of $10. From the storeowner's viewpoint, the ideal price was $50, but she could not find a buyer at that price. Therefore, the outcome was not satisfying to either party. In economics lingo, both you and the seller were out of equilibrium, or were in disequilibrium, and both of you were dissatisfied with the outcome.

The question is as follows: What is likely to be a satisfying outcome for both you and the seller? Obviously, both of you have to compromise and move away from your most preferred price. The seller has to lower her price to sell any T-shirts at all. In view of your demand curve, if she lowers her price to 40, she will sell one T-shirt and receive $40 from you;

if she lowers it further to 30, she will sell two shirts and receive $60 from you, and if she goes down to 20, she will indeed sell 3 shirts but her receipt will still be only 60.

Assuming that she wants to maximize her revenue while minimizing her cost, she will not reduce her price below $30. This price will then become the equilibrium price, and the exchange of two T-shirts will be the equilibrium quantity. You will both be satisfied with this outcome, which occurs at a point where your willingness to buy the shirts matches her willingness to supply them. In other words, an outcome satisfactory to both transacting parties requires that

$$\text{demand} = \text{supply}$$

This, then, is the equilibrium condition. In other words, when your demand matches the owner's offer, both of you are in equilibrium; you both are then in a state of rest, happy with the outcome, given your constraints. For you, the constraint comes from your income, for the seller, it springs from her own purchase cost. If your income were any higher, you could obviously afford to pay a larger price, and then the equilibrium price will be higher as well; on the other hand, if the seller's purchase costs increased, she might not be willing to lower her price below $40, and then you will buy only one shirt.

Thus, there is not one single level of equilibrium price and quantity, but many, depending on the constraints. When the constraints alter, the supply and demand curves shift and generate new equilibrium points, prices and quantities exchanged. Equilibrium values are useful because they are normally very close to the actual or observed values. Suppose a particular government policy enhances equilibrium employment, then it is also likely to increase actual employment. This way the notion of equilibrium plays a crucial role in economics.

10. Market Equilibrium

The way you and your seller arrived at the satisfactory outcome resulting in an actual transaction is repeated day and night in all markets, involving millions of buyers and thousands of sellers. Just like you two, markets arrive at equilibrium points through bargaining among transacting parties. Figure 4.4 illustrates the way a market arrives at such a point. Here DD is the market demand curve and SS, the corresponding supply curve. Where the two curves intersect determines the equilibrium point, such as E, because both demand and supply then equal OQ, generating a price of OP.

If the price were higher at point A, demand will be AB and supply will be AC. How do we know this? If you were to draw a straight line from B to the horizontal axis, the distance from the new point and the origin would exactly equal AB, and so on. At the higher price of OA, storeowners will be left with unsold goods equaling BC. This will induce them to announce sales in newspapers, radio or TV. Buyers will flock to the malls. How far will the price come down? Until the excess supply of goods, equal to BC, disappears, or until price falls to P.

If the price were at R instead, then there will be an overheated market. Sellers will soon realize that goods are selling faster than their ability to stock them. They will then demand a premium price, which will rise until the excess demand, equaling GT, vanishes. Thus, the market equilibrium arrives through bargaining among buyers and sellers. The bargaining may or may not be explicit, but it is inherent in the course of price movements.

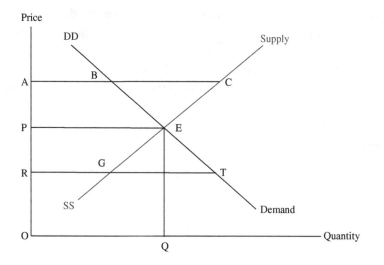

Figure 4.4:   Market Equilibrium

When stores announce sales to lure customers, they basically offer bargains, and consumers essentially do the same when they bid up prices through their increased purchases.

You should study Figure 4.4 again and again and master it thoroughly even though it deals with microeconomics, for in the classical world macro is just a giant version of micro. Most of the macro ideas of the classicists use similar graphs, as you will see in pages to come.

11. Summary

(1) Supply and demand together are the foundation stones of economics and represent Adam Smith's idea of an invisible hand guiding the markets.

(2) Other things remaining the same, you buy more of product as its price declines, and conversely. This is "the law of demand."

(3) Other things remaining, the same producers produce more of a product as its price rises, and conversely. This is "the law of supply."

(4) Market equilibrium occurs when demand equals supply, and both the buyers and sellers are satisfied with the prevailing price and quantity exchanged.

(5) The equilibrium is stable whenever a rise in price causes excess supply in the market, and a fall in price causes an excess demand. In both cases, the market price tends to come back to the equilibrium price.

(6) When variables listed on the two axes change simultaneously, then we move along the same curve. When only one of them changes owing to some other influence not listed along the axes, then the relevant curve shifts up or down.

(7) Shifts in one or both curves change the equilibrium price and quantity exchanged.

Chapter 5

The Classical Macro Model

Until now what you have studied is the classical version of microeconomics. The classical economists started out with a consumer's demand curve and a producer's supply curve. They then moved on to market demand and supply, and to the notion of equilibrium as explained in the previous chapter in Figure 4.4. From this they made a giant leap and argued that market demand and supply were just a miniature version of national demand and supply.

Thus, classical macroeconomics is simply a magnified version of classical microeconomics, even though the nation consists of millions of people of diverse minds, tastes, incomes and lifestyles.

Classical macro concepts were actually quite simple and that virtue made them extremely popular. In order to simplify their theories, macroeconomists commonly assume that depreciation and indirect taxes are each equal to zero, so that GDP equals domestic income, which in turn becomes national income if net factor payments from abroad are also zero. These are just simplifying assumptions, and not crucial to the questions under discussion. They imply that GDP equals national income. From now on, unless mentioned otherwise, GDP and national income will be regarded as the same.

1. National Demand

To begin with, what is demand at the national level? If you want to avoid the trap of adding apples to bananas, you have to find a denominator common to all purchases of final goods in a country. (Final goods were explained in Chapter 3.) Millions of cars and tons of food are bought in the United States every year. How do you add the number of car sales to tons of food sales? For this you have to find a common denominator. Is there one?

Yes, indeed. It is called spending or expenditure, involving a certain currency, checks and credit cards. National demand can be defined by the sum total of spending on all final goods newly produced in a country at a moment of time, say, a year. But spending involves both price and quantity, and if you just seek national demand, then spending has to be defined in real terms. Nominal spending has to be freed from the effects of changes in product prices to obtain real spending. As first explained in Chapter 3, this can be done by deflating nominal spending by the price level or the GDP deflator. *Thus, "national demand" is the purchasing power of total nominal spending in a nation.*

Some economists define an imaginary unit and call it an index of domestic demand that represents the demand for all newly produced final goods. They depict national demand in this way. Both concepts, the spending variety and an indexed variety, lead to the same outcome, but the spending concept is preferable, because it is used in the formulation of economic policy.

National demand comes from consumers, businesses and the government operating in a country. It equals aggregate expenditure and is given by the following:

$$\text{aggregate expenditure} = C + I + G$$

where C is real consumer spending, I is gross investment, or "desired, intended or planned" level of real investment spending, and G is real government spending. Thus, the concept of gross investment introduced here differs from that in Chapter 3, where investment also included any unwanted spending on unsold goods. Companies normally buy new capital goods to replace worn out machines or for business expansion. This type of spending is useful to them, but they have little use for any spending on unsold goods. *Therefore, unwanted inventories cannot be a part of desired investment.*

2. Aggregate Demand and Supply

National spending, however, may differ from total demand, because foreigners also spend money on home goods and generate American exports (X), whereas Americans spend money on foreign goods and create imports (M). The difference between the two is called net exports (NX) or the trade balance, which can be positive, negative or zero. Thus,

$$NX = X - M$$

When we add the trade balance to national demand, we obtain, what is often called "aggregate demand" (AD). Thus,

$$AD = C + I + G + X - M$$

National supply can also be defined in terms of a common denominator. The revenue earned by each firm producing final goods can be added to obtain the nominal aggregate revenue, which can be freed from the effect of product price changes through the use of the GDP deflator, to define real aggregate revenue. This real revenue gives us the concept of national supply. Thus, aggregate demand is the purchasing power of all spending on newly produced final goods, and "national supply" is the purchasing power of all revenue earned by firms producing final goods. The symbol commonly used for this supply is Y. Thus, in macro equilibrium, aggregate demand equals national or "aggregate supply" (AS) as follows:

$$AD = AS$$

or

$$Y = AS = AD = C + I + G + X - M$$

With GDP equaling national income, all output ends up as someone's income, so that Y also equals real income. People use their incomes for consumption, paying personal taxes (T) or savings (S), i.e.,

$$Y = C + S + T$$

which in view of the aforementioned context implies that

$$C + S + T = C + I + G + X - M$$

or

$$S + T + M = I + G + X$$

Here taxes are net of any transfers that households receive from the government, and S includes savings by households and corporations. This last equation tells us that in macro equilibrium, defined by the equality of AD and AS, "leakages equal injections." This is because savings, taxes and imports are all deductions or leakages of spending from the economy, whereas desired investment, government spending and exports are injections into the spending stream. Thus, *in macroeconomic equilibrium, when* AD *equals* AS, *injections match leakages.*

Matters can be simplified further, if we assume that for the time being the government budget and trade are in balance, so that $X = M$, and $G = T$.

This is the case of a balanced economy, which we assume for the time being. Here

$$AD = AS \text{ and } S = I$$

2.1. *Equilibrium GDP and Actual GDP*

What is determined when this balanced economy is in equilibrium? The real GDP, which is the same thing as output. In the case of macro disequilibrium, AD and AS are different from each other and so are S and I. More specifically, if savings exceed investment, then AD must fall short of AS, because then more funds are withdrawn than are injected into the system. In fact, we can even write that as follows:

$$AD - AS = I - S < 0, \text{ if } S > I$$

Thus, when savings exceed investment, aggregate demand falls short of aggregate supply. An interesting question may be raised at this point. What is the link between equilibrium GDP and the actual GDP that was defined and explored in Chapter 3? There you discovered that actual GDP was estimated in three ways, and that investment spending included unintended inventories as well. In equilibrium, AD = AS, so that there are no unexpected or "unintended inventories." In other words, in equilibrium, unsold goods do not pile up on the shelves of stores and malls.

Chapter 3 provides the estimate of actual GDP, which becomes the one prevailing in equilibrium, when there are no unexpected changes in inventory investment. When AD falls short of AS, inventories increase unexpectedly. Conversely, when AD exceeds AS, inventories fall by the unexpected surge in sales. Either way, the actual GDP is not at equilibrium, and the economy is not at rest. Whether or not it eventually comes to rest, or how long it takes to return to any equilibrium is a matter examined by a variety of macroeconomic theories.

3. Say's Law

The aforementioned concepts form the foundation of any macroeconomic theory, including the classical framework that you are about to explore. The classical model began with what is known as Say's law, named after Jean Baptiste Say, a French economist. Let us see what Monsieur Say had to say. Not much, because his theory had very few words, namely, "supply creates its own demand." It sounds like a slogan, and, in view of the stranglehold it had on the economist's mind later, it really became a slogan. Here supply means aggregate supply and demand means aggregate demand.

Mr. Say began with a barter framework, where goods are exchanged for goods not money, and argued that supply creates its own demand so that there is never any possibility of excess supply or overproduction. His logic was that people produce goods either for their own use or to exchange their production with goods produced by others. The very act of production creates demand for goods made by others. Thus, all supply generates its own demand, and overproduction of goods and services wherein AD is insufficient to absorb AS is impossible.

4. Savings, Investment and Overproduction

In a barter framework, Say's logic is impeccable. No one, after all, produces goods just for the sake of it, except to meet one's own needs or to exchange goods produced by others. Trouble may arise when goods are sold primarily for money, and some money gets parked into checking and savings accounts, because funds saved are funds not spent, so that there may be a shortage of AD and hence the potential of "oversupply." However, even in the realistic case of a monetary economy, it was shown in Section 2 that so long as investment matches savings there are no problems of "overproduction," or of unsold goods piling up on store shelves, because then AD equals AS.

Why is overproduction considered worrisome? When unsold products accumulate in malls, profits fall and businesses have to lay off workers, creating the problem of what is called "cyclical unemployment." If you or your parents own a company that is unable to sell all it produces, employees have to be fired, creating a mega headache for the macro economy. That is why the question of overproduction is at the center of many macro models.

So long as business investment, exclusive of unwanted inventory spending, matches savings, there is no possibility of overproduction or, what may be called, general excess supply. For instance, suppose initially companies use their own funds to produce goods worth $100. In the production process, they have used these funds to pay their rent, interest expense on any debt incurred in the past, and employee wages. Whatever remains is their profit income. Their production effort has thus generated an AS of $100 as well as incomes of $100.

Suppose further there is no foreign trade and government so that households and businesses are the only sources of aggregate demand and supply. This is done to make a point and avoid unnecessary complications. Out of the $100 of income generated by the firms, if 90 is spent on consumption goods, then the other 10 is saved and deposited in commercial banks. After all, people do save a bit for a variety of reasons. If businesses borrow the entire savings and use it to purchase investment goods, then AD also equals $100. Thus, in this case,

$$AS = \$100$$

and

$$AD = C + I = \$100$$

as well, so that the economy is in equilibrium, there is no overproduction, and no pile up of unwanted inventories. However, suppose companies borrow only $7 from banks for business expansion, in which case AD will be only $97 and there will be overproduction or unwanted inventories worth $3. Here the national product market is in disequilibrium, and

$$AS - AD = 100 - 97 = \$3$$

and

$$S - I = 10 - 7 = \$3$$

5. The Rate of Interest

Consider Figure 5.1, where the vertical axis displays the real rate of interest, and the horizontal axis, the real value of "loanable" funds. What then is the real rate of interest? The actual rate at which money is loaned out is called the "nominal rate of interest," which enhances the value of a lender's money. However, the purchasing power of the lender's loan shrinks by the rate of inflation. Therefore, the net or real interest income on a dollar loaned out is given by the real rate of interest, i.e.,

real rate of interest = nominal rate of interest − the rate of inflation

As with any transaction, the borrower actually pays and the lender receives the nominal rate, but they both may be inwardly concerned about the real rate. If you lend out $100 at the rate of 10 percent for a year, and the annual rate of inflation is 4 percent, then your nominal interest income at the end of the year is $10, but your real interest income is only $6, because inflation has lowered the purchasing power of your $100 loan by $4. Hence, the nominal rate of interest is 10 percent, whereas the real rate that you receive is 6 percent.

Let us now go back to classical thought. The classicists argued that the real rate of interest exerts a powerful influence on the spending behavior of consumers and companies. Specifically, since firms seek the lowest production cost to maximize their profits, they invest more at a lower interest fee and less at a higher interest fee. Consumers, by contrast, do

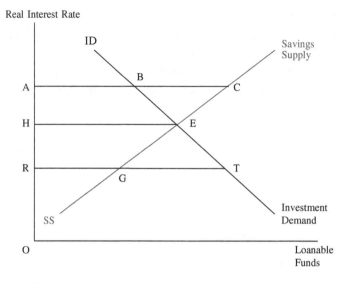

Figure 5.1:   The Classical Theory of the Interest Rate

the opposite. They save more to earn a higher interest rate, and less when the interest rate goes down.

Graphically, as in Figure 5.1, the relationship between investment and the real rate of interest looks like a consumer demand curve, ID, and the one between savings and the interest rate looks like a market supply curve, SS. If the interest rate is at point H, the loan market is in equilibrium at E, because then savings match investment, both equaling HE.

Only at a higher interest rate such as OA are savings in excess of investment, by the amount BC. Here the banks are able to lend only the amount AB, and have unused funds equaling BC. This induces them to lower their interest rate. Consequently, investment rises and savings sink until the two are equal at point E.

On the other hand, if the rate of interest happens to be at OR, there is a shortage of savings and an excess demand for loanable funds. Banks here lend only RG but the firms seek to borrow RT. This enables the banks to increase their interest fee, leading to a fall in investment and a rise in savings until the two are equal again at point E.

This is how classical economists argued that the interest rate variation in the market for loanable funds brings about an equality between savings and investment and corrects any disequilibrium in the product market. But this process requires time. Disequilibrium is indeed possible in the short run but not in the long run. Thus, now Say's law becomes *supply creates its own demand in the long run.*

Some economists subtract the "expected rate of inflation" from the nominal rate of interest to define the real rate in the belief that the lender is concerned with the inflation rate that prevails in the future. If you lend out $100 for 10 years then you are likely to be concerned about what inflation will be over the next 10 years, and not about what it is today. Nevertheless, the recent rate of inflation has a powerful influence on people's thinking about future inflation. Under most circumstances the two concepts come close to each other. Therefore, we will use the real rate concept that incorporates the actual rate of inflation.

6. The Theory of Employment

According to classical economists, *there is an automatic mechanism that ensures the full employment of labor in the national job market.* This mechanism has two pillars, of which one was just examined earlier, namely, the interest rate variations eliminate general overproduction, which is also the excess supply of goods as well the excess supply of loanable funds. In fact, to classicists, the excess supply or the excess demand for anything automatically disappears in the long run, because prices are flexible, both up and down. Goods and services bought and sold may differ from market to market, and fetch a variety of prices, but the demand–supply analysis is essentially the same.

In the job market, the price is the real wage, which is linked to labor demand coming from firms and to labor supply coming from households. Thus, demand and supply notions of Figure 4.4 in Chapter 4 come into play once again, except now the axes represent different items. Full employment occurs when labor demand is enough to absorb the labor supply at the prevailing real wage. Unemployment is impossible in the long run, because the real wage moves down to eliminate any joblessness, which equals the excess supply of labor. *The interest rate flexibility ensures that whatever is produced by the fully employed labor is sold out in the goods market.*

Let us go to Figure 5.2, which explores the national job market. Here LD is the negatively sloped labor demand curve, suggesting that employers hire more workers as the real wage falls, and fire workers as the real wage goes up. By contrast, LS is the positively sloped labor supply curve, implying that a higher real wage induces a higher offering of labor from households. Either those employed work harder or more people join the labor force in response to the higher pay.

You may recall that the real wage, displayed along the vertical axis in Figure 5.2, is the purchasing power of the nominal or the money wage. If the real wage is at point H, both labor demand and supply equal HE or OQ, the job market is in equilibrium, and the economy enjoys full employment. However, at a higher real wage such as OA there is excess supply of labor or unemployment equaling BC, because then labor demand is only AB but labor supply is AC. If the real wage remains stuck at OA, then unemployment will persist for a long time.

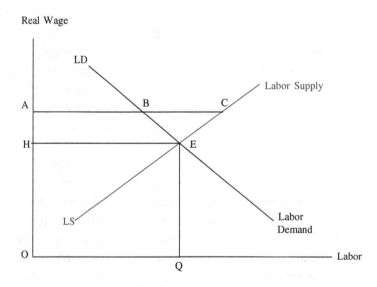

Figure 5.2:   The Classical Theory of Employment

This could happen, for instance, if labor unions are strong and they force a higher wage on employers; or if the government legislates a minimum wage, which cannot be lowered in spite of unemployment. *There are thus only two reasons for unemployment in the classical world — unions or a minimum wage legislation.*

However, if the real wage is flexible, i.e., it is free to move up or down in response to market pressures, then the joblessness is only temporary. Rather than remain without work and thus starve, unemployed workers accept a lower salary, which in turn brings the real wage down. This induces businesses to increase their hiring, while some workers drop out of the labor force. This way labor demand increases and labor supply falls, until the real wage sinks enough that employers are able to hire all those willing to work at the prevailing wage. In other words, the money wage drops until the real wage falls to point H, generating equilibrium and full employment again. *Thus, in the classical analysis equilibrium and full employment coexist. One cannot occur without the other.*

How long does it take for unemployment, if any, to disappear? In other words, how short is the short run in which unemployment can exist? It was the general understanding among classical economists that any joblessness would vanish within one or two years. *Thus, real wage flexibility and interest rate flexibility are the two pillars that automatically eliminate unemployment in the classical framework.* Interest rate variability also matters; otherwise, as shown just previously, there could be general overproduction and pileup of unsold goods, forcing layoffs and hence persistent unemployment.

6.1. *An Overview*

Let us summarize the classical ideas explored thus far. In the realm of microeconomics, product prices vary to erase excess demand or excess supply in any industry, until demand and supply are equal, and equilibrium returns. Similarly, in the realm of macroeconomics, the flexibility of prices ensures the equality of demand and supply in national markets. In the product market, price is essentially the rate of interest that varies to equate savings and investment or aggregate supply with aggregate demand. In the labor market, price is the real wage that moves to generate

full employment, which coexists with equilibrium. The classical economists assume that all prices are flexible, at least in the long run, so that
persistent unemployment is impossible in their world.

7. The Quantity Theory of Money

GDP, employment, the real wage and the rate of interest are the fundamental concepts of macroeconomics. You have seen how the real values of
these variables are determined in the classical model. But none of us deals
directly with real values; our dealings are with nominal or current-dollar
values. Your earnings in terms of rent, wages, interest or profits are all in
nominal terms, but subconsciously you are making calculations in real
terms, especially in the modern world, where average prices rise every year.

How do we move from real to nominal values in the classical framework? We do this with the help of a theory that determines the price level,
because the real values are simply nominal values deflated by a price
index. The price level (P) may be defined as

$$P = \frac{\text{GDP deflator}}{100}$$

The classical economists also offered a theory that determines the
price level in the economy. It is known as the quantity theory of money,
presented as follows:

$$MV = PY$$

Here P is the price level, Y the aggregate supply, M the supply of
money, and V, the income velocity of money. The concept of velocity
needs some explanation. It is the number of times a unit of money such
as a dollar bill changes hands. It is the turnover rate of money. For
instance, suppose you make a purchase with a $10 bill; that note moves
from you to a seller, who in turn uses that note to buy something else,
and so on. This way the total number of times a dollar bill is used in
transactions during a year is the velocity of that one bill. The velocity of
money is thus the number of times money changes hands in the course
of transactions.

In the quantity theory of money, *Y* is real GDP, not transactions. The implicit assumption here is that transactions are proportional to real national income, for the greater your income, the larger your number of purchases. The quantity theory of money is actually a tautology, because it is valid by the way its components have been defined. *PY* may be called the nominal value of transactions, which by definition equal the amount of money in the economy times its velocity.

You may note that *PY* is also nominal GDP that equals total spending; so *MV* equals aggregate spending, which requires the use of money. Each time a dollar bill is used, it adds to spending. Thus, the quantity theory depends on a truism or identity, which is valid at all times.

In the classical framework, *Y* or output becomes constant at the point of full employment. Let $A = Y/L$ be the average product of labor (*L*). Then

$$Y = AL$$

Since unemployment is temporary, the economy tends to return to the same level of employment (*L*). Therefore, *L* is constant at full employment. In terms of technology, the average product of labor, as we shall see in Chapter 6, is linked to the employment level as well. If *L* is constant, so is *A*. Therefore, *Y* is constant.

Similarly, *V*, the velocity of money, depends upon people's transacting behavior, which does not change easily, so that this is also invariant. Then it follows from the quantity equation, that *P* is determined solely by *M*; in other words, *the price level is strictly proportional to the supply of money.*

With *V* and *Y* unchanging, a rise in money supply must raise the price level in the same proportion, and *vice versa. Thus, money is purely a veil that has no impact on real variables.* If the supply of money falls, nothing else will fall except the price level. National output, employment and real values of investment, consumption, savings and the wage rate will be unaltered.

Money is then neutral in its impact on the real side of the economy. For as you saw in Figures 5.1 and 5.2, none of the curves shifts in response to price variations. Equilibrium values change only if one or all of those curves shift up or down. However, prices by themselves have no such impact. They do not influence investment, savings, labor demand and labor supply. Therefore, they have no influence on the equilibrium values of real variables.

The quantity equation aside, what is the process through which a monetary expansion translates into price escalation? Suppose the government prints extra money to finance its purchases. It then adds to aggregate demand. Since aggregate supply is constant under full employment, increased demand must contribute to higher prices, until the price level increases enough to bring the real value of spending down to the level of unchanged output. Hence, P must rise in proportion to the rise in government spending caused by the additional printing of money.

8. Full Employment

In theory, full employment occurs when labor demand absorbs all of labor supply at the prevailing real wage. Does it mean that all those seeking work must be always employed to reach the desirable goal of full employment? The answer is no, because there is always some amount of joblessness, no matter how strong the economy. Some people, for instance, work in areas that operate only a part of the year. Farming offers little work during harsh winter times, when snowdrifts or low temperatures make agricultural production impossible or uneconomical. Farm laborers are then without jobs, and suffer "seasonal unemployment," about which nothing can be done.

Professional athletes, who normally earn millions, are unemployed when their playing season is over. They may be without work but usually do not seek employment when out of season. All this suggests that just because someone may be without a job at any moment does not mean that they are unemployed. In fact, in economics lingo they are not even a part of the "labor force," *which is defined as those 16 or over and seeking a job.*

There are thus two requirements for you to be included in the labor force. You must be at least 16 and be looking for a job. Except for children, those employed, even if part time, are definitely a part of the labor force. But if you are without work, then you are included in the labor force only if you actively look for work.

Thus, the labor force excludes all students and retirees. It even excludes "discouraged workers" who at one time may have looked and looked for work but did not find any, and then stopped searching. They were part of labor supply when they actively sought a job but dropped out of the definition when they got tired of looking.

There are also those who are sometimes in between jobs. Students, just after graduating, may not find the right kind of work for a while. They may get job offers they do not like. They are then voluntarily unemployed and are part of what is called "frictional unemployment." Some people quit their jobs to find another line of work, or they take some time off before joining their new place of work. This type of joblessness is temporary and by choice, and also constitutes frictional unemployment.

However, there is a type of involuntary joblessness that may exist even in a strong economy. Owing to rapid technological change or to international trade, some skills become outdated. There are plenty of job vacancies but not for those with obsolete skills. Such people constitute what is known as "structural unemployment."

Computers were not in general use until the 1980s. Therefore, at that time those typists who could not use a computer or a word processor found themselves without work; they were structurally unemployed. There was a time, as in the 1950s and the 1960s, when TVs and VCRs were produced in the United States, but not anymore. Many workers so laid off could not find work in the 1970s and the 1980s; they were then structurally unemployed. Even when they found some low-paid work they were unable to use their old skills. They then became "underemployed."

Some people drop out of the labor force because they do not like their low salary; they may have enough savings or alternative means of support from relatives. They may have worked sometime at a higher pay but then quit when their salaries fell. Such people constitute "voluntary unemployment." Some housewives or homemakers may be voluntarily unemployed.

8.1. *Natural Unemployment*

The types of unemployment examined so far may be said to be normal or natural to any economy. Jobless persons comprising these categories may be regarded as "naturally" unemployed, because their existence does not imply a weak economy with insufficient vacancies.

As long as newspapers and some Internet websites advertise job offers that roughly match the number of job seekers, there is only natural unemployment, because evidently jobs are there but there is a mismatch of job seekers and vacancies. Jobs may be available in California, but the unemployed may be in New York, and so on.

There is one type of unemployment that is not natural. When the economy is so weak that it lacks enough vacancies to absorb all those seeking jobs at the prevailing wage rate, there is what is known as "cyclical unemployment." This type of joblessness is not by choice; it is involuntary and occurs because of falling aggregate demand. Goods pile up on store shelves, leaving firms little choice but to lay off some employees.

The rate of unemployment is defined as

$$\frac{\text{(the number of the unemployed)}}{\text{labor force}} \times 100$$

The unemployment rate, like inflation, is a percentage concept. It is the jobless fraction of the labor force multiplied by 100. Each month the department of labor sends out a survey to a sample of households, asks them questions about their job status and estimates the rate of unemployment. The survey, of course, does not include the various definitions of joblessness to avoid confusion. The estimated rate of unemployment also includes the job seekers that may be a part of just natural unemployment. Thus, in order to see whether the economy is not at full employment, the "natural rate of unemployment" should be subtracted from the official rate.

The natural rate may be comprehended in a number of ways. Some equate it to the economy's long-run rate of joblessness, where short-run fluctuations have worked themselves out. Others suggest that it is the rate at which inflation exceeds 3 percent and becomes a headache. Still others think it is the rate at which vacancies barely match the number of job hunters. Regardless of the definition, the natural rate of unemployment in the United States is understood to be in the range of 4 percent to 6 percent. We will set it at 5 percent.

The concept of full employment now becomes comprehensible. *The economy is at full employment if the officially estimated rate of unemployment is no larger than the natural rate, and there is no cyclical unemployment.* Normally, when joblessness is below the natural rate, there is no cyclical unemployment. But not always.

When president-elect George W. Bush was sworn into office in January 2001, the official rate of unemployment was just 4 percent. It rose over the next two years, because the demand for high-tech products fell sharply. Firms could not sell enough computers, cell phones, high definition TVs and so on. Cyclical unemployment thus appeared even though the official rate generally stayed below 6 percent. Looking at just the natural rate, some might say the economy still enjoyed full employment, but that did not capture the gloom of the public, which felt discouraged because hundreds and thousands of fired workers could not find work due to insufficient labor demand in some industries. In fact, in 2001 and 2002, nearly two million jobs disappeared. Another half a million vanished by May 2003, yet the jobless rate did not cross 6 percent.

When classical economists argued that unemployment is impossible in the long run, they referred to the cyclical component of total joblessness. Recall that the cyclical component arises from the lack of demand, which is ruled out by Say's law or the classical theory of the interest rate.

9. All Unemployment is Voluntary

As you have just seen, some types of joblessness are by choice. Frictional and even seasonal unemployment could be regarded as voluntary. But *classical economists insist that all unemployment is voluntary.* This is one of the most contentious theories, as you can well imagine. There is no such thing as involuntary or forced unemployment in the classical vocabulary.

The classical logic here is that everyone seeking work can find someone willing to hire them at a sufficiently small wage. What will a person not do when facing the desperation of starvation? In the extreme case, everyone must work or else perish. Thus, joblessness results from personal choice and not from a deficient system. To the classical faithful this argument may be harsh, but it is sound and reasonable, and we will explore it further in the next chapter.

10. Economic Policy

The classical model is quite simple and that may explain its longevity and popularity despite numerous challenges from alternative theories. Everything in the classical world is flexible, heals itself and requires no government intervention. The model preaches that *the government should keep its hands off the economy; in fact, the government intervention only makes matters worse.* The classical model, though simple and somewhat naïve, offers a variety of far-reaching prescriptions:

(1) no minimum wage,
(2) no or weak labor unions,
(3) no monetary policy,
(4) no government budget deficit,
(5) low taxation and hence low government spending.

Collectively, these policies are known as *laissez faire*. You have already seen that in the classical world full employment is the normal state of affairs; unemployment can persist only if the government legislates a minimum wage or if unions are strong enough to impose a real wage above the equilibrium wage. The classicists admit no business cycle; recessions and depressions are short-lived phenomena that heal themselves. State efforts to stimulate the economy through an expansion of money supply will only generate inflation in the end.

Government budget deficits are irresponsible, because a large government creates a large bureaucracy and productive inefficiency. Furthermore, Big Government intrudes upon people's rights in the pursuit of happiness and profit. The government should behave like a prudent household and spend no more than it earns through its tax revenues. Thus, *government budgets should be balanced year after year.*

Taxes should be kept low, because high taxes lead to big government, waste and bureaucratic inefficiency, and are not consistent with the spirit of private property and individualism. Thus, classical thought offers a wide variety of prescriptions that guided governments, especially U.S. presidents, in the 19th and 20th centuries.

11. The Economy in the 19th Century

Classical thought began to rule economic policy soon after the appearance of *The Wealth of Nations*, especially in the United States, where the classical ideal of small government appealed to the individualistic spirit of the freedom fighters. Many assumptions of the theory were satisfied with the advent of manufacturing in the new republic. The country had started out as an agrarian stronghold, but after the passage of the Tariff Act of 1816 that protected industries, it embarked upon rapid industrialization.

As start-up firms, American companies were small but numerous. They easily fit into the classical assumption of keen or perfect competition. Workers had few rights, and their wages were set by the pressures of labor demand and supply. Prices were also flexible, up and down. Thus, classical assumptions were realistic.

The classical framework has been denounced time and again, especially after the 1930s. Many have chided it for its faulty assumptions, but at least in the early part of 19th century America, classical requirements were more than met by industries. How did the model perform in its ideal setting? Miserably.

Oscar Wilde, the celebrated playwright, once said, "The well-bred contradict other people. The wise contradict themselves." You will now discover that the classical economists were extremely wise. In the classical world recessions and joblessness, if they ever come about, are short lived, lasting no more than one or two years. Of course, depressions, where business activity and employment remain depressed for a long time, say three years or more, are simply out of the question. Yet even a cursory look at 19th century America reveals something else.

There were two recessions during the 1820s, and one around 1835, which was followed by a seven-year-long depression of the 1840s. The 1850s saw only one recession, as did the 1860s, but the 1870s suffered another seven-year depression. While the 1880s experienced a deep recession, the 1890s suffered a deep depression. Thus, even though for much of the 19th century, classical assumptions were aptly fulfilled by the U.S.

economy, there were long periods of falling output and rising unemployment. Evidently, *there was something amiss with the classical logic, not with its assumptions.*

12. The Illogic of the Classical Model

Let us reexamine the classical logic, as set forth in Figure 5.1, which is reproduced in this section as Figure 5.3. The figure deals with the market for loanable funds, where loan demand comes from business investment and loan supply from households, who deposit their savings with commercial banks. The real rate of interest is the price in this market. The classical argument is a straightforward extension of the microeconomic formula of supply and demand, where the product price varies to equate them. In the market for loanable funds, for instance, the real rate of interest is the price that equates the investment demand for loans with the household supply of loans.

The equilibrium price is no fluke. Even if the price deviates from its equilibrium, it quickly reverts to this level, because of the self-interest of buyers and suppliers. As you saw in Figure 4.4 in the previous chapter, at any price above the equilibrium level excess supply appears in the market. In their self-interest, sellers announce a sale and reduce their prices, inducing buyers to increase their purchases while producers cut their output, until excess supply vanishes, and equilibrium returns.

In the opposite case, where the price is below equilibrium, there is excess demand, which forces buyers to bid up the price while firms raise their production, until the excess disappears. Thus, the product market is stable, and the price is either in equilibrium at E, or always has a tendency to return to that point.

Does this microeconomic logic of supply and demand apply to the national market for loanable funds? Classical economists say yes. Their argument goes something like this. At the equilibrium interest rate OH in Figure 5.3, the loan demand, or desired investment, equals loan supply, or savings. At a higher interest rate such as at A, there is excess supply of loanable funds, so that commercial banks lower the rate of interest to attract new customers for their loans. As the interest rate falls, savings go down, but investment expands until the two are equal again.

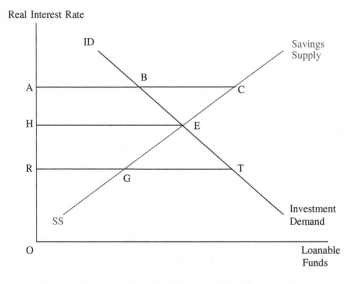

Figure 5.3:   The Classical Theory of the Interest Rate

If the interest rate is too low, as at R, there is excess demand for loanable funds. This enables the banks to raise the rate to the point that the excess demand vanishes, and *S* equals *I* once again.

However, the entire argument is flawed. Unlike micro supply and demand, the demand–supply concepts at the macro level are not independent of each other, and that renders the model unstable. First of all, do bankers face excess supply of loanable funds at the interest rate at A? The investment demand curve given by the ID-line represents planned or desired investment, and when desired investment equals savings, which is the case in equilibrium at E, unintended inventory investment equals zero. At point A, savings exceed desired investment by BC, which also happens to be the excess supply in the goods market, for, as you discovered in Section 4,

$$S - I = AS - AD = \text{unintended inventory investment}$$

In equilibrium, *S* and *I* are the same, and unintended inventory investment becomes zero. This is why, as Professor Robert Barro, one of the chief architects of classical economics today, points out, "the commodity market clears" at the equilibrium interest rate.[1]

---

[1] Robert Barro, *Macroeconomics*, 5th edition, Cambridge, Mass.: MIT Press, 2000, p. 333.

In equilibrium, when the interest rate is at H, both loan demand (or desired investment) and savings equal HE, and at the higher interest rate at A, savings exceed desired investment by CB, which also equals the excess supply in the goods market as well as unintended inventory investment. The loan demand then is not BA, but AC, of which AB is for desired investment and CB is for unintended or undesired inventory investment. The banks have no excess supply of loanable funds at the higher interest rate, so there is no reason for them to bring the rate down.

This is not like a fire sale that occurs at the micro level where, sellers, stuck with unsold goods, have to lower prices to clear their excess inventory. The micro logic does not apply to the interest rate, because macro demand and supply concepts are not independent of each other.

Let us continue with the numerical example first set forth in Section 4. Recall that the interest rate is such that in equilibrium,

$$AS = \$100$$
$$C = 90$$
$$S = I = 10$$

so that

$$AD = C + I = AS = 100$$

Now suppose the interest rate is too high, so that

$$S = 15, C = 85 \text{ and } I = 9$$

$$S - I = AS - AD = 100 - 94 = \$6$$
$$= \text{unintended inventory investment}$$

According to classical logic, loan demand is now $9 but loan supply is $15, and the banks, facing an excess supply of funds, are motivated to lower the rate of interest, inducing a decrease in savings or loan supply and a rise in investment or loan demand, until savings equal investment and AD equals AS again. However, loan demand is not just $9 at the higher interest rate but $15 that also includes unintended inventory investment of $6. Someone has to finance this accumulation of unsold goods, and businesses usually borrow money to finance their inventory spending as well.

13. Investment in a Recession

Clearly the classical logic is faulty, even after you grant their assumptions. However, the flaw in the classical argument does not end here. There is plenty more. Contrary to the textbook logic of the classical model, let us grant that the interest rate does fall when savings exceed desired investment, or AD falls short of AS. This is a state of recession, and interest rates do eventually come down in this situation. Firms trim production, unsold goods are gradually cleared away, so that inventory investment drops; consumer borrowing also falls for the purchase of durable goods. All this generates a fall in loan demand relative to loan supply, and the interest rate, after a while, begins to fall.

At this point, classical economists and their acolytes say that desired investment expands. This is also contrary to logic and common sense. First, there is a recession, where business and consumer confidence is low. Second, firms may still be stuck with some unwanted stock of unsold goods, even as the interest rate drops. Why would anyone want to expand their business under these conditions even if the real interest rate visibly comes down?

Reverting to the numerical illustration, suppose the rate of interest drops but unsold inventory is down from $6 to say only $3. Then, according to the classical analysis, desired investment starts to rise. But since unwanted inventories still remain, the recession is not over yet. Why should desired investment then increase? Thus, *the classical model requires that business investment expand in times of excess supply of goods or in a business downturn.* Has that ever happened? Professor Barro himself provides a clear-cut answer in the negative: "Broadly defined private investment accounts for the bulk of the fluctuations in real GDP, 93 percent on average. Thus, as a first approximation, explaining recessions amounts to explaining the sharp contraction in private investment components."[2]

---

[2] *Ibid.*, p. 314.

Barro also points the way to another flaw in the classical logic, wherein savings decline as the real rate of interest falls in a recession, which means that consumer spending rises in a recession to bring about the equality between *S* and *I*. But GDP data reveal that consumer spending behaves inconclusively in a slump. It has fallen in some downturns, risen in others.

Does it mean that desired investment or savings are unresponsive to falling interest rates? No. Ordinarily, with output or unintended inventory constant, savings and investment perhaps would respond quickly to interest rates in ways postulated by the old and modern classical economists. All we are saying is that *I* does not rise or *S* does not necessarily fall during a recession, where *S* exceeds *I*, even if the real interest rate goes down.

On the other side of the equilibrium, the classical model requires desired investment and consumer spending to contract just when business is booming under conditions of excess demand, where *I* exceeds *S*. Again that happens only in classical theory but not in reality. Ordinarily, investment would fall and savings rise in a static economy, as interest rates go up, but not when inventories have sharply fallen and new orders are multiplying.

Plainly speaking, we cannot blindly apply micro methodology to macro ideas, because micro demand and supply curves do not shift in disequilibrium, whereas the macro counterparts do. When *S* > *I* at a higher interest rate, the ID-line would shift to the left because of falling output, the *S*-line could shift to the right in the middle of the gloom, and the economy will not return to old equilibrium, or may not converge to any such point. Even if it does, it could take a long time, before it arrives at any equilibrium at all.

14. Instability in the Classical Model

Such contradictions have strong implications for classical prescriptions. First, all the conclusions reached by classical economists and their adherents are invalid, because their model is explosive and unstable. Please read the rule behind the curve shifts explained in the previous chapter. *When something relevant not mentioned on the two axes changes, then one or both lines shift up or down.*

For instance, consider the effects of an unexpected rise in savings, as in Figure 5.3. As before, E is the point of equilibrium at the interest rate OH. Now suppose consumer confidence sinks for some reason and savings rise, so that the savings-line shifts to the new savings line, NSS. At the old interest rate there is now an excess of savings over desired investment or an excess supply of goods equaling EB, and a recession occurs. At this point, according to the classical logic, the interest rate falls, *I* rises and *S* falls to bring about a new equilibrium at NE.

But since *I* declines in a recession, the investment demand curve moves to the left to NID, and at the old interest rate OH the excess supply expands to AB, which means a further fall in desired investment and another leftward shift of the ID-line, and then a further rise in excess supply. This will go on until investment becomes zero. In other words, once the equilibrium is perturbed, there is no coming back. The classical model thus is explosive: Logic suggests that *an ordinary recession becomes a depression in classical theory, which ironically holds that depressions are nearly impossible.*

All this happens, because the investment demand and savings supply curves are not independent of each other, unlike the case in micro models. Reverting to the numerical example, let us again start with the initial equilibrium as follows:

$$AS = \$100, C = 90$$
$$S = I = 10$$
$$AD = C + I = AS = 100$$

Now suppose savings rise to $15 at the old equilibrium interest rate, while investment stays at $10, generating an excess supply in the goods market of $5, and a recession. Businesses were planning to invest $10, but now that goods are piling up on their shelves, they will cut back their investment plans to say $8. The excess supply then rises to $7, which deepens the recession, which in turn implies another cut back in investment spending, and so on, until business investment falls to zero, and the excess supply balloons to $15. Here then the recession turns into a depression.

An unexpected increase in savings is one cause of recession; another, and in fact more frequent, cause is an unexpected contraction in investment resulting from uncertainty in the business environment. *Either way, the consequences are the same in the classical model, namely, an initial recession must turn into a depression.* In fact, that is what used to happen in the 19th century in the event of a significant expansion of savings relative to investment. Depressions at the time were frequent, and it would take a long time before excess supply of goods vanished and prosperity returned.

15. Standardizing the Graph

Please take a good look at Figure 5.3, which provides a graphical standard for the graphs in chapters to come. Wherever applicable point E will be the initial equilibrium point, with NE the new equilibrium point. A curve shift will be represented by the word "new" or the letter "N." Thus, NID represents the new investment demand line after the shift, and NSS is the new savings line. All this will be done to simplify the arguments.

With any graph, please first focus on the variables listed at the end of the two axes, because each line or curve represents a relationship between these variables. Then examine other relevant influences not explicitly mentioned in the figure, as they determine the shift of a line or curve. The initial equilibrium point E normally occurs at the intersection of the original demand and supply curves, and the new equilibrium point involves the intersection of one or both new lines. Wherever two lines intersect, the variables represented by them become equal at that point. With this standardization, the graphical analysis becomes easier to comprehend, because all that changes from one diagram to another are the variables dealing with various markets and theories.

16. Criticism by Keynes: Faulty Classical Assumptions

The classical model withstood the assault of reality for a long time, but began to crumble in the Great Depression that occurred in the 1930s. This cataclysm was too persistent and miserable for even the most diehard believers in *laissez faire*. Finally, in 1936, fully seven years after the start of the calamity in 1929, John Maynard Keynes published his treatise that denounced the classical tradition in scathing words.

Keynes took exception to various assumptions underlying classical theories. He doubted that savings and investment are very responsive to the interest rate. While investment in his view may indeed be negatively linked to the rate of interest, savings are determined mostly by national income. Even investment's interest sensitivity may be no more than mediocre. In terms of the savings–investment graph, Keynes's representation looks like that in Figure 5.4, where the investment line is drawn to be steep and the savings line is nearly vertical.

Graphically the degree of response between two variables can be displayed by the flatness or the steepness of the line representing them. In terms of Figure 5.4, the greater the flatness, the larger the response, and the greater the steepness, the shallower the response. The investment line in Figure 5.4 is somewhat steep, but the savings line is nearly vertical. This way Keynes demonstrates that the two lines may not intersect at a

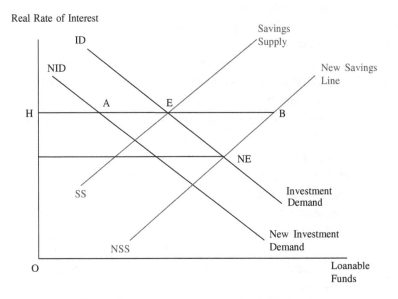

Figure 5.4:   Instability in the Classical Model

positive rate of interest, thus precluding the arrival of equilibrium for a long time. Even if the interest rate is as low as zero, there is excess supply of savings and goods equal to AB. This describes a bad case of overproduction, as during the Great Depression, which could not correct itself even seven years after the start of the depression.

Keynes also chastised the classicists for their analysis of the labor market. He conceded the accuracy of their labor demand curve, but not that of their labor supply curve. *Unemployment in the classical world is eliminated by the fall in the money wage that brings down the real wage.* Keynes contends that this self-corrective process may break down in two ways. First, the money wage may not fall at all or may fall a little because of the resistance of unions or individual workers. Second, even if the money wage falls sufficiently, the real wage may not decrease at all or sufficiently. For

$$\text{real wage} = \frac{\text{money wage}}{\text{price level}}$$

and the fall in the money wage is bound to depress consumer demand, which is already depressed by growing layoffs.

Falling consumer demand in turn lowers the price level. Therefore, a money wage decline does not ensure a decline in the real wage, which could stay constant or even rise, provided the price level decreases greatly as it did during the Great Depression. If the real wage fails to sink sufficiently, the classical self-correcting mechanism ensuring a rapid elimination of unemployment breaks down. In the context of the labor market, Keynes thus criticized the classical assumption that the real wage is flexible. It could take a long time before the real wage decreases enough to cure joblessness (Figure 5.5).

In short, Keynes denounced the classical framework on two counts. First, general overproduction may persist because the rate of interest cannot fall below zero; second the real wage may be rigid enough to preclude a return to full employment.

It may be noted that Keynes himself has not escaped criticism from the pupils of classical thought. Modern classical economists, using econometric models, contend that classical assumptions are indeed valid, at least in the long run. But you have already seen that even if these assumptions are fully granted, the classical logic is faulty, and general

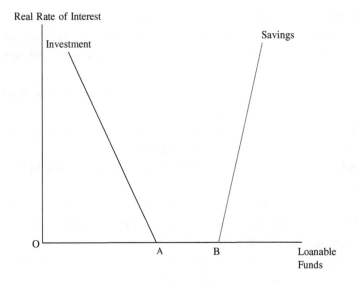

Figure 5.5:   Keynes's Critique of Classical Theory

overproduction and unemployment cannot be ruled out. "The classical model simply flaunts common sense." As Keynes used to say, in the long run we are all dead.

17. Summary

(1) Macro equilibrium occurs when aggregate demand equals aggregate supply, or when leakages equal injections. In the simplest model with balanced government budget and foreign trade, this happens when savings equal investment.

(2) The classical macro model operates in the same way as its micro counterpart. Specifically, the excess supply of anything vanishes with a fall in its price, whereas its excess demand disappears because of a rise in its price.

(3) Supply equals its own demand because a flexible interest rate brings about the equality of savings and investment.

(4) There is an automatic mechanism that ensures the full employment of labor. This mechanism is the flexibility of the interest rate and the real wage.

(5) Full employment occurs when the jobless rate equals the natural rate of unemployment, which in the United States is about 5 percent. The natural rate includes frictional, seasonal, voluntary and structural unemployment.

(6) All unemployment is voluntary, because a desperate worker can find some job at a sufficiently low salary.

(7) Unemployment arises only because of the minimum wage or union militancy that prevents a wage decline.

(8) Recessions are unlikely and depressions are impossible in the classical framework.

(9) Money has no effect on real variables. Thus, a rise or fall in the supply of money changes the price level in the same proportion without altering any real variable.

(10) Classical policy calls for *laissez faire* or the complete absence of government intervention in the economy.

(11) The classical model is illogical for two reasons. First, it requires the banks to lower the rate of interest even when they have no excess funds to lend. Second, it requires investment and consumption to rise in the middle of recessions and depressions, and that rarely, if ever, happens.

(12) Keynes denounced the classical model on two counts. First, savings may exceed investment even at a zero rate of interest, thereby generating overproduction. Second, the real wage may not fall in the presence of unemployment, thus keeping joblessness high for a long time.

Chapter 6

The Neoclassical Model

Despite its various flaws the classical thought reigned supreme for more than a century. It met a powerful challenge from Keynes during the 1930s and disappeared almost to the point of oblivion. But Keynes himself, and later his disciples, had committed some analytical errors that diluted the Keynesian revolution and enabled his critics to make a powerful comeback of their own.

But while their denunciation of Keynesian economics had some force, they did not offer a policy alternative. They simply returned to the classical policy of *laissez faire* with minor modifications. That is why the critics of Keynesian thought may be placed in the same group and called neoclassical economists. They have been exerting a strong influence on official policy since 1981, when Mr. Ronald Reagan became President. One way or another, they have offered the old classical wine in a new bottle.

The term "neoclassical" is occasionally used to include some pre-Keynesian writings, which reexamine classical theories in terms of highly abstract and mathematical models. Thus, neoclassical economics is a broad subject that pre-dates even Keynes's assault on the classicists.

1. What Is New in the Neoclassical Model?

The neoclassical framework raises some of the old questions in terms of a highly technical apparatus, especially in the realm of microeconomics. For instance, what is behind the labor demand and supply curves? Why does the labor demand curve have a negative slope and the labor supply curve a positive slope? The answers lie in the behavior of producers and consumers. Producers, facing keen or perfect competition and seeking to maximize their profits, engage in a cost–benefit analysis. They compare the benefits of hiring a worker with the related cost.

The cost of labor is simply the money wage (W), and the benefit is the value of output produced by a new worker. The output of the new worker is called the "marginal product of labor" (MPL), which is sold at a certain price (P). Thus, the benefit from the new worker is price times the worker's contribution, or $P \cdot \text{MPL}$.

Each firm goes through the following type of self-analysis in the course of its hiring or firing of a new employee. If

$W < P \cdot \text{MPL}$, cost < benefit, and the decision is to hire;

$W > P \cdot \text{MPL}$, cost > benefit, and the decision is to fire;

$W = P \cdot \text{MPL}$, cost = benefit, and the decision is to stop

The point where the firm stops is the point of equilibrium in its hiring, where its objective of profit maximization is achieved. Until then the firm makes its adjustments but stopping itself means that its goal has been satisfied. Thus, in its hiring equilibrium

$$W = P \times \text{MPL}$$

or

$$\text{MPL} = \frac{W}{P}$$

Assuming that all firms are alike, this condition is fulfilled at the national level as well, and P becomes the price level. W/P then defines the real wage. Thus, in the hiring equilibrium at the national level, the real wage equals the MPL.

The MPL follows an interesting property. The two important factors of production for a firm are capital and labor. In the short to medium run, the country's stock of capital is constant, because it takes some time, possibly three to five years, before this stock changes significantly.

The technology of production is such that when one factor is constant, the marginal product of the other factor declines with increased use. Thus, if a firm hires another worker, who has to share the machines with other employees, the new worker's output is smaller than the contribution of older workers.

In other words, with a constant capital stock, the MPL declines when more people are hired. Similarly, the marginal product of labor increases when some employees are laid off. This is known as the "law of diminishing MPL."

In Chapter 5, you first encountered the idea of labor productivity or the average product of labor (APL). The APL is the average output contribution of all employees, whereas the MPL is the contribution of a new employee. The two concepts are closely linked to each other. As the MPL falls, the APL must also fall with new hiring, although the APL, applying to all workers, old and new, will obviously fall more slowly than the MPL.

All these ideas are captured by Figure 6.1, where the APL curve lies above the MPL curve. Initially, the businesses face the real wage at OA; equilibrium arrives at point E, where the real wage line intersects the MPL curve; labor hiring is AE or OH. The APL in equilibrium is RH, and since

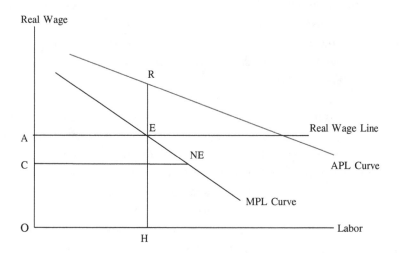

Figure 6.1: Labor Hiring in the Neoclassical Model

the amount EH goes to labor, the remainder, RE, goes to the other factor, capital.

If the real wage were to fall to OC, then the equilibrium point would move to NE, raising labor demand to CNE. Thus, Figure 6.1 explains what underlies the classical labor demand curve, namely, labor demand goes up with a real wage decline. In fact, the MPL curve itself is the classical labor demand curve, because at each equilibrium point MPL equals the real wage.

2. Labor Supply

The ideas about labor demand examined above pre-date Keynes, but those about labor supply are mostly the brainchild of modern economists such as Robert Barro, Arthur Laffer and two Nobel laureates, Robert Lucas and Milton Friedman. Their main thesis is that everyone is free to make a choice between work and leisure, and just like a firm an individual also engages in a cost–benefit analysis. Rational individuals seek to maximize their happiness or utility within the limits of their income and wealth. Happiness comes from leisure and consumption, but work generates unhappiness, for which a person must be compensated in terms of money.

The benefit from work is the real wage, and the loss is the unhappiness resulting from labor. The person works to the point where the benefit just offsets the discomfort of an extra hour of work. The number of hours worked is an individual's supply of labor. *At the national level, however, labor supply may be measured in terms of total working hours, the number of job seekers or both.*

In general, people require a rise in the real wage to induce them to forego extra leisure and either work longer hours or join the labor force. For this reason, marginal income tax rates are a strong deterrent to the work effort, because a rise in such a tax reduces the after-tax real wage and makes leisure more appealing. Other types of taxes such as the sales tax or the Social Security tax, which are low and have fixed rates, may have some negative impact on the work incentive, but the income tax rate, which is higher for most people and rises with the rise in income, has the maximum negative effect. In the decision to work more or less, the person compares the extra benefit of the after-tax income with the extra distaste for work.

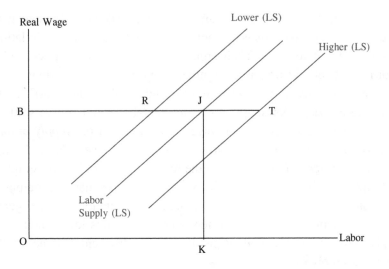

Figure 6.2: Labor Supply and the Work Incentive

In addition to the income tax, the work effort is also influenced by the real rate of interest. If the real interest rate rises, savings becomes more appealing, so that people like to earn more through harder work. Increased earnings will then enable them to increase their savings and thus enjoy the benefit from the increased interest rate.

All these ideas about labor supply are captured by Figure 6.2. At a real wage of OB the national supply of labor is BJ or OK. The labor supply curve itself has a positive slope, indicating that a higher wage attracts more people in the job market or induces some to work extra hours, and *vice versa*. If the marginal income tax rate goes up, the supply of labor falls, which is displayed by the leftward shift of the labor supply curve, so that at the same wage as OB, labor supply is now only BR. On the other hand, if the real rate of interest rises, the labor supply curve shifts to the right, eliciting a higher labor supply of BT from households at the same wage of OB.

3. The AD and AS Curves

As in the classical world, the neoclassical concept of aggregate demand is also negatively linked to the real rate of interest. This is because as the real interest rate rises both investment and consumption decline. The new twist added by the neoclassicists is that aggregate supply has a positive relationship with the interest rate. Their argument derives from the now-familiar labor market equilibrium, as in Figure 6.3, and proceeds as follows.

The initial equilibrium wage is OA, and employment is AE. If the interest rate rises, labor supply rises and the labor supply curve shifts to the right, generating a new real wage. *Since a rise in the supply of anything lowers its price, a rise in the supply of labor lowers the real wage, which is the price of labor.* A fall in the real wage in turn induces employers to increase their hiring to RNE, which then raises national output or aggregate supply. Conversely, a fall in the interest rate lowers the urgency to save, inducing people to work fewer hours and thus lower their labor supply. This raises the real wage, lowers employment and hence the aggregate supply.

Figure 6.4 illustrates the workings of the neoclassical analysis in terms of the AD–AS graph. There the AD curve is negatively sloped, so that AD is negatively related to the real rate of interest, whereas the neoclassical AS curve is positively sloped, so that output is positively linked to the interest rate. Equilibrium occurs at point E, where AD = AS,

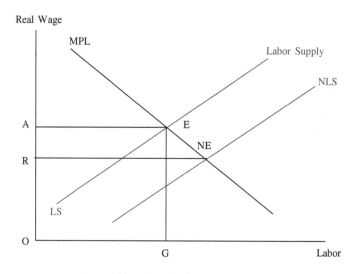

Figure 6.3:   Neoclassical Labor Market

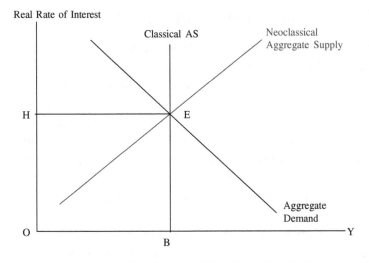

Figure 6.4: The Neoclassical Model of AD and AS

producing a real interest rate at OH and a real GDP of OB. By contrast, the classical AS curve is a vertical line, because in the classical model labor supply does not fluctuate with the interest rate.

Note that each point on the AS curve corresponds to an equilibrium point in the labor market graph. When the interest rate moves, equilibrium shifts in the labor market in a way that generates the positively sloped neoclassical AS curve. In other words, labor demand matches labor supply at each and every point of the AS curve, classical as well as neoclassical. Therefore, the macro equilibrium in Figure 6.4 occurs at full employment of labor.

Since the classical AS curve is vertical, output and employment cannot fluctuate in equilibrium. There is no possibility of the business cycle once the markets come to rest. However, the neoclassical model is not subject to this limitation. Its equilibrium values are not constant but vary with forces that impact the labor market, and only the labor market. In other words, anything that shifts the labor demand and supply curves can also cause employment and GDP fluctuations in the economy. However, money supply still plays no role in such fluctuations, because it has no effects on the labor market. Money continues to be neutral.

4. Supply Shocks and the Business Cycle

Neoclassical economists typically argue that business cycles are caused primarily by fluctuations in aggregate supply stemming from changes in technology, consumer preferences that determine savings, the work effort, and the real rate of interest, marginal income tax rates, prices of raw materials and energy, good or bad weather and so on. Such influences operate mainly from the supply side of the economy. By contrast, nominal variables, such as money supply and demand, nominal wages and the nominal interest rate that may create demand fluctuations have little impact on the economy. This viewpoint is now known as the "real business cycle (RBC) theory."

Suppose there is a sharp rise in the price of oil, which is governed by politics in the Middle East, where the Organization of Petroleum Exporting Countries (OPEC) has some leverage in setting the price. The OPEC has periodically succeeded in raising the oil price, especially during the 1970s. Oil is important as a raw material in chemical products as well as in the production of energy.

Consider the neoclassical AD–AS model of Figure 6.5. Faced with expensive petroleum, firms have to spend more on raw materials, so that at the current interest rate, output falls, and the neoclassical AS curve shifts to the left to NAS. Equilibrium moves from E to NE, the interest rate rises, but output falls, generating a recession.

In the labor market, an oil price increase causes a fall in the APL, because with the rising cost of energy and raw materials, the same level of employment now produces lower output. Since the average and marginal variables are interrelated, the MPL falls as well, so that the labor demand curve shifts to the left in Figure 6.6 to NLD.

The supply of labor, on the other hand tends to rise slightly with a rise in the interest rate, so that the end result is a fall in the real wage along with a drop-in employment. In Figure 6.6, the new labor supply curve intersects the new labor demand curve at NE to generate a real wage drop from OH to OR, while employment declines from HE to RNE. Of course, the fall in employment is consistent with the output decline in Figure 6.5.

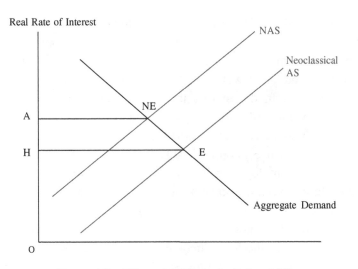

Figure 6.5: Effect of a Rise in the Price of Oil

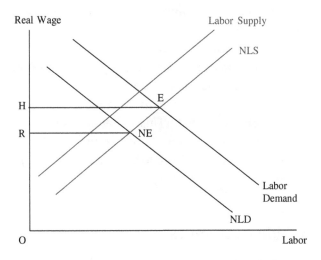

Figure 6.6: Expensive Oil and the Labor Market

What about the price level? The rise in energy cost raises the production cost in each industry, which in turn leads to a general increase in prices. The end result is a rise in the price level, which, if continued for a while, leads to inflation.

This is how the "RBC" theory explains the onset of a recession. The oil price rise is only one type of a supply shock to the economy. Another type can arise from extremely adverse weather that tends to destroy crops and thus lower output as well. The "RBC" model is then an improvement over the classical model in that it permits fluctuations in output and employment, while still remaining within the classical confines that the government should keep its hands off the economy.

The neoclassical economist has added a new twist to the classical belief that all unemployment is voluntary. The unemployed now enjoy leisure when not working, so being jobless is no longer painful. There is no stigma for being out of work, either, for you are only exercising your right to decide whether to work today or tomorrow. This is actually a novel reason, which the RBC theorists have offered for those who quit the labor force because of falling salaries. They call it "intertemporal substitution" of labor. The idea is that you work, when you are at your productive best, and command high incomes. Otherwise you wait for a propitious time.

Taxicabs are a case in point. A taxi driver finds from experience that his business picks up substantially on a rainy day. Therefore, he may choose to work fewer hours in a dry season, and wait for the rainy season to arrive, when he can be more productive, get more passengers and possibly command larger tips as well. This is intertemporal substitution of labor, wherein a person may even choose temporary joblessness over employment to enjoy complete leisure today in return for increased workload tomorrow.

5. Supply-Side Economics

However, there is an offshoot of the neoclassical system, which regards government intervention as salutary in curing recessions, inflation and unemployment. This is the supply-side version that became popular in the early 1980s. In this version, high taxes on incomes earned by individuals and corporations tend to depress employment and output in the economy. Therefore, the cure for joblessness lies in reducing corporate and individual income tax rates.

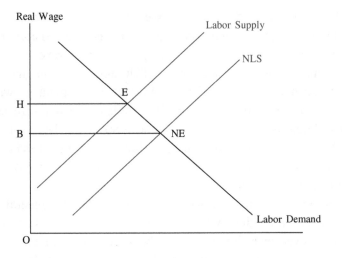

Figure 6.7: Supply-Side Theory

Figure 6.7 illustrates the supply-side viewpoint in the labor market, where each labor supply curve corresponds to a certain tax structure. The original equilibrium is at E. When the government lowers the income tax rate, the work effort rises and the labor supply curve moves to the right to NLS; as a result, the real wage falls from OH to OB, while employment increases from HE to BNE. This in turn raises real GDP. This then is a way to cure a recession and raise the level of employment, because a lower income tax motivates people to work hard or join the labor force, and a higher income tax induces them to trim their labor offer.

Another cure for a recession is to lower the corporate income tax. This will stimulate investment and, after a few years, raise the stock of capital. It takes time before increased investment gets realized into new factories and capital equipment. But once capital stock goes up, both the average and MPL rise, causing favorable effects on the economy. A corporate tax reduction is an antidote to the high price of oil. It reverses all the negative effects of rising energy costs that you have discovered in terms of Figures 6.5 and 6.6. It expands output, employment and the real wage, while lowering the interest rate and the price level. You can see all this by reversing the curve shifts in these diagrams.

Professor Arthur Laffer used the tax-cut ideas to devise what is known as the Laffer curve, wherein he claimed that the income and corporate tax reductions would generate so much prosperity and tax revenue that they would eliminate the federal budget deficit inherited from the 1970s. However, the hypothesis failed miserably, when the giant growth predicted from the income-tax cuts of 1981 failed to materialize and the country suffered from record deficits in the 1980s. Now the idea is appropriately known as the "Laugher Curve."[1] Hundreds of melodies have been written in praise of supply-side economics, but the theory can be demolished in just one paragraph.

When top-bracket income and corporate taxes fall, the federal budget deficit increases immediately by an equal amount. In order to finance its deficit, the government has to borrow back the same amount from the wealthy recipients of the tax cut. Therefore, the tax-cut beneficiaries only have IOUs from the State, but no extra funds. How can they possibly enhance their savings, investment and hence growth? Case closed.

This is all the supply-side tax cut does: the government hands out tax relief to the opulent with one hand, and then borrows it back with another. There is thus absolutely no benefit to the economy. However, future generations are saddled with the debt and interest payment. Supply-side economics is an indefensible dogma pure and simple, with no redeemable feature. (For more on the bankruptcy of this idea, see Chapter 11.)

5.1. Overview

In short, the neoclassical economists share a common ideology with the classicists. They are opposed to government intervention in the economy, except when it comes to lowering those taxes that disproportionately affect the wealthy. They have improved upon the classical inability to explain the recessionary part of the business cycle, but they generally oppose government activism to eradicate joblessness. The labor market in their view always remains at full employment. They also cling to the classical theology that the minimum wage laws hurt the workers by increasing unemployment.

---

[1] William Glasgall, "Laugher Curve," *Business Week*, May 8, 1995.

There are indeed variations in real GDP and employment, but they reflect the free choices of workers. Employment and output decrease whenever people choose to withhold their labor from employers, and soar whenever households rush into the labor force because of higher wages and interest rates or lower income taxes. They insist that this is the primary way in which the business cycle has operated in U.S. history.

There was a time when neoclassical economists vehemently opposed the government budget deficit, but in support of President George W. Bush and his multitude of tax-cut plans, they have recently mellowed and abandoned their passion. They now favor an income tax reduction regardless of the cost to future generations, who will have to pay off the government debt.

6. The Illogic of the Neoclassical Model

After all is said and done, you wonder whether the neoclassical economist, like his classical counterpart, should be taken seriously. But since conventional macroeconomics treats the neoclassicist with deference, let us take a closer look at the concepts and conclusions of his model.

To begin with, the neoclassical framework is vulnerable to the same logical objections as its classical precursor. The AD and AS curves in Figure 6.4 are just as independent of each other as their classical counterparts, and that is the chief source of the problem. At an interest rate above the equilibrium rate there is excess supply in the goods market, which is cleared only if the interest rate falls. This is unlikely to occur swiftly, because the excess supply of goods equals unwanted inventory investment that producers and retailers normally finance through their bank loans. Therefore, fully loaned out banks may feel no need to cut their interest fees until the inventory pile has eased, thereby delaying the return to equilibrium.

Even if interest charges come down swiftly, businesses will not expand their investment in a recession; consumers could possibly increase their spending slightly but it may not be enough to offset the investment reduction. Therefore, AD need not rise in spite of the fall in the real interest rate. On the supply side, the interest rate effect on labor supply is likely to be minimal. Few people change their work habits just because the rate of interest goes down. No one, to my knowledge, has reduced working hours just because the interest rate falls.

Therefore, if the supply of labor remains constant, AS will not respond to a falling interest rate. All this makes the neoclassical model just as explosive and unstable as the classical model. These analytical problems are the same as those that you discovered in Chapter 5.

The neoclassical model also does not permit any unemployment. It is true that employment and output can fluctuate in the new framework, but since labor supply always equals labor demand because of a flexible real wage, there is no scope for any unemployment. The model can indeed explain a recession, where output decreases, and employment is lower than before. Yet no one calls themselves unemployed in the model, because no one ever gets fired.

The job loss is purely by choice. The human being envisioned by the model is a highly dignified, self-respecting soul, who would rather quit than face a pink slip from the employer. In fact, in some neoclassical systems, there is no employer, as in a Robinson Crusoe type economy, where everyone is self-employed. In short, *neoclassical capitalism is a paradise, a dream world, where nobody is ever laid off.* How can it be taken seriously?

The neoclassical model, of course, has its critics, but even they concede that its analysis of the effects of changing oil prices has merits. History, however, reveals something else. The "RBC" version of the neoclassical model argues that as oil becomes expensive the average and marginal products of labor decline, generating a leftward shift in the AS curve and a decrease in employment. Did this occur between 1973 and 1975, when the petroleum price quadrupled in just two years, providing an ideal background for the RBC theory? Hardly.

According to the 1977 *Economic Report of the President* the index of output per hour in the non-farm business sector fell from 111 in 1973 to 109 in 1975. In other words, a nearly 300-percent increase in the international price of oil caused the average labor product to fall by about 2 percent. Furthermore, employment actually went up from 84.4 million to 84.8 million in the same period, while the rate of unemployment, because of new entrants to the labor force, jumped from 4.9 percent to 8.5 percent. Yet Real GDP dropped by 3.5 percent.

The "RBC theory" is refuted by these data even in the midst of an extraordinary rise in the price of oil. The fact that employment went up between 1973 and 1975, even though slightly, casts a shadow of doubt on the validity of the RBC model, which does not explain how output fell while labor demand went up. Another contradiction is that the rate of unemployment, which the model does not permit, jumped, although real GDP did decline. Clearly, the neoclassical explanation for a recession is dubious.

The oil price also soared in 1979, but once again the data were not kind to the "RBC model," because while output fell, employment went up in 1980 along with the rate of unemployment. The model is considered to be at its best while explaining the effects of a jump in the price of oil, but even there it fails. All it explains is that real GDP sank in the midst of booming inflation. However, the central model that we develop in Chapter 9 can explain all of the observed phenomena.

7. The Issue of Labor Supply

Neoclassical models typically assume a representative consumer or household, who behaves like an average person, consumer or worker. Does an average worker have free choice between leisure and work? Clearly, this type of freedom requires an employee to have a thick cushion of savings. A 1995 report published by the U.S. Bureau of the Census discovered that at any moment the median American family had about $1,000 in the bank. This means that half of all Americans had less than $1,000 and the other half had more. This happened when the economy was booming. What is a $1,000 today? Enough for a month's rent in New York? Perhaps. A Bank Rate study in 2019 reinforced the conclusions of the U.S. Bureau of the Census (https://www.cnbc.com/2019/01/23/most-americans-dont-have-the-savings-to-cover-a-1000-emergency.html).

The median American, perched at the middle of the population, certainly resembles an average worker. According to the neoclassical model, the average American worker, armed with $1,000 in the bank, is free to exercise a choice between consumption and leisure. He can quit his job at will, postpone the work effort to some propitious time in the future, and live in dignity without a care in the world. The average neoclassical employee worries not for food, apartment rent, clothing and medical care. She is either a retiree or a multi-millionaire.

This freedom-prone average worker is also motivated by a rising interest rate. She rushes to work hard to earn more, so she can save more. Never mind that the average rate of savings in America has been sinking since 1982, and nowadays hovers around mere 3 percent of disposable income, compared to over 10 percent for neighbors to the north in Canada and elsewhere.

In fact, an average neoclassical worker, as portrayed in modern neoclassical models, is constantly thinking about the future. He keeps a keen eye on the future MPL, future rate of interest, future consumption, future investment, future prices, future money supply, future taxes, future jobs, future government debt and so on. With a whopping savings rate of 3 percent, he cares more about his future income than current income, because if the current paycheck is not to his liking he will quit in a huff, thrive on "intertemporal substitution," and wait until his $1,000 is used up to start working.

The income tax also bothers the average American worker. She does not mind paying a high sales tax, a high Social Security tax, a high property tax, a high excise tax, a high Medicare tax, but, woe betide, if you were to raise her income tax, she would quit her job and exercise her birth right for leisure. It matters not that her low income is mostly exempt from the income tax bite. She suffers vicariously when she sees the wealthy pay the tax.

She also does not fancy the capital gains tax and the tax on dividends, but readily accepts other levies perhaps to do her patriotic duty to the government. Such is the average American worker of the neoclassical model. Which one of you can identify with him or her?

8. The Voluntary Unemployment Syndrome

The neoclassical model, like its classical predecessor, permits the presence of unemployment but only of the voluntary type. "All joblessness is by choice," its adherents declare with a straight face. One of the most prominent exponents of this view is Professor Robert Lucas, who won a Nobel Prize in 1995, coincidentally in the same year the U.S.

Census Bureau discovered that half of American workers had less than $1,000 in their bank account, whereas the average gross financial net worth, including some debt, was $2,700. This worker, according to Professor Lucas, can afford to make a choice between leisure and work.

Lucas's economic thought is sometimes called new classical economics. It is obviously new, because even the classical economists could not conceive that people, living from paycheck to paycheck, could quit work and enjoy leisure. The voluntary unemployment syndrome is not just a matter of semantics. It has profound policy implications.

If people choose not to work, why should the government do anything for them? Neoclassical economists have chosen their words with care. They are dead set against state intervention on behalf of the unemployed. That is why they permit no layoffs in their analysis. Nobody ever gets fired in their world, so no one deserves government help in securing a job. In *Models of Business Cycles*, Professor Lucas argues that the "decision to model unemployment as voluntary is subject to ignorant political criticism."[2] I guess it is ignorance to believe that some employees do get fired from their jobs.

In the neoclassical view, only employers, the job creators as they would call them, need and deserve the state help in terms of low taxes on their earnings, capital gains and dividends. For such a tax policy promotes the work effort, savings, investment and economic growth. Professor Samuel Morley explains the new classical logic in this way: "After all, they argue, if the labor force would accept a reduction in the money wages ... there need be no involuntary unemployment."[3] In other words, a manager who is laid off from Enron can always go to work at McDonald's for $7.25 an hour. He or she need not be jobless, and those who do not jump at this opportunity are voluntarily unemployed.

However, those who have been mangers all their life will hardly rush to accept wages suited for the unskilled. They will search and search in their own areas and be ready to take modest pay cuts. The idea of working for a fast food chain will come to them only as a last resort, when all their savings and credit card limits have been exhausted. Meanwhile they

---

[2] Robert Lucas, *Models of Business Cycles*, Oxford: Basil Blackwell, 1987, p. 66.
[3] Samuel Morley, *Macroeconomics*, New York: Dryden, 1984, p. 167.

could be without work for months, even years. Are they relaxing all this time and enjoying themselves? Hardly.

Professor Lucas is not the only Nobel laureate holding such beliefs. The dogma of voluntary unemployment was also backed by another Chicago economist, Professor George Stigler.[4] In this view, joblessness exists only because workers refuse to accept wage cuts. But is this really true? In 1996, *The New York Times* raised just such questions with those who were fearful about losing their job and came to this conclusion: "Worried that their grip on their jobs is loosening, most workers say they are willing to make concessions to employers if it would help to save their jobs."

Table 6.1 summarizes the responses to questions posed by *The New York Times* poll. The responses came from two groups: those who had been laid off recently and those who were still employed. Among those who had been fired, 59 percent said they would have accepted a wage cut to keep their job. They were laid off anyway and given no chance to do anything about it. As many as 95 percent would have gone for more training, and a slightly lower percentage would have worked longer hours and accepted smaller benefits.

In other words, more than half would have done anything dignified to retain their positions with their companies. But they were summarily dismissed. Were these people voluntarily unemployed, and did they enjoy the leisure of frantically engaging in a job search?

The Lucas tirade against unemployment has, of course, been challenged by economists. In an angry retort, Princeton Professor Albert Rees denounced the Lucas outlook: "Though scientific discussion is supposed to be dispassionate, it is hard for one old enough to remember the Great Depression not to regard as monstrous the implication that the unemployment of that period could have been eliminated if only all the unemployed had been more willing to sell apples or to shine shoes."[5]

It is not just at the practical level that neoclassical economics breaks down. There are serious logical flaws in its thinking. Most people would

---

[4] George Stigler, "The Economics of Information," *Journal of Political Economy*, June 1961, pp. 213–235.
[5] Albert Rees, *Journal of Political Economy*, 1970, p. 308.

Table 6.1:   Workers' Willingness to Make Concessions to Their Employers, 1996

Questions you will be asked	Yes: Replies among those who are working (%)	Yes: Replies among those hit by a layoff (%)
1 Get more training	93	95
2 Work long hours	82	87
3 Accept smaller benefits	53	69
4 Challenge the boss less often	49	66
5 Accept a smaller wage	44	59

Source: *The New York Times*, March 4, 1996, p. A9.

take a wage cut, and work harder to retain their jobs, rather than face the harshness, uncertainty and stigma of unemployment.

This means that work is valued far more than leisure. The neoclassicists believe that people have indifference curves between leisure and work and that they select a combination of the two that maximizes their utility without crossing the limit of their wages. The logical defect here is that, up to a certain level of income, work is far more important than relaxation because, without a job, survival may be at stake.

Note too that the neoclassical model assigns the same bargaining power to workers and their employers. In reality, the employers are in a much stronger position than their employees, especially in today's global economy, where factories can move abroad to low-wage countries, leaving workers with no jobs.

9. Corporate Taxes and Investment

According to neoclassical economists, especially the supply-siders, low corporate taxes stimulate business spending on plant and equipment. Such taxes include the corporation income tax, the capital gains tax and the tax on dividends that companies pay out to shareholders. When firms have more money, so goes the argument, they will have more to spend for their investment, which eventually improves technology and labor productivity. Supply-siders extend the same argument to individuals as well.

However, there is no earthly reason for investment spending to rise with a fall in individual and corporate taxes. No businessperson would risk money in a company unless they expect to sell the product. If demand is inadequate, no amount of tax incentive is enough for anyone to risk their funds in investment.

Investment expansion means business expansion. Would you expand your business if goods are piling up on your store shelves? Would you be willing to risk more funds if you cannot sell all you produce now? No, not at all. Capital spending plans are lubricated by demand, not tax rewards. That is why history shows that corporate giveaways since the 1950s have had little, if any effect, on business investment.

During the 1950s, the corporate income tax rate was 52 percent of profits. It was lowered to 48 percent in 1964, to 46 percent in 1978, to 45 percent in 1981, and then all the way to 34 percent in 1986. At present, it averages 21 percent. In addition, companies have been occasionally awarded subsidies for their capital spending in the form of investment tax credits.

Furthermore, some large corporations do much of their business in the United States but, on paper, base their headquarters in some foreign country to avoid American taxes. In this way, billion-dollar corporate incomes have escaped the tax bite completely. As William Greider, a best-selling author, remarks: "The tax code was so thoroughly gutted in 1981 that hundreds of profitable corporations became free riders in the American political system — paying no taxes whatever or even collecting refunds."[6]

Therefore, the impact of such practices along with the tax code changes should be examined by looking not at the tax rates but at the share of corporate taxes as a percentage of government revenue. This is what Figure 6.8 does; it displays the path of corporate tax share and the behavior of business investment as a percentage of GDP. If the neoclassical theory is valid, then the GDP share of investment should rise as the corporate tax share declines. The graph reveals that the corporate tax share indeed plunged from 1950 to 1995, but the GDP share of capital spending hardly budged. It was close to 10 percent in 1950, and about the same in 1995.

---

[6]William Greider, *Who Will Tell the People*, New York: Simon and Schuster, 1992, p. 91.

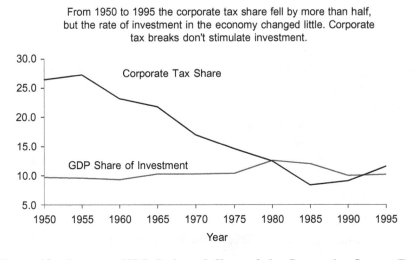

From 1950 to 1995 the corporate tax share fell by more than half, but the rate of investment in the economy changed little. Corporate tax breaks don't stimulate investment.

Figure 6.8: **Investment/GDP Ratio and Share of the Corporation Income Tax (in percent), 1950–1995**

Source: *The Economic Report of the President*, 1987 and 1996.

Through all this churning of corporate taxes, the rate of investment remained more or less fixed in the long run. This is because, as Professor Samuel Morley contends, "one significant determinant of profitability is the level of aggregate demand."[7]

The point is that if an investment project appears to be profitable before taxes, the firm will not abandon it just because of the high tax. If the project makes no money, you pay no taxes anyway. This is pure common sense, and history, not surprisingly, reinforces it. *Thus, corporate taxes and subsidies have had little impact on investment spending in the United States.*

Although the rate of investment generally hovered around 10 percent, it approached 12 percent in one decade — from 1975 to 1985. Why? The answer lies in the force of demand. The rate of inflation increased from 1974 on, suggesting that demand outpaced supply. When supply lags demand, firms know that their investment projects will find a ready

---

[7]Morley, *op. cit.*, p. 500.

market. This mitigates their risk of loss and spurs capital formation. The decade of 1975–1985 is the only post-WWII period when persistent inflation generated inflationary expectations. That period stands out in the otherwise dreary constancy of investment over the other four decades.

An exception to this conclusion occurred from 1995 to 2000, but as you will see in Chapter 10, nothing was normal in these five years because the United States then turned into a bubble economy that comes along once or twice in a century.

10. Summary

(1) The neoclassical model is essentially an old classical wine in a new but complex bottle. It still believes in *laissez faire* and the "neutrality of money."

(2) It is an improvement over the classical framework, because it permits fluctuations in output and employment, both of which are ruled out in the classical model.

(3) Such fluctuations are caused by variations in the supply of labor that responds to changes in the rate of interest. Specifically, a rise in the interest rate causes a rise in labor supply, employment and output, and conversely.

(4) In the neoclassical AD–AS model, aggregate demand has a negative relationship with the real rate of interest, and aggregate supply has a positive relationship with this rate.

(5) A rise in the price of oil causes a fall in output, employment and the real wage, but a rise in the price level, and conversely.

(6) Business fluctuations are caused by "supply shocks," including changes in technology, labor supply, income tax rates, weather and climate, and consumer preferences. This is known as the "RBC theory."

(7) All "unemployment is voluntary," and when workers quit work in response to the falling real wage, they enjoy leisure.

(8) No one is ever fired, and no one calls themselves unemployed in the neoclassical model.

(9) The average neoclassical worker can tolerate all taxes except those imposed on income, corporate profits, dividends and capital gains.

(10) A cut in the income and corporate tax rates shifts the aggregate supply curve to the right and brings about a rise in employment and output but a fall in the price level. This is known as "supply-side economics."

(11) Such tax cuts lead to a fall in government budget deficits.

(12) Contrary to supply-side claims, such tax cuts generated unprecedented federal budget deficits in the 1980s and the early 1990s. In fact, they have never resulted in a balanced budget. Today, the whole world is awash in government debt because of the dogma called supply-side economics.

Chapter 7

The Keynesian Model

In October 1929, something unexpected and unprecedented happened in the United States and set in motion a series of events that culminated in what today is known as the Great Depression. The New York Stock Exchange, after breaking a series of records during the 1920s, stunned its patrons and crashed. Almost immediately the economy went into a tail-spin of sinking output, investment and unemployment. The year began with great promise but ended with a recession, which, under the guidance of contemporary economists and classical economic theory, swiftly turned into a depression. Within two years, output, employment and prices plummeted, while joblessness and despair soared.

Leading economic theories in the United States have almost always sprung from Ivy League schools, especially Harvard, Yale and Princeton, but well-known economists have also taught at MIT, the University of Chicago and Stanford University. When the stock market crashed, prominent economists at these universities were astonished. They were caught napping in their idealized world. In fact, Irving Fisher, the most celebrated Economist of the era and a Professor at Yale, had proclaimed just a week earlier, "Stock prices have reached what looks like a permanently high plateau."

As share prices continued to dive amid spreading gloom, the Harvard Economic Society solemnly assured the public in November 1929 that "a severe depression like that of 1920–1921 is outside the range of possibility. We are not facing protracted liquidation."[1]

It is evident by now that the celebrity economists of the 1920s, advocating *laissez faire* and other supply-side prescriptions, had only a little knowledge of economics. But a little knowledge is a dangerous thing, as the world would soon discover. Ivy League professors masqueraded as economists but offered poison pills that quickly turned the recession into the worst depression in history.

During the 1920s they had spurred the government to cut the income-tax rates again and again in order to trim the budget surplus and stimulate economic growth, just what the supply-siders recommended in 1981 and 2001. But as soon as the share market plunged, the budget surplus of the 1920s vanished into thin air. Now a ballooning deficit was a stark reality that no neoclassical economist had foreseen. The scenario was reminiscent of what transpired in the early days of President George W. Bush's presidency, when a budget surplus, forecast for years to come, turned into a massive deficit by 2003.

1. The Classical Response to the Depression

Among the remedies that economists offered in 1930 were (1) do not panic and do nothing, (2) let the money wage fall and (3) balance the federal budget. The first remedy reflected their belief in the self-correcting features of capitalism, the second revealed their philosophy that fixing wages at some minimum generates unemployment, and the third displayed their undying faith in balancing the federal budget year after year.

Under the tutelage of classical ideology the government at first did nothing, then sharply raised the income tax rates to balance the budget, and finally, in the true spirit of *laissez faire*, failed to rescue the collapsing banks. The rest is history. By 1933 real GDP shrank by one-third, unemployment jumped by one-fourth and prices tumbled by 25 percent. Millions of formerly employed workers were now jobless. In the lexicon

---

[1] Ravi Batra, *Surviving the Great Depression of 1990*, New York: Simon and Schuster, 1987, p. 268.

of modern neoclassical economists, they had quit work to protest the falling real wage, or to enjoy leisure.

Classical assurances notwithstanding, the world was frightened, not of any natural calamity, nor of any war on which the public wrath could be focused, but of the man-made calamity with no escape in sight. Before writing a prescription, someone had to diagnose the illness, discard the poison pills and educate the public. This was a gargantuan task, because the century old classical dogma stood in the way.

In came a brilliant man bearing the name of John Maynard Keynes, a British Economist and an iconoclast by nature, unmoved by the classical rhetoric that supply creates its own demand. Touched by vast suffering surrounding him, Keynes set out to reshape economics, and in 1936 offered penetrating insight in his *General Theory of Employment, Interest and Money*, a full seven years after the start of the Great Depression. A radical overhaul of economic theory was the only way to rattle the economist's single-minded focus on supply. The engines of supply — factories, capital stock, new technology, job seekers — were plentiful, but the engines of demand, thanks to government inaction preached by the classicists, had been all but destroyed.

Keynes began by observing that businesses perform a two-pronged function: first, they supply goods, and second they pay incomes to households in the form of wages, interest, rent and profits (or dividends). The households in turn spend their incomes to buy goods from the companies. There is thus a "circular flow," in which money flows from producers to consumers, and then from consumers back to producers. As long as firms can sell all their output to consumers at a reasonable profit, the circular process continues smoothly, and the economy remains sound. However, if companies are unable to sell all they have produced, the circular flow breaks down, and so does the economy. This way Keynes underlined the importance of business sales or consumer demand in the process of production.

2. Keynesian AD and AS

Keynes took exception to the classical view that the rate of interest is the chief determinant of consumption and savings. Instead, he suggested that consumer spending and thrift are linked primarily to real national income, and only marginally to the interest rate. He called his relationships "consumption and saving functions," wherein real consumer spending and savings are positively linked to real national income. The idea is that if your income rises then you spend a part of the increase to meet your present needs and save the rest for future needs. On the contrary, if your income goes down, you try to maintain your lifestyle by reducing your savings so that your consumption falls only fractionally. Either way your consumption spending and savings move in the same direction as your income. In the form of a simple equation,

$$C = C^* + \text{mpc} \cdot Y$$

where C^* is called autonomous consumption, which is linked to non-income factors such as the interest rate, and mpc $\cdot$ Y is induced consumption, which is related to national income Y (or GDP) through a concept called the "marginal propensity to consume" (mpc). (Please recall our simplification that national income and GDP are equal.) Also, for the time being, let us ignore government spending, taxes and foreign trade.

Plainly speaking, the mpc is the fraction of new income consumed; technically speaking,

$$\text{mpc} = \frac{\Delta C}{\Delta Y} \leq 1$$

or it is a change in consumption divided by a change in income. What is "autonomous consumption?" Your spending also depends on your wealth as well as your ability to borrow money. People normally finance the purchase of expensive items such as cars and appliances. The rate of interest plays an important role in such purchases. Autonomous consumption then is that part of your spending that is linked to non-income factors such as your wealth, the rate of interest, etc. It may also be called minimum or subsistence consumption, which occurs when your income falls to zero. For when $Y = 0$, $C = C^*$.

There is also a "marginal propensity to save" (mps), which is simply

$$\text{mps} = \frac{\Delta S}{\Delta Y} = 1 - \text{mpc}$$

or the fraction of new income saved. Here, S is the amount of income saved by the households. *By definition, mps and mpc add to one.* Therefore, AD becomes as follows:

$$AD = C + I = C^* + \text{mpc} \cdot Y + I^*$$

where I^* is real "autonomous investment." An autonomous variable is considered to be constant, at least for the time being. It is not something that needs to be determined immediately by the model. Stated another way, an autonomous variable is a known number. Another term for the same concept is "exogenous." Therefore, the words "autonomous" and "exogenous" can be used interchangeably to capture the same idea. In equilibrium,

$$AD = AS = Y$$

which, in view of the aforementioned AD equation, suggests the following:

$$Y = \frac{C^* + I^*}{1 - \text{mpc}} = \frac{A^*}{\text{mps}}$$

Here, $A^* = C^* + I^*$ is total autonomous spending. Thus, *in equilibrium GDP equals total autonomous spending divided by the mps.*

Here is a revolution in the making. Unlike the classical framework, there is no direct role for the labor market in generating equilibrium GDP. The labor market is at the center of the supply side of the macro economy. In the Keynesian framework therefore, supply plays a passive role: output is mainly, some say purely, determined by aggregate demand. (We will come back to this point in Section 14, where we discuss what Keynes had to say about inflation.)

In the classical model, a fully employed labor, along with a constant level of capital stock and technology, produces a certain GDP, which in turn is completely sold out through the flexibility of the interest rate that equates savings to investment, and thus AD to AS. In the Keynesian framework, by contrast, GDP itself moves up or down to equate AD and AS, or to equate *S* and *I*. The equilibrium level of GDP in turn determines a certain level of employment that may or may not match the supply of labor. Therefore, in the Keynesian model equilibrium may arrive and persist at less than full employment, whereas in the classical as well as the neoclassical case, it can occur only at full employment.

Figure 7.1 illustrates the crucial difference between classical and Keynesian economics in terms of a 45° line. The chief property of this line is that every point on it displays equal horizontal and vertical distances. At a point such as E, for instance, the vertical distance is EH whereas the horizontal distance is OH, and the two are the same. Corresponding to another point such as F, the distance FM is equal to the distance OM.

Figure 7.1, which is called the Keynesian cross diagram, measures aggregate demand along the vertical axis and aggregate supply along the horizontal axis. First of all, let us note that "any equilibrium point must lie on the 45° line," because only then are AD and AS equal. In the classical case, you select that point which is generated by a fully employed labor in the labor market, such as point F, with OM being equilibrium GDP.

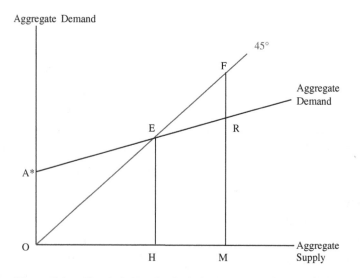

Figure 7.1:   Classical, Neoclassical and Keynesian Equilibriums

In the neoclassical case, equilibrium can be on any point on the 45° line depending on the supply of labor, which in turn depends on the rate of interest.

The "classical equilibrium is unique," because its labor supply is invariant to the interest rate, but not the neoclassical equilibrium, which may be at point F or on any other point, depending on the rate of interest, which in turn is sensitive to the economy's saving habits and investment needs.

The Keynesian equilibrium is also not unique. It depends on where the aggregate demand line intersects the 45° line. The AD line begins with $A*$ or total autonomous spending and then slopes upward with the rise in national income. This is because, as seen earlier, $AD = A* + mpc \cdot Y$. Therefore, when GDP is zero, AD equals $A*$ as in the figure, but as GDP rises AD marches along in proportion to the mpc. In fact, the slope of the AD line itself equals the mpc.

3. Stability of Keynesian Equilibrium

In Figure 7.1, the AD line intersects the 45° line at E, so that equilibrium GDP equals OH, which is AD as well as AS. Is this equilibrium stable? Unlike the classical and neoclassical equilibriums, it turns out that the "Keynesian equilibrium is indeed stable." Suppose the economy is producing a real GDP of OM instead of OH. At this higher GDP, AD is only RM, as point R lies on the AD line and also corresponds to OM. However, RM is less than FM, which equals OM. Therefore, when GDP is at OM, AD falls short of AS, and there is an excess supply of goods. Unsold goods pile up on store shelves, forcing businesses to lower their output and layoff some workers. This means that GDP declines and moves toward OH, and the leftward movement continues until the equilibrium level of output at point H returns. Thus, the economy has a tendency to move toward point E if this point is ever disturbed.

Similarly, you can see for yourself that if the actual output produced is below OH, there will be excess demand in the goods market, inducing companies to expand their output and employment. Therefore, the key differences among the Keynesian, classical and neoclassical framework in the following section.

3.1. *Overview*

The classical model permits no output and employment fluctuations, its equilibrium staying fixed at point F. The neoclassical model permits such fluctuations through variations in labor supply, but permits no unemployment, because its labor demand always matches its labor supply. The Keynesian framework permits output and employment variations through the medium of changing demand and is capable of handling unemployment as well. Its equilibrium may or may not be at full employment, depending upon the level of aggregate demand. If the AD line were to cut the 45° line at point F, then there would be full employment in the Keynesian model as well.

Why is the Keynesian model stable, while the other two are not? The reason is that the other two are governed by micro methodology, where the demand and supply curves are independent of each other. But the Keynesian system is true to the circular flow, where AD is linked to AS, and the two concepts are interdependent. The micro methodology may or may not work in the macro framework.

In short, in the Keynesian system AS always falls or adjusts to the level of AD, whereas in the classical and neoclassical frameworks AD always rises or adjusts to the level of AS through the operation of the market for loanable funds. This market plays no role in the adjustment process of the Keynesian equilibrium.

4. Savings and Investment

Unlike the classicists and their progeny, the neoclassicists, savings and investment in the Keynesian system are equated by movements in national income. This becomes clear from Figure 7.2, where the savings line starts out from the negative quadrant, suggesting that at a zero level of national income people survive by dissaving an amount equal to ON. In fact, savings are negative, until national income increases beyond OG, and then become positive, and rise further with the rise in GDP.

The investment line is horizontal and starts with the point I*, which, being exogenous, is a known number. The savings–investment equilibrium occurs at point E, where the savings line intersects the investment

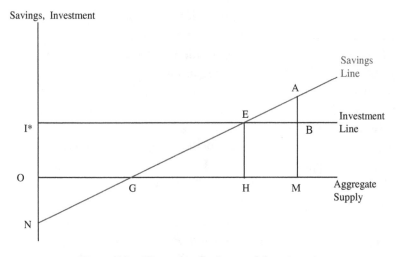

Savings, Investment

Figure 7.2:   Keynesian Savings and Investment

line. At a GDP level of OM, investment is still at MB but savings are at AM, exceeding investment by AB. This excess supply of savings equals the excess supply of goods, which vanishes only with a fall in output and the movement of point M toward point H, until savings and investment are equal again. *Thus, the movement in GDP generates the saving–investment equilibrium in the Keynesian model.* Recall again that in classical and neoclassical frameworks the role of restoring the equilibrium point belongs to the real rate of interest.

5. The Paradox of Thrift

In the summer of 2001, government policymakers and the news media — newspapers, radio and TV news channels — worried aloud that the American consumer, concerned by mounting layoffs at high-tech companies such as Nokia and WorldCom, would increase their rate of saving and hurt the macro economy. The next year the main topic of discussion was how the American consumer had kept the economy alive by not giving in to the urgency of saving, thus keeping the rate of saving as low as it had been in recent years. Why was thrift considered so bad at the time? The answer lies in what Keynes called the paradox of thrift, whereby an increase in savings can be harmful to the nation.

Suppose gloomy consumers decide to raise their savings out of current income, so that the savings line in Figure 7.3 shifts to the left to the new savings line. The level of saving, out of the current equilibrium income of OH, rises from EH to HR. The immediate result is an excess supply of goods equal to the difference between saving and investment, which forces companies to lower their output. The economy then moves from its initial equilibrium point of E toward NE, where savings fall to the old level of investment. As GDP declines savings also decline. In the new equilibrium output is lower at OB, but savings are the same as before.

This is the paradox of thrift in which a nation's attempt to increase the level of savings is frustrated by the fall in GDP. This is the syndrome that most experts feared in 2001 and 2002; it thrives in uncertain and gloomy times, where rising savings are not matched by a rise in investment. Note that if the investment line also shifted up by the same distance as the savings line, as would happen in the classical and neoclassical models, there would be no fall in GDP. But Keynes rightly argued that investment does not shift up to the level of savings in the midst of a recession's despair.

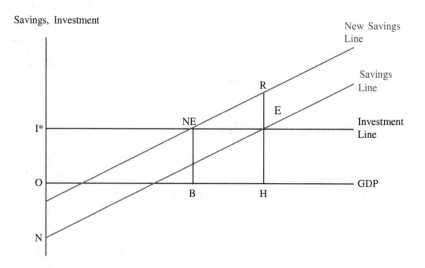

Figure 7.3:   Saving–Investment Equilibrium

During the slump of 2008, the savings rate went up, and then the recession turned into the Great Recession. The paradox of thrift afflicted the American and global economy at that time.

6. The GDP Multiplier

Another new idea that Keynes introduced is known as the GDP multiplier or simply the multiplier. It is, in fact, inherent in the equilibrium GDP equation presented in Section 1, where the

$$\text{GDP multiplier} = \frac{1}{\text{mps}}$$

or the inverse of the mps. Equilibrium GDP is actually autonomous spending times the multiplier. Since the mps is a small fraction, the multiplier number is significantly greater than one. Suppose the mps equals 0.1 or 10 percent. This implies that 10 percent of new income is saved. Here then the multiplier equals 1/0.1 or 10. If the mps is 5 percent, then the multiplier is 1/0.05 or 20. *Thus, the smaller the mps, the larger the size of the multiplier.*

In reality, the economies are much more complex than the one envisioned here, so the multiplier is not this large. There are several leakages in the spending stream that reduce its value. Tax rates, the nation's tendency to increase its imports with rising incomes are some of the leakages that substantially lower the multiplier. A realistic number hovers around 3. In other words, GDP is about 3 times the size of autonomous spending. Stated another way, autonomous spending is about one-third of aggregate demand. The remaining two-thirds is called "induced spending," i.e., spending that is related to national income. Thus,

aggregate demand = autonomous spending + induced spending = GDP

As mentioned earlier, spending is either linked to national income or to non-income factors such as the rate of interest, credit availability, national wealth, etc. Equilibrium GDP is then a magnified version of autonomous spending, as indicated by the formula:

$$\text{GDP} = A^* \cdot \text{multiplier}$$

Any change in autonomous spending also then generates a larger change in equilibrium output. Suppose business investment goes up and raises A^*. This will immediately increase aggregate spending, which will be matched by an equal rise in production on the part of firms, provided there are some underutilized resources available to raise production.

A rise in output means a rise in people's incomes, of which a fraction equaling mpc will be spent, and another fraction equaling mps will be saved. *Therefore, the rise in autonomous spending generates a rise in induced spending.* The combined increase in spending, or AD, includes the rise in autonomous spending plus the rise in induced spending. Therefore, the final increase in GDP will be more than the initial increase in output caused by the rise in autonomous spending. *This then is the process underlying the multiplier, whereby an exogenous increase in spending is translated into a magnified rise in AD and GDP.*

Unfortunately, this happy outcome is reversed in the case of a decline in autonomous investment. The immediate result is a fall in output and national income by an equal amount. But now there is an induced fall in consumption, which is matched by an equal fall in GDP, leading to another induced fall in consumption, and so on. The end result is that GDP sinks by much more than the initial fall in investment.

This is how Keynes argued that the recession of 1929, which began with a fall in investment resulting from business uncertainty and the stock market crash, turned into a cataclysmic depression through the insidious process of the multiplier. The GDP multiplier thus plays a significant role in Keynesian economics. It makes the economy fundamentally unstable and underlines the interdependence of AD and AS once again.

7. Government Spending and Taxes

Let us add a dose of reality into the model by introducing government spending, taxes and the budget (B). The State offers a variety of services and transfer payments (TR) to the public. Its spending includes the outlays for final goods (G), TR and interest payment on its debt, i.e., its past borrowings from the private sector. Government spending then equals total government spending $= G +$ TR $+$ government interest

Government earnings equal total tax revenue and a variety of fees such as a driver's license fee, passport application fee among others. The State budget is then given by the following:

$B =$ total government spending $-$ total government income

Let us define T as taxes plus fees net of transfer payments and government interest. Then we may write

$$B = G - T$$

which furnishes the government budget. B is a measure of the budget deficit, or surplus when B is negative. If $B = 0$, the budget is in balance.

A simple way to introduce the government budget into our analysis is just to add B to the concept of aggregate demand. The idea is that T lowers consumer spending by an equal amount and G adds to aggregate spending by an equal amount. A complex way would be to add G and subtract mpc $\cdot T$ from AD in the belief that taxes lower disposable income and thus both consumption and saving, so consumption falls only by the amount of mpc times the tax payment.

Unless otherwise specified we work with the simpler way because in almost all cases the conclusions remain unchanged. The simpler way also describes reality today. When the household rate of saving in the United States is extremely low, near zero in recent years, any increase in taxes must come mainly from the fall in consumption, and any tax reduction will go primarily into consumer spending. In light of this discussion

$$AD = C + I^* + B^*$$

where B^* is the autonomous level of the budget deficit. Introducing State expenditures and taxes in this way leaves the basic features of our analysis unchanged. The equilibrium GDP equation is still

$$\text{GDP} = \frac{A^*}{\text{mps}} = A^* \cdot \text{multiplier}$$

except that now $A* = C* + I* + B*$ is autonomous spending, which equals private sector's autonomous spending plus the State budget deficit.

Any change in $B*$ affects the GDP in the same way as a corresponding change in private spending. An increase in taxes (T) unmatched by a rise in government spending will lower $B*$ as well as GDP, and a rise in government spending (G) unmatched by a rise in taxes will raise $B*$ and GDP. In all cases,

$$\Delta\text{GDP} = \Delta A* \cdot \text{multiplier}$$

where autonomous spending can change from a change in autonomous levels of consumption, investment and the budget deficit. The change in $A*$ is sometimes called the "initial change in spending." The point of this analysis is that when the economy suffers from unemployment, a rise in the budget deficit or $B*$ will raise the output back to the full employment level of output. You can even calculate the desired increase in the budget deficit. From the earlier equation, we can write

$$\Delta B* = \frac{\Delta\text{GDP}}{\text{multiplier}}$$

while setting $\Delta B*$ equal to $\Delta A*$. Thus, if the multiplier is 3, and the desired increase in GDP is \$90, then the desired increase in the budget deficit is 90/3 or \$30.

8. The Balanced Budget Multiplier

You may have noted that a rise in taxes tends to lower equilibrium GDP, whereas a rise in government spending tends to raise it. What happens if G and T rise by the same amount and there is a balanced budget type of change in the economy. In the American economy today where any tax increase would lower consumption almost equally, the effect would be close to zero. But if the mps is substantial, as it used to be until the end of the 1980s, there would be some positive effect on GDP.

A rise in government spending on final goods adds to aggregate spending. If net taxes (T) rise then people's disposable income falls by an equal amount, but consumption falls only by mpc times the tax increase, which equals the fall in disposable income.

Suppose the government raises its taxes and spending each by $50, and the mpc is 0.9, so that the mps is 0.1. Then aggregate spending rises by full $50, but consumption falls by only 90 percent of the tax rise, i.e., by $45. There is a net increase in autonomous spending of $5. Since the inverse of the mps is 1/mps or 1/0.1, the multiplier equals 10. Because of the slight increase in autonomous spending, GDP will rise in this case and the rise, as usual, will equal the initial rise in spending times the multiplier. Therefore, GDP will rise by

$$5 \times 10 = \$50$$

In other words, the rise in GDP equals the rise in *G* and *T*. The *balanced budget multiplier thus equals one regardless of the size of the mps.* Stated another way, when *G* and *T* change by an equal amount, GDP also changes by the same amount. This is the balance budget multiplier theory. However, when the mps has been close to zero for some time this effect disappears, because then people have no cushion of savings out of which to pay the increased tax. Their autonomous consumption, in fact then falls by the full amount of the tax rise.

9. Output and Employment

In the Keynesian model, GDP determines the equilibrium level of employment. The process is actually very simple but requires a new concept, namely, the production function. A production function for a firm defines an engineering or a technological relationship that links the firm's output to its factors of production such as capital, labor and land. The function can also be defined for a nation, wherein aggregate supply is linked to the nation's capital stock, employment and land. However, land may be disregarded for its relatively low contribution to GDP, and capital may be considered fixed in the short to medium run. We may write such a function as

$$Y = F(K_0, L)$$

The equation simply says that national output depends on capital and labor through the medium of technology represented by the symbol "F." Here, Ko is the fixed amount of capital and L is labor demand or employment. Figure 7.4 presents a typical production function, OEA, which is drawn for a certain stock of capital. The axes display output and labor utilization. The curvature of OEA reflects the law of diminishing marginal and average product of labor (APL) examined in the previous chapter. At point E for instance, output is EB and employment is OB, so that the APL is EB/OB, which in turn is the slope of the line OE. At another point such as A, the APL will be the slope of the line OA. Clearly, OA has a smaller slope than OE, indicating that as more labor is hired the APL declines.

But the APL can decline only if each new worker produces a smaller output than the old worker, so that the marginal product of labor (MPL) falls. Thus, the curvature of OEA reflects both the falling APL and the MPL. *You may note that MPL also equals the slope of the OEA curve at any point.*

Once equilibrium output has been determined by the level of aggregate demand, employment can be easily read off from Figure 7.4. Suppose

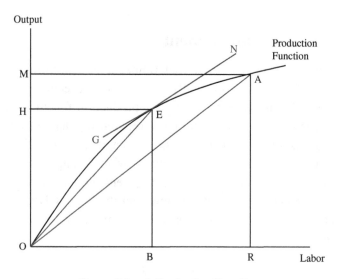

Figure 7.4:   A Production Function

the equilibrium GDP is OH; then equilibrium employment is OB; if AD and hence output rise to OM, then employment rises to OR. Clearly, the labor market plays a passive role in Keynes's system.

Equilibrium output and employment also determine the real wage, which equals the MPL. Here, Keynes accepted the classical and neoclassical theory of labor demand examined in the previous chapter. Suppose E is the point of equilibrium in Figure 7.4; then the real wage equals the slope of the curve OEA at point E, i.e., the slope of the line GN, which is drawn tangentially to the production function.

If the labor supply in the economy is OR, then there is unemployment of BR that equals the excess supply of labor. Unlike the classicists, Keynes did not believe that the real wage affects labor supply. He argued that workers do not quit work if prices rise and the real wage falls. True, they would like to restore their purchasing power in the face of inflation and might even make their wishes known to their employers, but they do not force the issue if their boss does not comply. Therefore, the supply of labor remains more or less fixed at a certain level regardless of the real wage. *Thus, full employment occurs only if the demand determined output is large enough to absorb all the job seekers ready to accept the prevailing wage.*

The classical economist at this point would like to raise a question. What prevents the system from eradicating this unemployment? Joblessness in the classical model triggers a fall in salaries or the money wage; the fall continues until the real wage declines sufficiently to generate enough new jobs for all the job seekers. Keynes argues that the "money wage is more stable than the real wage," because workers tend to resist wage cuts even in the middle of excess supply of labor, so the money wage may not decline in the short run or may fall only a little. Even if the money wage falls, there is no guarantee that AD will rise at all, and unless that happens output, and hence employment, cannot increase.

A money wage fall is likely to depress consumer spending, which in turn would cause a further decline in AD and hence employment. Falling AD will depress the price level and tend to raise the real wage, because

$$\text{real wage} = \frac{\text{money wage}}{\text{price level}}$$

is the purchasing power of the paycheck. If the real wage rises in the face of job losses, the self-healing classical mechanism breaks down, even if the money wage declines somewhat.

10. Labor Market

Keynes's analysis of the labor market complements his analysis of the product market presented earlier. He accepts the classical idea that profit maximizing producers facing intense competition hire workers until the real wage equals the MPL. That is

$$\text{MPL} = \frac{\text{money wage}}{\text{price level}} \text{ or}$$
$$\text{money wage} = \text{price level} \times \text{MPL}$$
$$= P \cdot \text{MPL}$$

where P is the price level. This last equation suggests that labor hiring stops when the money wage equals the value of the MPL. For instance, if a new worker builds 5 chairs for a furniture factory, then her MPL is 5, and if a chair sells for $20, then the value of her contribution is $100. If the money wage is also $100, then she will be the last employee hired by the company, because the law of diminishing MPL ensures that the contribution of another new worker will be less than $100 and the money wage.

However, Keynes rejects the classical idea that labor supply is positively linked to the real wage, simply because workers do not quit work if the price level goes up, while the money wage is constant, so that the real wage falls. His labor supply curve is a horizontal line at the prevailing money wage as in Figure 7.5. Unlike the classical framework, the vertical axis now displays the money wage, not the real wage.

The labor supply curve starts out from point H, which is the prevailing money wage in the labor market. Until point BN, called the "bottleneck point," the money wage is constant, and the maximum labor supply at that wage is OR, or HBN. The bottleneck point arrives when there is a shortage of some exceptionally skilled workers, so that the average wage rate begins to rise even before full employment is reached. Thus, the labor supply curve has a kink at point BN and becomes positively sloped

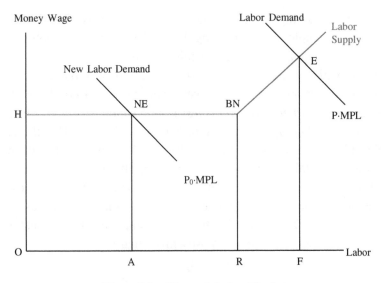

Figure 7.5:   Keynes's Labor Market

thereafter. *Contrary to popular impression, Keynes did not assume that the money wage and the price level are constant until full employment* (see Section 14 for details).

The Keynesian labor demand curve is negatively sloped just like the classical counterpart, but is given by the marginal value product curve, not just the MPL curve. This is because with Keynes the money wage equals $P \cdot \text{MPL}$. Initially, the labor demand curve intersects the labor supply curve at E, which is then the full-employment equilibrium of the classical model.

The equilibrium money wage is FE and employment is OF. Now suppose consumer and business confidence sinks, because of, say, the stock market crash, so that both consumer and investment spending decline. As AD falls, the price level falls to P_o and the $P \cdot \text{MPL}$ curve shifts to the left to the new labor demand curve given by $P_o \cdot \text{MPL}$. The new equilibrium point is given by NE, and employment falls all the way to OA, while the money wage falls from EF to OH.

Several points are noteworthy. First, there is now large-scale unemployment even though the money wage has declined. Second, there is voluntary unemployment equal to RF, because as the money wage falls RF amount of the labor force quits the labor market. This portion comes from the upward sloping part of the labor supply curve. Third, there is involuntary unemployment, equaling AR, which occurs when job seekers outnumber labor demand at the prevailing wage of OH.

At the market wage of OH, labor demand is only OA, but labor supply is OR, so that AR amount of labor seeks work but fails to find one. *Thus, in the Keynesian framework joblessness is both voluntary and involuntary, although the voluntary portion is rather small.* When AD falls, some people indeed quit work because of the shrinking paycheck, but many more are simply laid off even when they are ready to accept pay cuts.

This is the central message of the Keynesian model. The message itself is not profound, but its theoretical demonstration is, because until Keynes's *General Theory* no one had even come close to demonstrating the obvious, namely, layoffs are mostly involuntary.

11. Investment

Keynes accepts a number of ideas from his precursors. The theory of labor demand is one such idea; another is the theory of investment, although he modifies the argument slightly. In the classical world, business spending on capital goods is negatively related to the rate of interest. The same is true in the Keynesian model as well. This way we may write an investment equation as follows:

$$I = I^* - hi$$

which is known as the investment function. Investment now has two components, one autonomous (I^*), and the other linked negatively to the rate of interest (i). Here, h is a known number that links the rate of interest to the level of investment spending, and the minus sign indicates that the relationship is negative. However, to Keynes investment is not overly sensitive to interest rate variations and may have profound consequences for the stability of the economy. For, as we saw in Chapter 5, a low interest-sensitivity for capital spending, coupled with a nearly vertical savings line, means that even at a zero rate of interest savings exceed investment or AS exceeds AD. This is a recipe for overproduction and layoffs (see Figure 5.4).

Note that unlike the classicists, Keynes generally makes no distinction between nominal and real interest rates. Inflation in his system is either negative or low until full employment arrives, and the nominal interest rate moves parallel to the real rate. At times he assumes price stability; at others, he does not. (We will return to this point later.)

The autonomous component of investment captures all variables other than the interest rate that could also impact capital spending. For instance, the level of profit, new technologies that raise the productivity of labor and/or capital, an increase in the price of oil that necessitates new oil-saving equipment, environmental laws that motivate companies to install pollution-removing machines, etc., are some of the other forces that could impact capital spending and raise I^*. On the other hand, sagging business confidence, increasing uncertainty, corporate scandals such as the unprecedented bankruptcies of Enron, WorldCom, Global Crossing among others, a stock market slide, etc., may demoralize businesspeople, hurt investment and lower I^*.

As with the classicists, Keynes paid little heed to the current level of demand as a major determinant of investment. He did not think that current income impacted capital spending in an important way. His emphasis was on future profitability of investment projects, and the rate of interest was a significant factor in determining such profitability.

Keynes *regards investment spending as highly volatile that tends to sow the seed of instability in the economy.* Unlike consumer spending, capital spending makes aggregate demand unstable and leads the business cycle. In boom times, investment soars faster than output, and then sinks faster than output during recessions. Thus, investment tends to magnify economic fluctuations via the process of the multiplier.

12. The Rate of Interest

Having discarded the classical theory of interest as the foundation underlying aggregate demand, Keynes set out to offer a theory of his own. His thesis is known as the "liquidity preference" or the monetary theory of interest. Keynes considered the rate of interest as the price of money, and like any price it is determined by the forces of demand and supply.

Except that now we deal with the money market, where money is bought and sold like any commodity, generating the concepts of money demand and supply. Here Keynes starts out with a simple question.

Money earns no or little interest income; so why do people hold or demand money, when they could be holding income-yielding assets? He offers three motives for this purpose — the "transactions motive," the "precautionary motive" and the "speculative motive." It is true that money begets no income, but it offers a quality that the income-yielding assets such as bonds and stocks lack.

This is the quality of liquidity, whereby everyone accepts money to make transactions. Nobody would ordinarily accept other assets in the process of exchange. You would have to sell them first for money and then acquire something. Thus, other assets lack the liquidity or transactional ability that money possesses.

People also like to hold money for emergencies. What if you or someone in your family suddenly fall sick, or you have an accident? You may then need money in a hurry, leaving little time to sell your assets. This is money demand for precautionary purpose.

People generally hold their money in the form of cash and checking and savings accounts. Whatever they keep in cash and checking accounts is usually for money demand for purposes of transactions and emergencies. These two are linked to individual and national income. The higher your money income, the larger your value of transactions, and so the greater your money balances held in checking accounts.

A rich man, for example, goes after an expensive car, and keeps plenty of funds in the checking account for a larger down payment. A man of meager means, on the other hand, keeps smaller balances in his checking account. *Thus, money demand for transactions and emergencies varies positively with a person's income as well as the price level.*

13. Speculative Demand for Money

But people also hold money in other forms — such as saving accounts and certificates of deposits (CDs). Keynes describes these holdings as the speculative demand for money. Why do people hold this type of money that brings a lower return when they could buy stocks and bonds, which generally yield a larger return? The reason lies in the risk factor associated with non-money assets.

Companies can declare bankruptcy, and thus default on their shares and bonds. Bond and stock prices can also sink in asset markets and wipe out their owners. At the same time, they can soar and bring great joy to asset holders. It all depends on how much risk and uncertainty you can stomach. To simplify the analysis, Keynes makes an assumption that all non-money assets can be lumped together as bonds.

A bond is a piece of paper that contains a borrower's promise to pay a certain rate of interest in return for a loan. Thus, a bond is sold by a borrower to a lender. Most of the bonds are issued by companies and the government, although households also borrow money, especially to finance the purchase of homes, cars and appliances. Therefore, there are corporate bonds, household bonds and government bonds that mature over certain years. In general, a high interest rate tends to lower the speculative demand for money, because then people have to forego a greater reward from bonds. In fact, as the rate of interest rises, the speculative demand for money falls, and as the interest rate declines the speculative demand for money goes up. In light of all this, we may write the money demand function as follows:

$$MD = kPY - qi$$

where k and q are known numbers that respectively link (MD) to nominal GDP, equaling PY, and the rate of interest (i). The equation shows that the rate of interest has a negative influence on MD, whereas nominal GDP has a positive influence.

The other force operating in money market is money supply (MS), which consists mostly of cash, funds that people hold in bank accounts, and loans made by the financial institutions. We will explore these factors in detail in Chapter 13. For now, let us assume that the supply of money is exogenous and determined by a monetary authority such as the country's central bank, which in the United States is known as the Federal Reserve System (or the Fed in short). In the money market equilibrium,

$$MD = MS$$

This equilibrium condition determines the interest rate, as in Figure 7.6. The axes now list the rate of interest and money. MD is the money demand curve, which has a negative slope, until a minimum interest rate is reached at the Min. point, suggesting that the interest fee has a floor below which it cannot drop. The MD curve shows that a fall in the interest rate leads to a rise in money demand until the Min. point, where the MD curve becomes horizontal because the interest rate cannot decrease below that point. Nominal GDP, the other determinant of money demand, plays a role in the position of the MD curve. A rise in GDP tends to raise MD and shift the MD curve to the right, whereas a fall in GDP has the opposite effect.

By contrast, the money supply curve is vertical at its existing level that is determined by the central bank or the Fed. The MS line shows that money supply is constant regardless of the interest rate. The point where the MS line cuts the MD curve is the point of equilibrium, E, that sets the interest rate at OG. Keynes goes on to argue that at this interest rate, savings may not equal investment, because the rate of interest is determined in the money market and not in the market for loanable funds. The interest rate so determined may not be low enough to equate

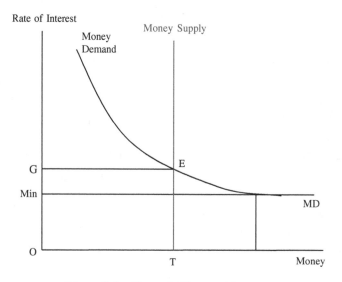

Figure 7.6:   Keynes's Theory of Interest

investment to savings. His theory of interest is thus the last straw that buries the classical model.

14. Inflation

During the 1930s when prices fell year after year, it would be the height of lunacy to be concerned about inflation. But Keynes was interested in offering a general analysis and his *General Theory* tackled the question of inflation as well, though not as extensively as the case of joblessness and full employment. There is a lot of misconception among experts in this regard.

For over four decades the critics have denounced Keynes for assuming a fixed price level until full employment is reached, because in actual practice the CPI has been rising annually since 1940. The critics have also taken him to task for assuming a rigid money wage that, with a fixed price level, generates a rigid real wage. But Keynes did no such thing. He did not assume that money and real wages are fixed until full employment; nor did he assert that the price level is constant until joblessness disappears. See for yourself what he said about the behavior of prices.

> Hence, in general, supply price will increase as output from a given equipment is increased. Thus increasing output will be associated with rising prices, apart from any change in the wage unit .... It is probable that the general level of prices will not rise very much as output increases, so long as there are available efficient unemployed resources of every type. But as soon as output has increased sufficiently to begin to reach the "bottle-necks," there is likely to be a sharp rise in the prices of certain commodities. (*General Theory*, p. 300)

Thus, Keynes states in unmistakable terms that prices are stable at a high level of unemployment, and output at that point may rise without an increase in prices. But once some, but not all, resources are used up and the bottle-neck point arises, further increases in output call for an increase in prices. What could cause such prices to rise? Demand pressure. As Keynes puts it,

> Thus a moderate change in effective demand, coming on a situation where there is widespread unemployment, may spend itself very little in raising prices and mainly in increasing employment; whilst a larger change ... will spend itself in raising prices. (*General Theory*, p. 300–301)

Many well-known experts have made a claim to this hypothesis. Others would call it the modern theory of employment, wherein prices and output generally move in the same direction. Sorry, it was first discovered by Keynes. But to Keynes, this is not "true inflation," which occurs, as in the classical framework, when full employment arrives.

> When further increase in the quantity of effective demand produces no further increase in output and entirely spends itself on an increase in the cost-unit fully proportionate to the increase in effective demand, we have reached a condition, which might be appropriately designated as one of true inflation. (*General Theory*, p. 303)

Here cost unit refers to the cost of production. There are then two sources of increasing prices. One is the cost pressure that may arise long before full employment arrives, because some resources become expensive, and the other is the pressure of effective demand (AD in our terminology) that comes into play after the arrival of full employment? This sounds like a general theory of inflation, not depression.

14.1. *The Money Wage*

What about the other frequent charge leveled against Keynes that he assumed the rigidity of wages. As Professor Barro writes: "Keynes's analysis and some subsequent treatments focused on 'sticky' nominal wage rates and the resultant lack of balance between labor demand and supply."[2] Thus, Professor Barro, like other critics, continues to misinterpret Keynes and base the Keynesian unemployment analysis on the

---

[2] Robert Barro, *Macroeconomics*, 5th edition, Cambridge, Mass.: MIT Press, 2000, p. 758.

rigidity of the money wage. Did Keynes make such an assumption? Read what he writes:

> We shall assume that the money-wage and other factor costs are constant per unit of labor employed. But this simplification, *with which we shall dispense later*, is introduced solely to facilitate the exposition. (*General Theory*, p. 27, italics added for emphasis)

Here the rigidity of the money wage is purely a simplifying and provisional assumption, which Keynes relaxes later and argues that the relaxation makes little difference to his chief conclusion that insufficient effective demand may create a less than full-employment equilibrium. In fact, he devotes an entire chapter, entitled "Changes in Money Wages," to the effects of wage cuts. It is mind boggling to know that critics have denounced Keynes time and again for assuming that the price level is constant until full employment and that the money wage is inflexible. As you can see clearly, he did no such thing, and his demolition of the classical model was done under the most general of assumptions.

Then how did this misconception come about? It is well known that Keynes had a lot of detractors. He himself had denounced his peers, for good reason, and included their names in his tome. Moved by vast human suffering during the Great Depression, Keynes chastised his contemporaries who, under the safety of tenured positions at Ivy League schools, would not budge from their ideology of *laissez faire*. They and their theories had helped the rich get fabulously richer during the 1920s, and now frowned upon any government attempt to ease public suffering, recommending, of all the things, cuts in the money wage amid plunging demand.

Therefore, it should not come as a surprise that the classical and neoclassical economists went to the point of misleading their students and the public about Keynes's views. Ironically, some of them later laid claim to ideas that Keynes himself had discovered.

15. What Caused the Great Depression?

More than anything else, Keynes wanted to answer the question: What caused the Great Depression? His answer was that there was a strong expansion of investment in the business boom during the 1920s in Britain and the United States. Investment opportunities, however, were exhausted by the end of the decade, so that capital spending began to decline. Then came the stock market crash, and that triggered an investment collapse in both countries. The crash also hurt autonomous consumption slightly. The result was a strong downward drift in autonomous spending, which, with the help of the multiplier, turned an initial recession into a debilitating depression.

Keynes's analysis also implied that "American fiscal policy was perverse," as the income tax rate soared for all income classes, and further reduced private spending. Consequently, even though the money wage fell by a third between 1929 and 1932, a shallow depression turned into a Great Depression.

The Classical self-correcting mechanism had no chance of success under these conditions. The money-wage fall only made matters worse. In fact, the wage decline continued into 1933, when as much as 25 percent of the labor force was unemployed in the United States. In other words, in terms of Keynesian economics, there were three reasons for the Great Depression in America — collapse of investment, a mega tax rise, and a sinking money wage.

16. Economic Policy

When the economy is stuck at underemployment equilibrium, i.e., it cannot move out of the sorry state of joblessness, what should be done? Keynes gave an answer that was diametrically opposite to that of his peers and precursors. He suggested that the government would have to step in. Since the system was not self-correcting, someone from outside would have to lend a helping hand to cure, or just shorten, the pain.

What could the government do? It would have to do something to raise aggregate demand in a recession or depression, and, by implication, lower aggregate demand in a situation of true inflation. Here Keynes offers two types of measures, namely, fiscal policy and monetary policy.

"Fiscal policy" involves the adjustment of government spending and/or tax rates. In a depression when AD is lowly, the State should raise its spending on public works and build roads, railroads, bridges, health-care facilities, parks and so on. Increased state spending on public works provides a direct stimulus to AD. Alternately, the State can trim its tax rates, especially those that burden the poor and the middle class, to increase the public's disposable income. This will indirectly increase AD, as larger disposable income raises consumption in proportion to the mpc. Thus, the state should raise its spending, cut tax rates or do both. The idea is to augment autonomous spending, which, through the multiplier process, would sharply raise AD, GDP and employment. Obviously, the rise in employment is larger when the economy is in the throes of a depression, because then the price level is more or less constant. But in a recession, where joblessness is moderate, the rise in employment is small, because a part of increased demand could just raise the price level and thus bite into the State's ability to raise real spending.

For instance, suppose the government increases its spending by $100 and the price level remains constant. Then the entire increase will be realized into a rise in real spending. But suppose the price level rises by 5 percent at the same time; then the rise in real spending will be much smaller. Thus, fiscal policy is exceptionally effective in its objective of creating jobs in a depression, but not in a recession.

This is Keynes's "expansionary fiscal policy" in action. It obviously calls for government budget deficits, which were fiercely opposed by classical economists. Under the classical influence, President Herbert Hoover had sharply raised the top-bracket income tax rate from 23 percent to 65 percent in order to balance the federal budget. Even low incomes were not spared by the tax rise. This to Keynes was just the opposite of what was required to combat unemployment. This is the kind of perverse economic policy that had moved him to denounce his peers, because their beliefs were actually adding to public agony, not alleviating it.

Of course, the budget deficit should not be permanent. In times of high employment, when prices increase sharply or "true inflation" emerges, Keynesian analysis calls for a budget surplus. *Thus, Keynes recommends balancing the government budget over the business cycle, though not each year.*

16.1. *A Progressive Tax System*

Keynes also revealed his preference for a progressive tax system, wherein the tax rate rises with rising income. This would have the effect of raising the mpc and lowering the mps. As Keynes wrote, "If fiscal policy is used as deliberate instrument for the more equal distribution of income, its effect in increasing the propensity to consume is all the greater" (*General Theory*, p. 95). The resulting increase in aggregate demand would then generate increased employment opportunities. It is well known that the poor spend almost all of their income for living, while the rich, although spending more in terms of dollars, save a substantial portion of their earnings.

Suppose an income tax cut of $100 is granted to the poor and is financed from an equal increase in tax on the affluent. Then spending would rise by almost the same amount. For the poor would likely spend the entire tax cut to meet their unmet needs, whereas the rich would maintain their lifestyle and pay the tax mainly out of their savings. At most their consumption will decline slightly. For the economy as a whole autonomous consumption would climb, lifting up the level of AD. Here then Keynes' model offers a way out of the depression without any rise in the budget deficit, because the tax cut for the poor is matched by an equal increase in the tax on the wealthy.

16.2. *Monetary Stimulus*

Fiscal expansion may be complemented by expansionary monetary policy. Here Keynes recommends that the central bank raise the supply of money so as to bring down the interest rate. How this might be accomplished is explained in Figure 7.7. The intersection of the money demand curve with the money supply line generates an equilibrium interest rate of ET. When the money supply line shifts to the new line NMS, equilibrium moves from point E to point NE, and the interest rate decreases to HNE. This will spur investment spending, even though slightly, raise autonomous spending and thus AD and output through the process of the multiplier.

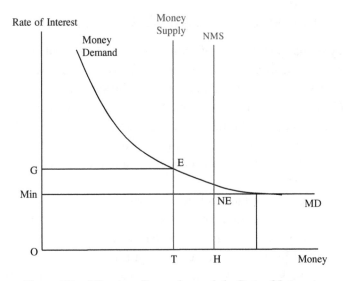

Figure 7.7: Monetary Expansion and the Rate of Interest

However, Keynes cautioned that monetary expansion might not be effective if the interest rate had already reached its minimum point. This could happen, for instance, in a depression, though not in a recession. Someone later called this case the "liquidity trap." Here monetary ease is useless because no amount of monetary expansion will reduce the interest rate, and thus stimulate investment. This way Keynes revealed his preference for fiscal stimulus over monetary ease in combating unemployment.

There is no problem of a liquidity trap, when "true inflation" vexes the nation. Monetary contraction is then a straightforward action that could be combined with fiscal restraint to bring AD in line with AS at full employment. The rate of interest would rise, triggering a fall in investment and thus aggregate spending. This would be a way to ease demand pressures in the economy.

Keynesian economic policy is thus a complete reversal of classical hands-off policy. Keynes wants the government to keep a watch over the economy, and counter the business cycle, raising AD during contractions and restraining it during booms, when inflation threatens to get out of hand.

17. An Assessment of Keynes's Contribution

That Keynes has a vast horde of critics is unquestioned, but even today he perhaps has more admirers than detractors. Those who take Keynes to task also use the same new vocabulary that he introduced and popularized. When *General Theory* first came out, the reaction among economists was harsh and predictable. Some said there was nothing new in the tome; others chastised Keynes for penning a wordy potion of homilies with confusing anecdotes. Still others denounced him for his seemingly contradictory statements.

There is no doubt the book was poorly written; it was repetitive at places, unnecessarily complicated at others. A case in point is the idea of involuntary or cyclical unemployment that Keynes himself regarded as the pivotal point of his entire volume. In plain English, the idea refers to an excess of job seekers over vacancies available at the prevailing wage. But see what Keynes wrote in emphatic italics:

> *Men are involuntarily unemployed if, in the event of a small rise in the price of wage-goods relative to the money-wage, both the aggregate supply of labor willing to work for the current money-wage and the aggregate demand for it at that wage would be greater than the existing volume of employment.* (*General Theory*, p. 15)

I am embarrassed to confess that I do not understand what this passage really means. Fortunately, Keynes clarifies the concept on p. 289: "when effective demand is deficient there is under-employment of labor in the sense that there are men unemployed who will be willing to work at the existing real wage." These words are comprehensible.

Thus, Keynes's volume does not make an easy reading, and at places is very confusing. It has no graphs at all; they were introduced later by those who admired Keynes's contribution. Yet, the work overall is simply brilliant. It is no joke to demolish a century-old dogma even in the best of circumstances, which, of course, were just right at the time *General Theory* appeared. Karl Marx, among some others, had tried to dethrone the classicists, but had failed.

Keynes's singular contribution is in the demonstration that supply may not create its own demand in spite of wage-price flexibility, because savings and investment are not sufficiently sensitive to the rate of interest, leading to persistent unemployment. The rigidity of nominal wages helps but is not crucial to this demonstration. Once supply comes to exceed demand, State intervention may be indispensable for a return to prosperity. The classical economist would wait for the system to cure itself in the long run. But how long could you wait during the 1930s before succumbing to hunger? Keynes was fond of saying, "In the long run we're all dead." This was not said in jest either, because at the time death and hunger stalked the lands of America, Europe and developing countries.

In the 1930s, with the classicists still entrenched in the government, Keynes's prescription fell on deaf ears. But soon circumstances would prove him right. Ironically, what Keynes could not accomplish during peace came to pass in the war-drenched decade of the 1940s, when nation after nation resorted to giant budget deficits for survival, only to see unemployment vanish in a hurry.

18. Summary

(1) Keynesian economics is the anti-thesis of classical economics.
(2) Deficiency of aggregate demand results in involuntary or cyclical unemployment, which occurs when job seekers exceed vacancies at the market real and money wage.
(3) The Great Depression occurred in the United States, because the fall in investment following the stock market crash led to a sharp decrease in aggregate demand. It was made worse by a falling money wage and a perverse fiscal policy that sharply raised the income tax on all sections of society.
(4) In macro equilibrium, real GDP equals autonomous spending times the multiplier. The multiplier is the inverse of the mps.
(5) The mpc establishes a link between national income and consumer spending.
(6) An initial fall in spending produces a greater fall in aggregate demand because of the multiplier, so that even a small investment decline may cause a large decline in output and employment.

(7) The rate of interest is determined in the money market by the twin forces of money demand and money supply. Money demand falls with a rise in the interest rate but rises with a rise in nominal GDP.

(8) A rise in money supply generates a fall in the interest rate, except when the economy is in the "liquidity trap," where the interest rate has already reached its minimum.

(9) Expansionary fiscal policy that calls for a large government budget deficit is the best cure for a depression.

(10) Both types of expansionary policies — monetary as well as fiscal — can be effective in a recession.

(11) A "progressive tax system" raises the mpc and may produce a moderate increase in employment without a budget deficit.

(12) Fiscal and monetary policies should be contractionary in the case of inflation.

Chapter 8

The Neo-Keynesian Model

With the world plagued by depression, and everyone groping for answers, Keynesian logic made a lot of sense in the 1930s. This was common sense macroeconomics par excellence. Keynes appealed to the heads of State to expand their budgets and spend profusely on public works projects, but his words could not budge them from their faith. Their advisers stood in the way of humanitarian programs. Only as a last resort will men and women of letters discard their obsolete dogmas. Throughout history intellectuals as a class have been the last to accept new ideas in their own fields. During the 1930s, in spite of the Great Depression, the classical theology that depressions are unlikely in a market economy was discredited but not discarded. Its demolition occurred in the 1940s.

Earnest pleas by Keynes to President Franklin D. Roosevelt (FDR) to follow his prescriptions proved abortive. Classical luminaries, who were advisers to the President, had always championed balanced budgets in order to avoid market intervention and inflation. Keynesian economics did not move them one bit.

President Herbert Hoover had already erred by more than doubling the income tax rate in 1932. FDR compounded the error by further raising the tax in 1934 and then again in 1935 and 1937. The results were predictably disastrous. The depression lasted all through the decade, and even in 1939 the jobless rate was as high as 17 percent.

Only during WWII, when the Western world was forced to adopt deficit budgets, did Keynesian economics replace classical thought. Europe and the United States had no choice except to spend massive amounts of money for armaments and defense production. Soon, unemployment that had bedeviled America for an entire decade disappeared, and by 1942 gave way to spot shortages of workers. What the nation could not accomplish in 10 years was forced upon it in a matter of two to three years. Keynes was right after all. Fed by massive budget deficits, demand was creating its own employment. No longer did Keynes have to plead for attention. Experts now paid homage to his views, marveling at his genius. The Keynesian revolution had finally swept the classical dogma aside. Unfortunately, Keynes did not live long enough to relish his celebrity, as he passed away in 1946.

1. Automatic Stabilizers

First the depth and persistence of the depression, and later the triumph of Keynesian economics, changed the economic landscape forever. Several state institutions in the United States had already undergone surgery from what is known as the New Deal that FDR had invoked in the 1930s. This program established the Federal Deposit Insurance Corporation (FDIC), the Securities and Exchange Commission, the Social Security Administration among others. It also introduced a minimum wage, unemployment compensation, agricultural subsidies and a host of other measures designed to stabilize the economy. Even though the New Deal by itself produced little increase in government expenditures, it set a precedent for government intervention, though not of the Keynesian variety.

A principle had been established. Henceforth, the government would be called upon constantly to repair a faltering economy. The New Deal also started the tradition of transfer payments, which were low at first, but grew substantially after the war. Another sweeping transformation occurred in the tax system, which became progressive as never before. Under FDR the top-bracket income tax rate rose to 81 percent by 1940 and to as high as 90 percent in 1944.

Macroeconomic theory could not but take note of the new economic landscape, which had instituted what are known as "automatic stabilizers." Transfer payments and the progressive tax system are the chief pillars of these stabilizers. While they started out under the New Deal, they were sharply expanded by President Lyndon Johnson in 1965 as a part of his plan for the Great Society. They were designed to create a calming influence on aggregate spending so as to tame the business cycle.

Whenever the economy slows and a recession threatens, these stabilizers come into play. When incomes decline, the progressive income tax reduces the government tax bite on the public. At the same time rising joblessness increases government payments for unemployment compensation, food stamps, Medicaid and other types of welfare. The end result is that the spending decrease and the recession are shallower than they would be otherwise. Furthermore, the FDIC insures deposits to infuse public confidence in the banking system. All this reflects Keynes's imprint on economic policy.

In a booming economy, the built-in stabilizers play an opposite role. They then slow the rise in aggregate spending and output. As for the government budget deficit, it tends to soar in a recession and shrink in a boom. In fact, after 1995, the federal budget even turned into a surplus as unemployment fell to levels not seen in three decades.

2. AD–AS Again

Unfortunately, every sound idea seems to fall into the hands of extremists, who tend to abuse it and eventually bring discredit to its originator. Keynes had advocated massive government spending to fight the depression, not to combat low levels of unemployment. Furthermore, he wanted the government to make up for the budget shortfall with a budget surplus in times of boom or inflation. But his followers, known as neo-Keynesians, called for monetary and fiscal ease even when joblessness rose slightly in the economy. In reality, they applied his medicine to bypass the laws of labor demand and supply, and lower the rate of unemployment permanently. This was not to be, and the end result was massive inflation that brought disrepute not only to neo-Keynesians but also to their mentor.

Neo-Keynesians first started the myth that Keynes had assumed a rigid nominal wage and price level until the arrival of full employment. They then claimed to discover models that would display the coexistence of inflation and unemployment, even though *General Theory* had already made similar arguments. Nevertheless, the neo-Keynesians did produce a new technical apparatus with which to handle the question of GDP equilibrium amid a variable price.

Few consecutive decades display as striking a contrast as the 1930s and the 1940s. While the 1930s witnessed sinking prices, money wages, interest rates, employment and output, the 1940s saw everything reverse itself. There is a difference of night and day between two time periods in the history of the United States as well as the world. One displays agony, hunger and despair, the other brims with energy, hope and triumph. Someone who lived with the depression in the 1930s, would marvel at the complete social transformation that occurred by the late 1940s. Gone was the depression and its multi-sided suffering. What prevailed now were prosperity and reveling.

But this prosperity inflicted a heavy toll in terms of roaring prices. The 1940s turned out to be another peak decade of inflation (see Chapter 3, and Figure 3.3). Keynesian economics had replaced the classical orthodoxy, but its models were in need of some refinements, which sprang from the pens of neo-Keynesians.

Aggregate demand and aggregate supply had already entered the lore of economics, and they were here to stay. But they needed alterations to explain the new phenomenon of a rising price level amid moderate unemployment. In the neo-Keynesian model, AD and AS are linked to the price level, and the two together determine the GDP equilibrium. It is not that real income no longer matters in the case of consumer spending and AD, only that the price level now receives a prominent role. Keynesian concepts of consumption and saving functions are still important, but they are now in the background, not the forefront.

2.1. *The AD Curve*

In terms of the new model, aggregate demand depends negatively on the price level. In its broad definition presented in Chapter 5,

$$AD = C + I + G + X - M$$

where, as before, C is consumer spending or demand for consumption goods, I is planned investment or demand for investment goods, G is State spending or the government demand for final goods, and $(X - M)$ equal net exports, all expressed in real terms. When the price level changes, three effects come into play. They may be called the consumption effect, the investment effect and the foreign trade effect.

What does a changing price level do? First, it alters the purchasing power of your cash balances, and money that you hold in your checking and savings accounts. Second, it tends to change the nominal rate of interest, which is essentially the price of credit. In terms of the Keynesian theory explored in the previous chapter, a fall in the price level lowers the transactions demand for money, so that the interest rate decreases. This is because if the demand for something declines, so does its price, which in the money market is the rate of interest. *A rise in the price level, by contrast, tends to raise the rate of interest.* A changing price level then affects consumption in two ways. Suppose the price level falls. First, the resulting decline in the interest rate stimulates the demand for expensive items that people normally buy on credit, possibly using their credit cards. Thus, a decrease in the interest rate spurs the demand for cars, appliances, furniture and so on. Second, if the price level falls, the purchasing power of your cash rises, enabling you to buy more goods. All this happens even if your salary or income does not change.

In the opposite case, where the price level rises, the rise in the interest rate lowers the demand for expensive goods, sometimes called consumer durables. Consumer spending also declines because your cash holding now buys fewer goods. *Since C is a part of AD, a fall in the price level raises AD, while a rise in the price level lowers AD.* This is then the "consumption effect," which results from the change in the interest rate and the real value of your cash balances.

The effect of a price fall on total investment, however, is uncertain. Broadly speaking, there are two types of investment. One includes business spending on new factories and machines; the other includes household spending to purchase new homes and apartments. When the price level falls, home buying becomes attractive on two counts — lower price and the lower rate of interest. Houses are expensive, so most people borrow money to buy new homes, and low interest rates play a crucial role in this regard.

However, business purchases of plant and equipment usually decline with a fall in prices. If you own a company then you don't like to see your prices go down. People do not like to expand their business in an environment of falling prices even if the interest rate goes down. From 2001 to 2003, the interest rate plunged, but so did business investment because many industries — computers, cell phones, telecommunications, autos — saw their prices fall substantially. The same thing happened during the recession of 2007 and 2008. Thus, the overall "investment effect" of a price fall is uncertain, because while households buy more new homes, companies buy fewer machines.

Similarly, if the price level rises, household investment for homes declines because of higher home prices and interest rates, but business investment goes up, as it did from 1975 to 1985 (see Chapter 6, Section 10). *On the whole the investment effect of a price change is likely to be miniscule. We shall assume it to be zero.*

The price change influences AD in yet another way. As the U.S. price level falls, domestic goods become attractive relative to foreign goods. Both Americans and foreigners then buy more American goods and less foreign products. Therefore, American exports rise and imports fall, causing a rise in net exports. This is the "foreign trade effect." Since net exports also constitute AD, a fall in the price level stimulates a rise in AD from this source as well. Similarly, if the price level rises, net exports fall, and so does AD.

The sum total of the three influences is the price effect on AD, although the overall impact is likely to be small, because the investment effect is paltry. Therefore, the AD curve of Figure 8.1, though negatively sloped, is very steep, in fact nearly vertical. The GDP data tend to confirm this view.

The bulk of consumer spending is linked to disposable income. Recent data show that Americans normally spend 95 percent of their disposable income for consumption expenditure and 2 percent on other personal outlays that include the financing cost involved in buying goods with credit cards, so that the total personal outlay is 97 percent of disposal income. This suggests that almost the entire consumer spending is explained by the disposable income, and that wealth and interest effects on consumption are miniscule.

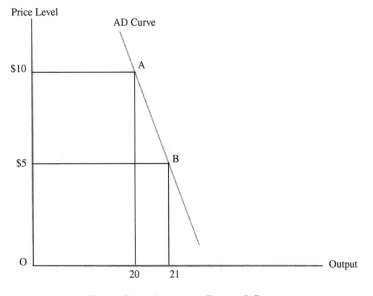

Figure 8.1: Aggregate Demand Curve

Since the investment effect is puny anyway, the overall effect of a change in the price level is extremely small, and the AD curve is nearly vertical. This means that even a large fall in the price level generates a small rise in AD, or a large rise in the price level produces only a minor fall in AD. In Figure 8.1 as the price level falls from $10 to $5, AD rises from 20 units to 21. Here the unit of measurement is either aggregate spending in constant dollars of a base period, or some assumed index of commodity output.

3. The AS Curve

While the AD curve is nearly vertical in Figure 8.1, the AS curve is not. The AS curve of the neo-Keynesians closely resembles that suggested by Keynes, namely, at first output may rise without any increase in the price level. Any further rise in output requires the price level to go up, until full employment arrives, and then a price increase produces no rise in output. Thus, the curve RBFK in Figure 8.2 displays Keynes's AS curve.

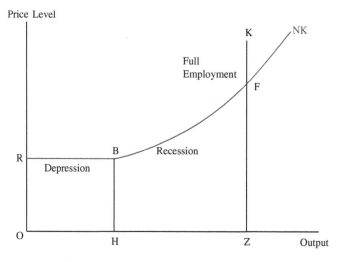

Figure 8.2:   Keynesian and Neo-Keynesian AS Curves

Around point R, where output is very low in a depressed economy with huge unemployment, the AS curve is horizontal; then it has a positive slope between points B and F, indicating a positive relationship between output and the price level. This may be regarded as the range of recession, where the rate of unemployment is high, but not catastrophic. Finally, after point F, the point of full employment, the AS curve becomes vertical. The neo-Keynesian AS curve, given by RBFNK, overlaps with much of the curve verbally explained by Keynes, except beyond point F.

In the neo-Keynesian case, output may rise even beyond point F, because employers may be able to squeeze increased work from their employees through generous overtime pay. A lucrative real wage may induce workers to toil for longer hours and thus raise production beyond the point of full employment. This way the neo-Keynesian AS curve remains positively sloped even after full employment is achieved.

The shape of the AS curve is dictated by how the cost of production behaves at various levels of output. At low levels between zero and point H, additional units of production require no increase in marginal cost (MC), which is the cost of producing an extra unit of output. Thus, for the output level of OH, MC is constant, and so is the price. As output increases above OH, MC rises along with the price. Point Z gives us the output level at full employment, beyond which MC and price rise sharply with a small rise in production.

Another way of analysis looks at the marginal product of labor (MPL) and the money wage (*W*). You may recall from Chapter 6 that for producers facing perfect competition labor demand is determined by the real wage and the MPL. Labor hiring occurs until the point where the real wage equals MPL. That is,

$$\text{MPL} = \frac{W}{P} \text{ or by } P \ \frac{W}{\text{MPL}}$$

Let us assume, for the time being, that the "nominal wage is constant." At low output, the MPL is also constant, because there is plenty of unused equipment, and the MPL does not fall as more workers are hired to enhance production. Thus, at extremely low output levels, the price level (*P*) remains unchanged.

As output rises, further hiring of workers tends to lower the MPL, because when more employees operate on a constant level of capital stock, production efficiency suffers. Machines then need frequent repairs; they tend to break down more often, leading to a loss of time and effort. The MPL decline resulting from rising output thus tends to raise *P*. Thus, if the money wage is constant, the output rise above a low point calls for a rise in the price level. This is what eventually creates a positively sloped supply curve from what is known as the "cost effect."

Neo-Keynesians cite another reason for the AS curve to be positively sloped in the short run. If *P* rises and *W* is constant, then a firm's profit goes up and that tends to raise output as well. Conversely, if *P* declines then profit tends to fall and the firm has to lower output. This is known as the "profit effect."

What happens if the money wage, as it should, rises with the price level? For workers are likely to demand higher pay when prices go up. In fact, as the neoclassical economists argue, if *W* rises in the same proportion as *P* so that the real wage is constant, then MPL and hence output cannot change, and the AS curve becomes vertical. On the flip side, if the price level declines, the employer is likely to lower the money wage in the same proportion so that the real wage is constant, and again output cannot change.

Whether or not the AS curve is vertical or positively sloped depends upon how much time elapses between the change in the price level and the change in the wage rate. In the "short run," the nominal wage may be assumed to be constant in terms of the labor contracts already signed between workers and employers. A one-year contract sets the salary for a year; a two-year contract may have a built-in wage increase in the second year in proportion to a price rise, and so on.

Therefore, if the price level rises unexpectedly, then at least for a year the wage rate is given, so that the real wage declines and output goes up. After one year, with higher output and employment, workers will be in a position to demand a higher wage and the real wage will return to the old level, and so will output.

In the opposite case, if the price level declines, with wages set for two years, the real wage rises. Therefore, labor demand and output must fall. But after two years, the employer will insist on paying a lower salary to bring it in line with the lower price level. The real wage will go back and so will output. Thus, the AS curve is positively sloped in the short run but is vertical in the medium to long run.

But is it vertical at full employment output? The answer is yes, because in the long run the rate of unemployment in the United States has averaged 5 percent, which defines full employment or natural employment.

How do we move from the short run to the long run? In the short run, the money wage is constant, and the AS curve normally has a positive slope. In the long run, the money wage changes in the same direction as the price level, so that the short-run AS curve shifts to the left when the money wage rises, and to the right when the money wage falls. More will be said on this aspect of the AS curve in Section 8.

4. Macro Equilibrium

In equilibrium, AD = AS, as at point E in Figure 8.3, generating an equilibrium output of HE and an equilibrium price of OH. The first question we must raise is this: Is this equilibrium stable? You may recall that we have been asking this question in all the models we have explored so far and discovered that only the Keynesian system is stable. The classical and

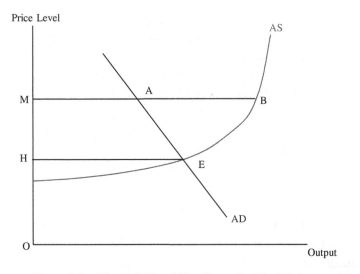

Figure 8.3:   The Stability of Neo-Keynesian Equilibrium

neoclassical models turned out to be unstable because, unlike the micro system, macro demand and supply are not independent of each other.

The circular flow between consumers and producers ensures the element of interdependence. This problem did not occur in the famous Keynesian cross diagram, wherein AD and AS depend on each other.

The neo-Keynesian model essentially reverts to the classical method-ology. AD and AS curves, linked to the price level, are treated as indepen-dent once again. Fortunately, the model does not fall prey to instability, but needs some additional assumptions, which may be considered reasonable. Let us ask the question: If the price level deviates from its equilibrium, does it come back to a state of rest again?

Suppose price is at point M so that an excess supply of AB afflicts the economy, producing a recession. This is precisely the method we used with the neoclassical AD–AS model, and the classical saving–investment graph. The excess supply in the goods market leads to a fall in price, as retailers stuck with unsold inventories resort to sales and to price mark-downs. Unlike the neoclassical system where the interest rate may not fall immediately in a recession, because the banks have to finance the accu-mulation of unexpected inventories, in the neo-Keynesian model the price level responds quickly.

As the price level declines, AS moves down from point B toward point E. What about AD? Does it rise toward the level given by the old equilibrium? First of all, it does not have to. Even if the AD line is vertical and AD remains constant in the wake of the price decline, the economy can still return to point E because of the fall in output. Second, if the AD curve is steep but not vertical, then AD has to rise slightly.

Can this happen in a recession? In the neoclassical model, it cannot, but in the neo-Keynesian framework, indeed it can. The neoclassical model requires investment to rise in a recession — which has never happened — but the neo-Keynesian model does not, because we have already assumed the investment effect to be paltry. Even consumption does not have to rise. The foreign trade effect, not present in the neoclassical model, may itself ensure the rise in AD with a price fall, even if investment declines a little. *Thus, the neo-Keynesian system is stable. Unlike the classical and the neoclassical counterpart, it does not require investment and consumption to rise in a downturn.*

5. Fiscal Policy in the Short Run

What is the effect of Keynesian policies in this new setting? In the short run, the AS curve does not shift with a change in P. Expansionary policies, such as fiscal and monetary ease, tend to shift the AD curve to the right. If government spending goes up, AD increases by the same amount at the current price level. On the other hand, a decrease in taxes raises disposable income by the same amount, and nearly increases spending by the amount of the fall in the tax revenue. In both cases, the AD line shifts to the right, with the shift equaling the initial rise in spending times the multiplier. For, as you saw in Chapter 7, the total increase in AD equals the initial rise in spending times the multiplier.

Output and employment consequences of the AD-shift depend on the current state of the economy.

In Figure 8.4, initial equilibrium is at point E, where the AD line intersects the neo-Keynesian AS curve at its horizontal portion. If the rightward shift of AD is slight to NAD line, output rises from RE to RNE without any rise in the price level. This is the case of a depression

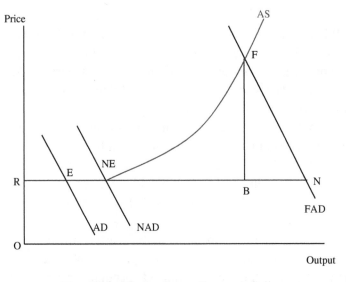

Figure 8.4: Expansionary Economic Policy

economy. If the AD-shift is large, then the new equilibrium point lies on the AS curve on any point beyond NE. Indeed if aggregate spending rises enough to shift the AD line to FAD, full employment is reached with output rising all the way to RB; but now the price level rises by a large amount of BF, and inflation occurs. Needless to say, any further rise in spending will be extremely inflationary with slight benefit in output.

If the price level were constant, the initial rise in spending to attain full employment equals EB divided by the multiplier. If the price level rises, as in the real world, then the initial rise in spending equals EN divided by the multiplier. This is because, from the multiplier formula, we can see that

$$\Delta GDP = \Delta AD = \Delta A^* \cdot \text{multiplier}$$

Therefore,

$$\Delta A^* = \frac{\Delta AD}{\text{multiplier}}$$

where ΔA^* is the initial change in spending resulting from economic policy. When prices are constant, ΔAD equals BE for the arrival of full employment. Otherwise, it equals EN. This shows that the required rise in government spending, or the required fall in taxes, is larger when prices tend to rise. *In other words, a larger budget deficit is needed to get to full employment in an inflation prone economy.*

This conclusion holds even when some joblessness remains. If the AD curve were to cut the AS curve at any point between F and NE, then the policy of fiscal ease would lead to a rise in the price level and output, but the increase in employment would not be enough to employ all those seeking jobs at the existing wage. Some unemployment would remain.

What if the economy is operating at the nearly vertical portion of the AS curve, where it is afflicted with roaring inflation? Fiscal restraint is then the right policy. A cut in government spending, or a rise in tax rates would then shift the AD curve to the left and bring down the price level with a minor fall in the level of output.

5.1. *Crowding Out*

The neo-Keynesian model, of course, has its critics. One of them, Professor Milton Friedman, points out that large budget deficits tend to raise the rate of interest and thus lower private spending, especially investment. Suppose the government borrows money from the private sector to finance its deficit. This will raise the interest rate because the State will add its own needs to private loan demand. The result is a fall in investment that dampens the rightward shift of the AD line. If investment spending is highly sensitive to the interest rate, the rightward AD shift will be very small. In the extreme case, the shift will be zero. Here then fiscal expansion is totally ineffective, and the crowding out is complete.

Of course, crowding out is not possible in a depression, where investment is low to nil, and cannot fall any further. But in a recession, it can certainly dilute the expansionary impact of fiscal policy. However, complete crowding out, is unlikely, and fiscal policy in a recession may be somewhat effective.

6. Monetary Policy in the Short Run

Expansionary monetary policy, by contrast, first lowers the rate of interest, and then raises investment and consumer spending, which in turn increases AD. Thus, expansionary monetary policy also generates a rightward shift in the AD curve, unless the economy is caught in the "liquidity trap," where the rate of interest has already reached its minimum and cannot fall anymore. Barring this exception, a policy of monetary ease operates in the same way as the policy of fiscal ease.

The required increase in the supply of money is larger in an inflation prone economy than where prices are constant. Here, the multiplier concept applies to the rise in investment resulting from the decreasing interest rate, and you can calculate the desired increase in investment spending by the same method as explained earlier.

In the case of soaring inflation, with the AD curve cutting the nearly vertical portion of the AS curve above point F, "monetary restraint" would raise the interest rate, lower investment, consumption and AD, and thus be the right policy. Prices would come down, with little fall in output and employment. Of course, monetary contraction would have to be just enough to shift the AD curve leftward to point F and no more. Otherwise, the price fall would be accompanied by sharply rising unemployment.

7. Economic Policy in the Long Run

In the long run the AS curve is vertical, and economic policy, fiscal and monetary, has no effect on output. How does the economy evolve from the short run to the long run? This is displayed in Figure 8.5, where SRAS is the positively sloped neo-Keynesian AS curve in the short run, and LRAS is the vertical one in the long run. The figure omits the horizontal portion of the AS curve for graphical simplicity. Initial equilibrium prevails at point E, which lies on the three curves — AD, SRAS and LRAS. The economy then produces at full-employment output or natural-employment output.

Suppose the government follows a policy of monetary and/or fiscal ease, thereby shifting the AD curve to the right. In the short run, the new point of equilibrium is at TE, and output rises by BE, while the price level

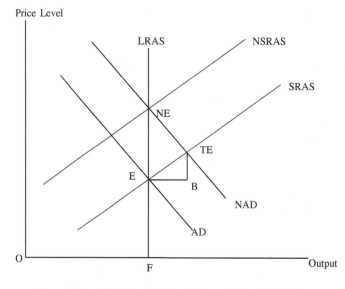

Figure 8.5:   The Short-Run and Long-Run Equilibrium

goes up by BTE. As time passes, old contracts expire, and workers demand a higher wage, so that the cost of production for each dollar of output goes up. The firm has to lower output at the current price, and the SRAS curve shifts to the left. Since in the long run the real wage is constant, so that the unemployment rate and output are also constant, the SRAS curve will shift to the left to the NSRAS line and intersect the NAD line at NE. The price level will rise further, and output will be unchanged at the natural or full employment level.

Thus, *in the short run the money wage is constant while the real wage falls with a rise in P, and in the new equilibrium both price and output are higher. Or the real wage rises with a fall in P, and in the new equilibrium both output and price are lower. In the long run, however, the money wage rises with a rise in P and falls with a fall in P, but the real wage is constant, and so are output and employment.*

8. An Initial Shift of the AS Curve

The AS curve may also shift in the economy initially, provided something alters the cost of production. This could happen, for instance, if powerful labor unions impose higher wages on employers, or if the price of oil goes up or down.

The AS curve shifts to the left if oil becomes expensive or the union power rises to sharply lift the money wage. For then MC increases at the current level of operations, so that the current price level supports a lower level of output. The consequences are depicted in Figure 8.6. When production costs increase, the SRAS curve moves leftward to the NSRAS line. Initially, the equilibrium point rests at E that lies on the intersection of AD and AS curves, and output is at the full employment level of OF. As the AS curve shifts leftward to NSRAS, equilibrium moves to TE. Output falls a little by BE but the price level rises by a sharp BTE. Here we have the worst of both worlds: employment declines and inflation leaps. Such a state of economy is called "stagflation." The price level then soars in a recession.

The sharp rise in the price level even in a recession reflects the inflationary bias that has been observed in the American economy since 1940. It arises from the near verticality of the AD curve. Prior to 1950, prices in America rose only during war decades, and then came down swiftly after the end of hostilities. But since that year, the CPI has been increasing with

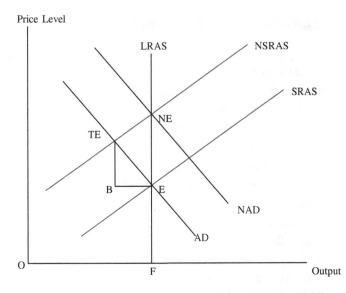

Figure 8.6: Union Militancy or a Rise in the Price of Oil

or without a war. This is the inflationary bias of the economy, for which one reason is the steepness of the AD line.

Another reason lies in the changed State attitude toward unemployment. In 1946, Congress passed the Full Employment Act, which committed the federal government to the goal of full employment by means of its economic policy. The legislation had unexpected consequences in terms of union militancy. Secure in the knowledge that politicians were committed to maintaining a high level of jobs, organized labor became aggressive in its salary demands, and occasionally succeeded in imposing unreasonable wage increases on employers. The results were continuous increases in the price level.

Let us take another look at Figure 8.6. When union militancy shifts the AS curve to the left, both output and employment decline in the short run, while the price level rises. Now the government steps in and adopts expansionary policy by expanding the budget deficit or the supply of money, and shifts the AD curve upward to NAD, which passes from NE, lying on the long-run AS curve. Output and employment return to old levels, but the price level rises, once again. Clearly, society maintains full employment but with constantly increasing prices.

9. The Inflation–Unemployment Tradeoff

Thus, high employment comes at a cost in terms of persistent price escalation. This is what the neo-Keynesians realized during the 1950s. They also discovered that expanding budget deficits led to a slow rise in the rate of interest, which threatened to derail the goal of full employment. They then decided that monetary expansion should accompany budgetary expansions to maintain a stable interest rate. The 1950s experienced two recessions. Both were short and shallow, especially the one in 1958, when the budget deficit and money supply were expanded briskly, and output fell less than 1 percent. Thus, the goal of full employment required both monetary ease and fiscal ease.

By the end of the 1950s, neo-Keynesians came to believe that there was a tradeoff between inflation and unemployment. The tradeoff started out as the Phillips curve, which was named after a New Zealand Economist, Professor A. W. H. Phillips. He discovered the relationship in

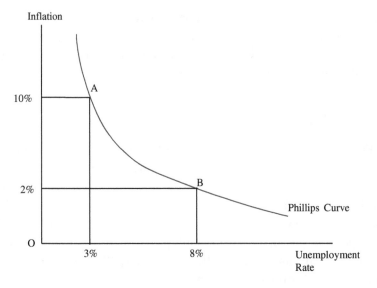

Figure 8.7:   The Phillips Curve

1958 in an econometric study, which found a negative correlation between the rate of unemployment in Britain and its wage inflation, which in turn is linked to price inflation. From this correlation, Professor Phillips and others concluded that the cost of a low unemployment rate is high inflation, and the cost of a low inflation rate is high joblessness.

Figure 8.7 displays the Phillips curve, which has a negative slope in terms of what the two axes represent, namely, inflation and the rate of unemployment. Suppose, the inflation rate is high at 10 percent, then unemployment is lowly at 3 percent. When unemployment rises to 8 percent, inflation falls to 2 percent. From this negative correlation, the followers of the Phillips curve concluded that joblessness could be permanently lowered by the government if society were to accept a certain rate of price escalation. Thus, was born the dogma of deficit financing, which would eventually hurl the world into a major crisis of stubbornly high inflation as well as unemployment.

As you have just seen in the aforementioned paragraph, this viewpoint also accords with the theoretical apparatus of the neo-Keynesian model.

Neo-Keynesians were not daunted by the prospect of price instability. They argued that high inflation is the evil that we have to endure to escape the greater evil of layoffs. Persistent price increases were just a small price that developed economies had to pay to avoid recessions that had afflicted workers in the past. All you needed was deficit financing wherein high levels of money growth finance the budget shortfalls.

9.1. *The Flaw of the Phillips Curve*

The Phillips curve hypothesis appears suspect on its face. This was a myopic theory, pure and simple. If it is so simple to banish joblessness and poverty permanently, all a country has to do is to print money to pay for its budget deficits. You do not have to be a genius to see the flaws of this doctrine. How easy is it to erase poverty from Earth? Just turn on your money-printing pump, asserts the Phillips curve. It is perhaps this thesis that moved film star Woody Allen to remark, "Money is better than poverty, if only for financial reasons."

But the Phillips curve had been discovered by a well-known economist, and that too through econometrics. How could common sense prevail now? The inflation–unemployment statistics were there for all to see, but, as Mark Twain had warned a long time ago, statistics can be damned lies.

In the 1960s, expansionary monetary and fiscal policies were tried all over the globe. The jobless rate in the United States came down from close to 7 percent in 1962 to just 3.5 percent in 1969. This was the heyday of neo-Keynesian economics. Inflation indeed had soared from about 1 percent in 1962 to above 5 percent by the end of the decade, but was that not expected? The creed of deficit financing, so suspect on grounds of common sense, brought international acclaim, even Nobel Prizes, to some of its authors.

However, in the end econometrics kills econometrics. By the end of the 1960s, some statistical studies threw cold water on the sanity of the Phillips curve. Backed by such discoveries, Professor Friedman, among others, argued that the jobless rate cannot be lowered permanently, because there is a natural rate of unemployment in every economy. Once inflation comes to stay, workers start expecting it and add to their wage demands, causing a continual leftward shift in the short-run AS curve. Therefore, in order to maintain full employment, the budget deficit, money supply and the rate of inflation have to increase continuously. Eventually inflation soars high enough to become socially unacceptable, at which point society has to suffer both high inflation and high joblessness.

Friedman did not have to wait long to see his prophecy come true. After 1969, both inflation and unemployment began to increase, but the neo-Keynesians clung to their theology. They came up with new econometric studies: the Phillips curve had merely shifted up, they claimed, and you could still permanently maintain full employment by just accepting a higher but stable rate of inflation.

Such obstinacy from the neo-Keynesians offered neoclassicists a wide opening to attack not just their peers, but also Keynes himself, who, as you can see, had nothing to do with this dogma. He had sought to balance the government budget, not annually but over the business cycle. He would have been alarmed to see his ideas twisted so brazenly by his followers.

10. The Neoclassical Resurgence

The worst was yet to come. In 1973 and again in 1979, thanks to OPEC, the price of oil soared. Oil went up from $2.60 per barrel to $10 in 1973, to $12 in 1976, and then all the way to $35 in 1980. The AS curve shifted leftward all over the globe, inflicting the trauma of stagflation around the world.

The Great Depression had resulted from tumbling demand, the stagflation from tumbling supply. When aggregate supply falls relative to aggregate demand, Keynesian strategy alone can become self-destructive. Keynes, after all, had tackled the deficiency of demand, not supply. Deficit financing had already generated high inflation; the supply shock of oil pushed prices into the stratosphere. Stagflation was now at its peak.

The government policy, still in the hands of neo-Keynesians, offered the same old remedy of deficit financing even though circumstances had changed dramatically. The result was persistent joblessness with high inflation, which peaked at 13.5 percent in 1980, and coexisted with a jobless rate of 7 percent.

During the 1970s, the neoclassicists came out firing against Keynesian economics. The assault was led by two Chicago experts, Professors

Friedman and Lucas. Professor Friedman pioneered what is known as "monetarism," which argues that the source of most business fluctuations is the monetary and not, as Keynes believed, the investment-goods sector. While to Keynes the deficiency of investment relative to savings is the catalyst for recessions, to Friedman the causal factor is the deficient supply of money, whose growth has declined prior to every recession in the United States. Furthermore this shrinkage, Friedman claims, sprang mostly from the ineptness of monetary authorities or the intrusion of politicians. Therefore, it is not possible to fine tune the economy and expect it to remain healthy.

Monetarism differs fundamentally from Keynesian thought, which regards the economy as basically unstable, requiring constant government watch in terms of monetary and fiscal policies. Monetarists, by contrast, suggest that the economy is basically stable, and the State should limit itself to maintaining a uniform growth rate of money, equal to real GDP growth, which approximates 4 percent per year. This is because when money and output grow at the same rate, the rate of inflation becomes zero. Otherwise, high money growth designed to permanently maintain high employment only spawns inflation, at least in the long run.

There is one exception to the uniform monetarist rule. During an emergency such as the Great Depression, the government may intervene by sharply raising the growth of money; but even their fiscal expansion could backfire because of the phenomenon of crowding out discussed previously. *Thus, monetary policy, according to monetarists, takes precedence even in an emergency.*

11. Rational Expectations

Professor Lucas's assault on Keynes is more broad-based than Friedman's. He seeks to rejuvenate the entire classical thesis but offers views that border on the ridiculous. Friedman would at least permit some government intervention in an emergency like the Great Depression. Lucas would not. He rationalizes the entire classical potion, but in a new package. You are already familiar with this package from Chapter 6. Now you have a chance to see some more.

Professor Lucas believes that workers have rational expectations, especially about future prices. Except when the economy is in depression, employment expansion in the Keynesian model requires that the real wage fall following the increase in the price level. Keynes himself acknowledged this much. Lucas argues that rational workers would not permit the fall in the real wage even in the short run. Therefore, any kind of economic policy aimed at promoting employment is bound to fail.

When workers see repeatedly that government actions raise prices, they associate expansionary policies with higher inflation. Therefore, whenever the government announces its intention to follow such a policy by means of deficit financing, workers expect higher inflation in the near future, and immediately demand higher wages, rather than wait for expected inflation to materialize.

If the money wage rises to match the rise in the price level, there is no fall in the real wage, in which case output and employment cannot increase. Therefore, economic policy is totally ineffective even in the short run. Government policy can be successful only if workers misinterpret it. Rational workers, however, cannot be misled.

Some neoclassicists regard rational expectations as a revolutionary idea, surpassing even the depth of Keynes's thought. The idea indeed makes good sense in an inflationary environment, but not in general. It is one thing to say that workers equate deficit financing with higher inflation when they have lived with an era of rising prices, and quite another to say that deficit financing always creates expectations of rising prices.

When the government resorted to deficit financing in the recessions of 2001, few expected the resurgence of inflation. This is because inflation had already cooled for a full decade. The federal budget was in surplus that year but went into a massive deficit exceeding $350 billion by 2003. At the same time the Federal Reserve expanded money supply briskly and cut the interest rate 12 times in just 18 months. This was the fastest jump in the rate of deficit financing in U.S. history. But no one expected the revival of inflation. Where were those rational expectations?

Professor Lucas's idea is not a general theory and applies only to the realm of persistent inflation. You already know that there is a long-run cycle of inflation in the United States, wherein inflation peaks every third decade in normal circumstances. Therefore, Lucas's viewpoint applies to only one decade out of every three. It is far from a revolution.

The rational expectations hypothesis is purely ridiculous for another reason. Suppose you ask your employer for a raise as the government announces an increase in deficit financing. The theory assumes that the employer will immediately grant your request. We know that real wages of production workers have been falling since 1972. Nowadays, the American employer does not raise wages even in the long run, even if your productivity rises. Thus, the Lucas theory flies in the face of reality.

11.1. *Professor Lucas's Average Worker*

You have seen in Chapter 6 how wealthy the average worker is in Lucas's framework. How he is never laid off, is focused on the future, and hates the income tax and so on. Now you see that Lucas's average worker is also a savvy economist and econometrician. He is informed and well versed in statistical techniques. He is also a forecasting genius. There is a well-known joke that for every four economists gathered in a room there are eight forecasts. When the experts themselves make constant errors in forecasting, how can an average Joe foresee inflation accurately?

Because of the cycle of inflation, with its peaks and valleys, few have ever anticipated inflation. To my knowledge no-one foresaw the fall of inflation that occurred in the 1980s and the 1990s, or the stock market bubble that spanned two decades, or the stock market crash that started in the new millennium. To paraphrase Mark Twain once again: It is very difficult to make predictions, especially about the future. Yet, the average worker, asserts Lucas, is astute enough to foretell the future. If she cannot, then government intervention may lessen unemployment in the short run.

However, Professor Lucas has rightly denounced the idea of the inflation–unemployment tradeoff. What then is left of the Phillips curve? Not much. After 1983, both inflation and unemployment fell together until 1986; then inflation picked up, but joblessness moved erratically. Similarly, from 1993 all the way up to 2000, inflation rates were either constant or on the decline, while the rate of unemployment kept up its downward march. None of these events accords with the idea of the Phillips curve. It is surprising, and indeed a testimony to the numbing influence of econometrics, that such nonsense became popular, and swayed policymaking for a long time.

Today, the neo-Keynesian model is still on the defensive, at least among academic economists, even though many government policies continue to display Keynes's imprint, especially since the Great Recession of 2007–2008. The neoclassical framework, in spite of its overt irrationality, dominates macroeconomic thinking, especially in the realm of tax policy that focuses on the income tax. Both schools of thought have logical flaws, of which some have been pinpointed. Some others will be noted in the next chapter, where we perform a blending of the two systems and remove the defects to obtain a truly general theory.

12. Summary

(1) In the Neo-Keynesian model aggregate demand is linked negatively and the aggregate supply positively to the price level.

(2) In a depression, expansionary monetary and fiscal policies raise output and employment without causing inflation.

(3) In a recession, expansionary monetary and fiscal policies raise output, employment as well as the price level.

(4) If the aggregate supply curve shifts to the left because of a rise in the price of oil or sharply rising wages, output and employment fall and the price level goes up.

(5) Stagflation is a state of rising inflation as well as unemployment.

(6) There is a tradeoff between inflation and unemployment and is known as the Phillips curve.

(7) According to the Phillips curve or the creed of deficit financing, which means that State budget deficits are financed primarily by money creation, joblessness can be reduced permanently. Needless to say, such painless and simple way of eradicating unemployment is false.

(8) According to monetarism fluctuations in money supply are the main cause of business fluctuations so that the monetary authority should

follow a uniform rule whereby money supply grows at the rate of long-run GDP growth, approximating 4 percent.

(9) Rational expectations mean that workers use all available information to form their future expectations. Specifically, expansionary economic policies cause them to believe that inflation is about to rise.

(10) The policy of deficit financing followed in the recession of 2001 failed to create expectations of future inflation.

Chapter 9

A Classi-Keynesian Model

Both the neoclassical and neo-Keynesian systems have a good deal to offer in the realm of macroeconomics and economic policy, but they also have their defects, of which a few have been noted before. At the risk of repetition, some of their major flaws are noted as follows:

(1) Classical and neoclassical models are unable to explain "involuntary unemployment," which has afflicted the world time and again.

(2) They regard money as neutral as far as real variables are concerned, but experience shows that small injections of monetary stimulus lead economies out of recessions, so that real GDP and employment rise. Thus, money and monetary policy are far from neutral and may have beneficial effects on the real side of the economy.

(3) The neo-Keynesian framework can indeed explain the phenomenon of involuntary unemployment but may need wage rigidity. It is not a market-clearing system in the sense that not all its markets have to be in equilibrium simultaneously. For instance, there may be excess supply in the labor market while the goods market is in equilibrium. In addition, the real wage in the Keynesian system is set arbitrarily and not determined by the forces of demand and supply.

(4) Another problem is that in the Keynesian system the real wage falls in a booming economy with soaring employment, whereas experience and common sense suggest the contrary. When labor demand climbs,

the real wage should increase, not fall, because a rise in the demand for anything tends to raise its price. Economic data also reveal that the real wage generally moves up with a rise in employment, but in the classical, neoclassical, Keynesian and neo-Keynesian systems the real wage is the lowest at full employment.

Since both the classical and Keynesian systems deal with the same subject, it should not be difficult to construct a hybrid of the two models that does away with their flaws while retaining their merits. This is what we will do now and call the hybrid a classi-Keynesian model.

The "classi-Keynesian" system can accommodate both wage-price flexibility and wage rigidity, and yet demonstrate that money may or may not be neutral, depending upon the state of the economy. Even with perfectly flexible wages and prices, the alternative model explains the onset of unemployment in recessions, which can be eliminated by monetary injections, although around full employment of all resources, a monetary stimulus will only generate inflation. In other words, *the new model demonstrates precisely what seems to have been corroborated by empirical experience. But it does all this in a basically classical framework, not in terms of the Keynesian system, although the conclusions remind you of what Keynes sought to accomplish.*

Our point of departure lies in introducing the concept of capacity utilization (CU), which varies across the business cycle. History suggests that a booming U.S. economy utilizes about 90–95 percent of its productive capacity, as in the 1960s, whereas in a stagnant or contracting phase of the economy this utilization falls sharply. Indeed, it fell to as low as 50 percent during the Great Depression.

The classical model generally believes that capital stock is either fully utilized or its rate of usage is constant regardless of the state of the economy, while the use of labor input varies depending on the level of output. In reality, as documented by scores of studies, the rate of capital utilization and labor demand move together. When employment is high, capacity use is also high, and when employment is low, capacity use is also low. We generalize the simple classical framework by explicitly incorporating the proportion of capacity usage in the production function.

1. The Fixed Price Case

Let us begin with the simplest case of a fixed price level. Here marginal cost is constant and the firms base their production completely on what are called "factory orders." When such orders increase, companies expand their output; when they go down, output falls. The firms receive these orders primarily from retailers, who, in turn, sell goods to households and government agencies.

Factory orders and aggregate demand move together. The orders expand with a rise in AD and contract with its fall. They have a direct and immediate impact on capital stock utilization. When factory orders increase, output first responds through an increased usage of productive capacity, not through enhanced hiring. Only when firms are convinced that the increase in aggregate demand is permanent, do they expand their employment. The main idea is that AD first affects CU and then jobs. Similarly, on the supply side, output in the short run varies in two ways — first through the fluctuating usage of existing capital, and then through changes in labor demand.

A rise in AD raises the usage of capital at the current level of employment. This raises the average and hence the marginal product of labor (MPL), enabling the firms to increase their hiring. If AD falls, output decreases and the capital usage decline immediately, thereby lowering the MPL as well as employment. Thus, aggregate demand does not have a direct impact on labor demand; it influences employment indirectly, through its impact on CU. This seems to be a minor point of departure, but it turns out to have profound implications for macroeconomics, because it erases the flaws of conventional theories.

Take the case of a fall in AD, so that CU declines along with the MPL. This forces the firms to lay off workers, even though the real wage, equal to the MPL, has also declined. You can see this easily in the now-familiar classical graph of the labor market, where the fall in the MPL will shift the labor demand curve to the left, generating sinking employment and the real wage. (Please also see Figure 9.3). Thus, employment shrinks in spite of a flexible real wage. Of course, if the real wage is rigid, the job decline will be even stronger.

In the opposite case of expanding AD, CU rises first and then the MPL, enabling businesses to increase their hiring and offer a higher real wage. The main point is that once CU is considered explicitly, aggregate demand determines employment and the real wage even in the classical model. It alters the character of the entire argument. Keynesian rigidities are no longer needed to explain unemployment. Such rigidities may indeed be present in the economy, but they do not have to be invoked to explain joblessness.

You may also see *that a rise in employment now coexists with a rise in the real wage, and joblessness coexists with a fall in the real wage*, something that common sense dictates. In addition, economic policy that impacts aggregate demand comes to play a significant role in business stabilization in spite of the real wage flexibility.

2. The Variable Price Case

The flaws in the neoclassical and Keynesian systems arise from their treatment of the supply side of the economy, and this is what we will now address. Let us continue to assume that firms face keen or perfect competition, and hire the factors of production, capital and labor, in a way to maximize their profits, so that the marginal value product of each factor equals the factor cost. That is,

$$W = P \cdot \text{MPL}$$

and

$$i = P \cdot \text{MPK}$$

where MPK is the marginal product of capital, and, as before, W is the money wage, P the price level and i the nominal rate of interest. Both factors are combined technologically to generate the output in terms of a production function as

$$Y = F(K, L)$$

and

$$K = \text{CU} \cdot K\text{o}, \text{CU} \leq 1$$

where, as before, Y is output or aggregate supply, Ko is the constant stock of capital, and CU is a fraction that stands for capacity utilization. You have already seen in Chapters 7 and 8 that if P rises then labor demand goes up, provided the nominal wage is either constant or fails to match the price rise. In the same way, from the capital-hiring condition, you can see that the demand for capital will also go up if the interest rate fails to match the price rise. But capital stock is constant; so, what actually rises is CU, up to its limit of one.

On the other hand, if P declines then the demand for capital will fall, so long as the interest rate responds sluggishly. But with capital stock constant in the short run, CU has to fall in a downturn. This is what we normally observe in the economy, but the classical and Keynesian models generally ignore it. Thus, the output fall in a recession arises not only from a decline in employment but also in CU. By contrast, in the phase of expansion, the output rise stemming from a price rise comes from a rise in employment as well as in CU.

3. Price Level and the Interest Rate

The Keynesian theory of interest can be used to show that an increase in P increases the nominal interest rate but not in the same proportion. In Figure 9.1, the equilibrium interest rate appears at the intersection of money demand and supply curves, or at point E. Here money demand is related negatively to the rate of interest. Money supply, by contrast, is positively linked to the interest rate, because in general it is determined not only by central-bank authorities but also by the behavior of financial institutions, such as commercial banks, savings and loan associations and brokerage houses.

A rise in the rate of interest induces the banking system to increase their lending and thus increase the supply of money. This is how the banks maximize their income, a behavior pattern that is captured by the positively sloped money supply curve. (More on this in Chapter 13.)

Now suppose the price level goes up to shift the money demand curve to the right to line NMD. Rising prices induce people to increase their transaction and precautionary demand for money, which goes up in proportion to the rise in P. This shift equals EA. Since a rise in the demand

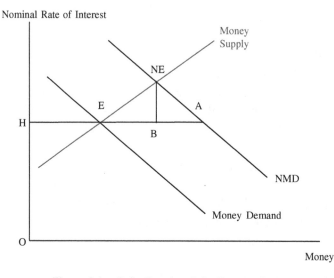

Figure 9.1:   Price Level and the Interest Rate

for anything raises its price, the rate of interest, the price of money, rises in the new equilibrium by an amount equal to BNE, which is clearly smaller than EA. Thus, the rise in the nominal interest rate is likely to fall short of the rise in *P*.

This analysis implies that a rise in inflation lowers the real rate of interest, and a fall raises the real rate, because the

real rate of interest = nominal interest rate – the rate of inflation

Figure 9.2 confirms this conclusion historically. The upper part of the figure displays the track that followed the rate of inflation, as measured by the percentage increase in the GDP deflator, whereas the lower part depicts the path of the real rate of interest. Their trend lines that represent the average behavior of the two variables move in the opposite direction. One has a positive slope and the other has a negative slope. This means that as the rate of inflation rises, the real rate of interest falls, and as the inflation rate declines, the real interest rate increases. In fact, during the 1970s, the real rate of interest even became negative when inflation soared, as in 1974 and 1975.

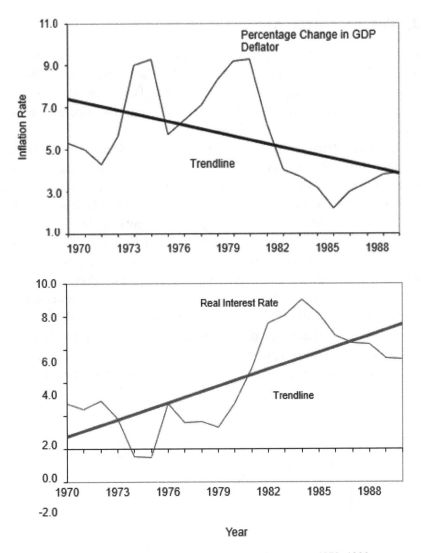

Figure 9.2: Inflation and the Real Rate of Interest: 1970–1990

This section then reinforces what we have argued earlier, namely, a rise in P tends to raise the rate of CU up to its limit because the nominal interest rate fails to match the price rise. Similarly, a fall in the price level lowers CU as the real interest rate rises.

4. The AS Curve Again

It is now clear that if *P* rises the real rate of interest falls. Let us now assume perfect wage-price flexibility, so that the nominal wage rises or falls in the same proportion as the price level. Here then labor demand equals labor supply, as in the classical model, and by this definition, the economy is always at full employment.

Suppose *P* rises, say, under the pressure of increasing aggregate demand. This raises CU until its limit, and even if labor demand is constant, the level of output rises up to the limit. This, in turn, enhances the average product of labor as well as the MPL. As a result, labor demand and employment also rise, so that output climbs once again.

The argument becomes clear in Figure 9.3, which is the same type of figure as used in Chapter 5 to illustrate the classical theory of the labor market. As before, the axes depict the real wage and labor. The initial equilibrium point is E, which is the product of intersection between labor demand and labor supply curves, generating a real wage of OH.

In the classical model, a rise in *P* produces no change in the figure, so that the real wage and employment are also unchanged. But if CU goes up because of a rise in the price level, then MPL rises and the labor demand

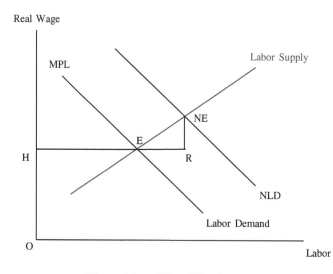

Figure 9.3:   CU and Employment

curve shifts up to NLD, generating a new equilibrium at NE. Clearly then, employment climbs from HE to HR, and the real wage rises by RNE.

Aggregate supply then rises because of a rise in CU as well as employment, of course, up to the limit of CU.

If the price level falls, CU falls; then MPL falls, employment declines and so do output and the real wage. This can be seen by a leftward shift of the MPL curve in the figure (not shown). The AS curve so generated looks like the one in Figure 9.4. It has a positive slope between point B and FC (full capacity), and then it becomes vertical. The shape of the AS curve suggests that output goes up with an increase in the price level until the exhaustion of productive capacity, and then becomes constant. With *each point on the AS curve, labor demand equals labor supply, and employment rises until the FC point.* The equality of labor demand and supply is guaranteed by the classical assumption of wage-price flexibility.

Let us now redefine the concept of joblessness. *Let us suppose that full employment of labor occurs when the economy operates at full capacity.* Therefore, even though labor demand and supply are equal at all points on the AS curve, full employment arrives only at point FC. This is because the higher the level of CU, the higher the level of employment. Herein arises the importance of aggregate demand in the case of a variable price level.

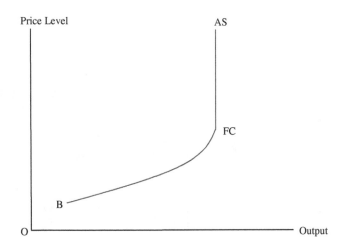

Figure 9.4:   The AS Curve in the Classi-Keynesian Model

Since 1970 the rate of CU has been generally below 90 percent, even when the jobless rate hovers around 5 percent. But at the end of the 1960s, when CU exceeded 90 percent, the rate of unemployment was merely 3.5 percent. This suggests that at the full capacity point, where CU approximates 95 percent, the employment level is at its maximum. Therefore, the full capacity point defines the full employment of all resources — labor and capital. *In the classi-Keynesian model, full employment occurs when output and employment levels available from all resources are at their highest point. Similarly, unemployment prevails, when the economy operates below the full capacity level of output.*

5. Macro Equilibrium

In Figure 9.5, the aggregate demand curve cuts the AS curve at point FC, the full capacity point, generating an equilibrium output of OG as well as full employment. If the AD curve were to cut the positively sloped portion of the AS curve, output will be below full capacity, and there will be a recession and some unemployment. Now the question is: Is this jobless-ness voluntary or involuntary? It is both, even though the labor market equilibrium is generated by the intersection of labor demand and labor supply curves.

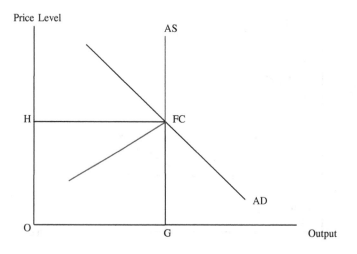

Figure 9.5:   Equilibrium in the Classi-Keynesian Model

Let us go back to Figure 9.3 and start with point NE as the point of full employment. Suppose aggregate demand decreases and lowers the utilization rate of existing capital stock. Output declines at the constant level of employment. Therefore, the average product of labor and the MPL also declines. In Figure 9.3, the NLD curve shifts to the left to the MPL line, equilibrium moves to point E, the real wage falls by RNE and employment by RE.

As the real wage falls, some people quit work, but most do not. The higher real wage improves a family's lifestyle, which is not easy to give up. Let us examine a typical two-earner family today. With higher income, the family has bought a bigger house with a bigger mortgage, possibly sends its children to private schools, and gets accustomed to vacationing out of town.

Suppose now the real wage falls, and one of the two earners has a choice between neoclassical leisure and work. The worker will be unwilling to leave her job because this could require the sale of the house, moving children to inferior schools and giving up joyful vacations. The benefit is the extra leisure, but for most families the cost in terms of the changed lifestyle is prohibitive, because few like to uproot their children from their home and schools. Therefore, the worker will be happy to swallow the bitter pill of a reduced real wage while keeping her job. But if she is fired anyway, her joblessness is involuntary.

Since labor demand at the real wage of OH is HE in Figure 9.3, while the labor supply at that wage is somewhere between, HE and HR, there is some involuntary unemployment. *The neoclassical labor supply curve depends on household preferences, but these preferences change once a family comes to enjoy the lifestyle of a higher income.* If the lifestyle had not changed, perhaps most workers would have left at will with the fall in the real wage. But the upper-income lifestyle alters the household's preference function, and the fact of employment itself increases an employee's preference for work over leisure. Therefore, when labor demand falls, there is involuntary unemployment in our model.

Joblessness is therefore both voluntary and involuntary. Those who quit work are voluntarily unemployed, but those who are laid off even though they are willing to work at the lower wage of OH are involuntarily unemployed.

6. Monetary Policy

Let us begin with a situation of recession, where output is below its full capacity level, and employment is below its maximum. Can monetary policy be used to cure the problem? The answer is yes.

Take a look at Figure 9.6, where the initial equilibrium is at point E that lies on the intersection of AD and AS curves, and output is HE, which is less than the full capacity output of HB. This is a situation of recession. If the central bank increases the supply of money, a chain reaction follows. First, the interest rate comes down, and then consumer spending, household investment, some business investment and hence aggregate demand, all go up.

The AD line shifts up to the NAD line, which in turn cuts the AS curve at point FC. Full employment returns, output rises by EB, while the price level goes up by BFC. Here, then, money is no longer neutral. But if monetary expansion is overdone, the new AD curve is given by the line HAD; so output still rises by EB but the price level soars by BR. *Monetary expansion becomes neutral once full capacity output is realized.*

Thus, money is neutral so long as the AD curve intersects the AS curve at its vertical portion. Otherwise it is not. The effects of

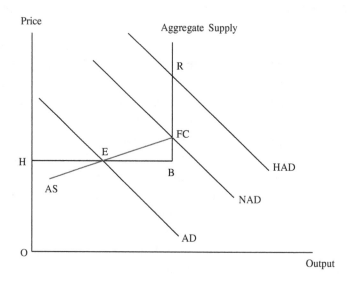

Figure 9.6:   Neutrality and Non-Neutrality of Money

expansionary fiscal policy, subject to crowding out, can also be analyzed in Figure 9.6. The conclusions are similar to those applying to monetary policy.

7. Employment and the Real Wage

What happens to the real wage when employment goes up? It no longer falls. This is because as AD expands, CU goes up, and so does the MPL. This in turn raises employment as well as the real wage. You can confirm this from Figure 9.3. Unlike the Keynesian model, there is no decline in the real wage with growth in jobs.

It is not that we have given up the law of diminishing MPL. In the Keynesian framework, the rise in employment occurs along the MPL curve, but in our model, it occurs because of the upward shift of the MPL curve resulting from rising CU and output. The rise in CU itself produces an increase in the MPL, employment and real wage, something that occurs neither in the neoclassical nor in the neo-Keynesian system. In fact, when the economy operates at full capacity, employment and the real wage are at their maximum in our model.

Similarly, in a recession, the MPL curve shifts to the left because of falling output and CU. The result is a fall in both equilibrium employment and the real wage.

8. A Rise in the Price of Oil

How does a rise in the price of oil interact in our model? In order to understand this phenomenon, let us rewrite the capital-hiring condition as

$$i + \text{energy cost} = P \cdot \text{MPK}$$

This suggests that capital hiring increases until its marginal contribution equals its true cost, which includes not only the cost of borrowing money (i) but also the energy cost incurred in operating machines. A rise in the oil price raises the energy cost and tends to reduce the use of capital (K), but since $K = \text{CU} \cdot Ko$, then, with capital constant, it is CU that ends in a fall. This itself tends to lower production at the full-employment price

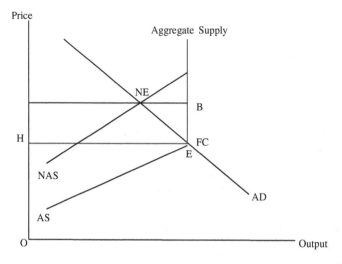

Figure 9.7:   Oil Price and Stagnation

level of OH and shift the AS curve leftward in Figure 9.7 to NAS. The full capacity output level is constant, but equilibrium output falls by BNE, whereas the price level goes up by EB.

What happens to employment? In the labor market, the MPL curve shifts to the left, reducing the MPL and hence the real wage. However, something unexpected may happen to employment because of the rise in the price level. Initially, as CU and the MPL decline, employment falls, as in Figure 9.8, where the fall in the MPL pushes the labor demand curve LD backward to the TLD line. Here, the axes represent the nominal wage and labor. The equilibrium point moves temporarily to TE, and the money wage falls by BE. The real wage also falls by this amount, because so far, the price level has been kept constant.

Now comes the effect of the leftward shift of the AS curve so that the price level goes up by BFC or BE in Figure 9.7. This rise tends to shift the new labor demand curve back toward the old one, and if the price rise is in proportion to the initial fall in the MPL, the labor demand curve comes back to where it started. Here employment is unchanged at the level HE, and the money wage returns to its old level.

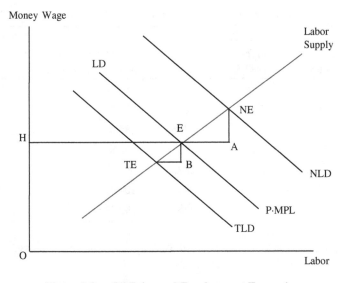

Figure 9.8:   Oil Price and Employment Expansion

9. The Employment Paradox

It is also possible that the increase in the price level outweighs the initial
fall in the MPL, so that the labor demand curve settles above the initial
LD curve, at the NLD line. The final equilibrium in Figure 9.8 is then at
point NE, and employment actually rises by EA. This effect may be called
the "employment paradox," which occurs when in the new equilibrium
output falls while employment goes up. The money wage rises further but
by less than the rise in the price level, so that the real wage falls again.
Here is one case in our model, where the real wage falls in the wake of a
rise in employment.

The employment paradox resulting from a rise in the price of oil is not
just a theoretical novelty, but a fact of life that occurred twice in the oil-
induced recessions in the United States. Take a look at Table 9.1, where
the effects of expensive oil are listed for two time periods — 1973–1975,
and from 1979–1982.

The Organization of Petroleum Exporting Countries (OPEC) raised
the international price of oil sharply during the 1970s, but domestic

Table 9.1:   Fuel Prices and Recessions in the United States; 1973–1982

(1) Year	(2) Fuel Price Index	(3) Real GDP (billions of) 1987 $	(4) CU Index	(5) Employment (thousands)	(6) GDP deflator	(7) Real Wage Index
1973	19*	3,269	88	85,064	41	99
1974	25	3,248	84	86,794	45	98
1975	31	3,221	75	85,846	49	98
1979	57	3,797	86	98,824	66	102
1980	69	3,767	82	99,303	72	99
1981	85	3,843	81	100,397	79	99
1982	100	3,760	75	99,526	84	100

Note: *All figures have been rounded.

Source: *The Economic Report of the President*, February 1995, Council of Economic Advisers, Washington, D.C., pp. 276, 278, 314, 328, 333, 348.

American prices did not rise as fast. From 1973 to 1975 the domestic fuel price index (column 2) jumped from 19 to 31, or roughly by 63 percent. Consequently, real GDP (column 3) dropped from $3,269 billion to $3,221 billion over two years. The fall in output came mainly from the decline in CU (column 4), which fell from 88 to 75, or by 15 percent, because employment (column 5) in 1975 was actually higher than in 1973. The reason was the sharp rise in the GDP deflator (column 6), which rose from 41 to 49, or by almost 20 percent. Finally, the real wage (column 7) fell a little.

The picture is more or less the same in terms of the recession that started in 1979 and essentially lasted all the way till 1982, even though in 1981 output rose slightly. However, the entire period may be regarded as contractionary, because the 1982 output was below the 1979 output.

There were two culprits here. One, of course, was the sharp rise in the fuel price over the entire period, leading to a decrease in CU, while employment generally continued to rise along with the GDP deflator. Another was the policy of monetary restraint that the Fed adopted in 1981 to fight raging inflation. During this downturn, as in the period between 1973 and 1975, the real wage fell slightly.

It may be noted that the "employment paradox" occurs only when the economy is hit by a supply shock such as the soaring price of oil.

A demand shock stemming, say, from a fall in autonomous investment does no such thing, either in theory or in practice. For instance, in the recessions of 1953–1954 and 1957–1958, investment decreased first, causing a fall in aggregate demand, output and employment. The same thing happened in the more recent recessions of 2001 and 2007.

The classi-Keynesian model thus explains the entire spectrum of economic activity during the 1970s and 2000s, whereas other models do not. Even the "Real Business Cycle (RBC)" theory, which is designed specially to tackle the case of expensive oil, fails to account for the paradox of sinking output along with rising employment. What is missing in other models is an explicit role for CU, which makes it possible for output to fall even as labor demand goes up because of surging inflation.

Then what about all the horror stories you hear of high unemployment during the 1970s and in the recession of 2001? The unemployment rate indeed soared in 1970s, only because labor supply soared owing to the rising tax burden on the poor and the middle class, and not because of a fall in the number of jobs (see Chapters 10 and 12 for more on this point). On the whole, there were no layoffs, only new job seekers met with disappointment. Indeed, the jobless rate was 8.5 percent in 1975 and a prickly 9.7 percent in 1982, yet the culprit was a lack of hiring, not a jump in firing.

10. Summary

(1) The "classi-Keynesian" model is a blending of the classical and neo-Keynesian models.

(2) The hybrid system retains the assumptions of the classical framework but derives Keynesian conclusions. Thus, employment is determined by aggregate demand, while the real and nominal wage spring from the labor-market equilibrium. Nevertheless, Keynesian rigidities can also be accommodated in the new framework.

(3) Even though, thanks to wage-price flexibility, labor supply and labor demand are always equal along the aggregate supply curve, full employment occurs only when the economy operates at the "full capacity" point. This occurs because both employment and the real wage can rise until the full capacity point.

(4) A rise in the price level raises CU, because of a fall in the real rate of interest. A fall in the price level does the opposite.

(5) The real wage is the highest at the full capacity point. Contrast this with various classical and Keynesian systems, where the real wage is the lowest at the point of full employment.

(6) Monetary and fiscal expansion generate a rise in CU, employment, output and the real wage, so long as the economy is in recession, i.e., it is operating below the full capacity point.

(7) Beyond the full capacity point monetary and fiscal expansion cause nothing but inflation.

(8) During the two recessions of the 1970s, when the international price of oil soared, output fell but employment rose slightly. This "employment paradox" can be explained only by the classi-Keynesian model, because CU shrank so much from the rise in energy cost that output fell despite a rise in labor demand, which itself resulted from a sharp rise in the price level.

(9) Unemployment is both voluntary and involuntary because the work preference increases once a person becomes employed, so that with falling aggregate demand and the real wage some workers quit work, while others with changed preferences are laid off against their will.

Chapter 10

The Anatomy of Stock Market Bubbles and Crashes

The classi-Keynesian model explored earlier removes some of the flaws from conventional macroeconomics, but a major drawback remains. The orthodox theories are unable to explain the rise and fall of stock market bubbles, which have traumatized the world in recent years. Ever since 1987, the year of the worst stock market crash in history, share prices have fascinated people at all income levels, yet macro texts have mostly winked at them, offering just a casual treatment. This is unfortunate, because speculative bubbles or manias generally precede depressions, poverty growth or persistent employment stagnation, and until the bubbles are properly explained by the macroeconomic model, depressions and poverty will remain a mystery. Conventional ideas do an adequate job of accounting for recessions, but not for a catastrophic slump of the kind that plagued our planet in the 1930s. The following questions remain unanswered:

(1) Why do stock markets not always rocket in a boom?
(2) Why do all sky-high share markets crash eventually?
(3) Why do such crashes generally breed depressions or prolonged stagnation?
(4) What is the role played by macroeconomic policy in first generating the market bubbles and then erasing their aftershocks?

(5) Why is the world currently plagued by huge budget deficits and trade imbalances?

(6) Why has income and wealth inequality soared all over the world?

These are the questions on which our macro model will now focus. U. S. history reveals that there were two time zones in which share prices escalated sharply — during the 1920s, and then from 1981 all the way up to 2019. Other decades saw paltry rises in stock markets even though some of them displayed much greater prosperity.

The 1960s were thriving times for American business and labor, yet the Dow Jones Index of stock prices (the Dow in short) rose just 40 percent. The economy grew at the rate of 4.4 percent per year, and the Dow failed even to match that growth rate. By contrast, the 1980s saw a sluggish growth rate of 2.8 percent, while the Dow almost tripled. From 2010 to 2019, annual economic growth was even more mediocre at 2 percent, but that did not stop the Dow from reaching an all-time high. Therefore, what did recent decades have that the 1960s lacked?

1. What Is a Bubble?

During the 1990s the Dow broke all bounds and jumped from about 2,500 in 1990 to its peak of 11,700 in January 2000. Was this a bubble, a word that implies irrationality? Look at it this way. The Dow Jones Index was first compiled in 1885 and following 1982 it permanently passed 1,000. The Dow took nearly 100 years to cross the 1,000 mark, and then in the next two decades it surpassed 11,000. This was not an ordinary bubble, but a bubble of the millennium.

The Nasdaq stock index flew even higher, from about 300 in 1990 all the way up to 5,049 on March 10, 2000. Even as late as 1996, the index stood near 1,000, but then in the next six years it crossed 5,000.

What is a speculative bubble? When the law of demand for assets breaks down completely, a speculative bubble or mania is born.

By instinct people do not like to buy goods when they are pricey, but in a ballyhooed environment surrounding bubbles they purchase assets simply because their prices have already surged and are expected to surge more. On the flip side, the public shuns these assets even as their prices fall.

When Nortel sold for $80 per share, Wall Street analysts cajoled investors to buy even more. When it crashed all the way to $2 in 2001, they advised, "don't buy it." Price Line.Com once sold for $170 per share, and still had a lot of seekers. When it sank to $1 per share, it had few takers. Such is the stuff of which bubbles are made. People become irrational and the law of demand falls apart completely, first when prices of speculative assets rise, and then again when they fall.

2. Wages and Productivity

In all our models so far, we have assumed that the real wage equals the marginal product of labor (MPL), which in turn is linked to its average product or labor productivity. This is not a bad assumption and applies to much of American history. In fact, you saw in Chapter 2 that from 1874 to 1950 the real wage generally kept up with rising productivity (Figure 2.5).

There are, however, times when the strong, positive relationship between the real wage and productivity breaks down. Why this occurs does not concern us at this point and will be examined later. Whenever this happens, however, something unique and unexpected transpires; something that enthralls the public for a while, and germinates a speculative mania, but is followed by a devastating crash. Society gets drunk overnight, only to face the hangover that comes the day after.

Whenever the real wage trails productivity, a wage gap develops in the economy. Therefore, the concept of the wage gap may be defined as the following:

$$\text{wage gap} = \frac{\text{productivity}}{\text{real wage}} \geq 1$$

In a two-factor world of capital and labor, unless profit or capital income is zero, the wage gap is always present. This is because the fruit of productivity generally accrues to both labor and capital, so that the wage-gap ratio exceeds one. In the extreme, when profit vanishes altogether, the ratio equals one.

The wage gap grows if productivity grows faster than the real wage and falls in the opposite case. When wages just keep up with productivity, the gap remains constant. Take a close look at Table 10.1, which describes the wage–productivity relationship in the United States for two time periods — first the 1920s and then from 1970 to 2019.

If we divide the index of output per hour in the business sector by the index of real employee compensation, both available from various issues of *The Economic Report of the President,* we obtain a measure of the

Table 10.1: The Wage Gap in the United States for Selected Years: 1970–2018 and 1919–1929 (in percent)

Year	Prod/Wage*	Year**	Prod/Wage
1970	65	1919	111
1975	69	1921	128
1980	70	1923	130
1985	75	1925	148
1990	77	1927	154
1995	81	1929	156
2000	82	—	—
2010	99	—	—
2018	101	—	—

Notes: *Column 2 furnishes the wage-gap index, which is obtained by dividing two other indexes, one dealing with output per hour or labor productivity in the business sector, and the other with real employee compensation or national real wage.

**The wage-gap indexes in columns 2 and 4 are not comparable because of differences in the definition of wages.

Source: *The Economic Report of the President,* 2019, B-49; *Historical Statistics of the United States,* 1975.

wage gap in the United States. If real incomes rise in sync with labor productivity, which is the same thing as hourly output, then the figures in column 2 should be more or less constant. In 1970, the wage-gap index stood at 65, and rose steadily thereafter, at first slowly, and then in a torrent to reach an all-time post-WWII high of 101 in 2019. Clearly, real wages trailed productivity over time; in four decades the wage-gap index soared about a third.

What is interesting, however, is that from 1970 to 1980, the wage gap was fairly constant, ranging from 65 to 70, but after 1980 it began a steady rise. The wage-gap index in column 2 relies on an overall wage, which is highly aggregated and does not truly represent the general public in the United States, because it also includes the compensation of the CEOs of the Fortune 500 corporations.

These bigwigs have seen a vast jump in their salaries since 1980 and their presence tends to distort the size of the real wage data pertaining to the public. We can get a better measure of the wage gap by using the average real wage of the non-supervisory or the production worker that you first met in Chapter 2. The message, however, remains the same, namely, that after 1970 the wage gap rises and then soars after 1980.

The other time zone in Table 10.1 refers to the 1920s. There the wage gap climbed from 111 in 1919 to 156 in 1929, or about 40 percent in one decade. This jump is comparable to the jump in column 2. It is clear that the decades following the 1980s have something in common with the 1920s, namely, that wages badly trailed productivity in both cases.

There are more similarities in the two time periods than meets the eye. Profits, stock prices, consumer debt and business mergers soared in both cases. Then, as now, governments adopted a non-interfering approach to company behavior. The general belief was what is good for big business is good for America. In both cases, macroeconomic policy emphasized industrial and financial deregulation. Taxes were cut repeatedly to benefit the affluent in the 1920s, just as in the 1980s. In both periods, leading economists argued that such tax cuts foster efficiency and promote social welfare. Figures 10.1 and 10.2 display how

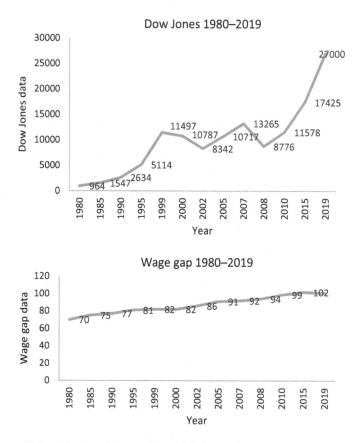

Figure 10.1:   The Dow Jones Industrial Index and the Wage Gap, 1980–2019

the rising wage gap coexisted with stock market bubbles in the 1920s and from 1980 to 2019. In 2019, for the first time in history the Dow crossed 27,000.

Then, as now, income and wealth inequality jumped, while the State stood idly by. Finally, of course in both cases, the share markets crashed. To be sure, there are also striking differences in the two time periods. But differences are only natural over time. The element of surprise lies in all the similarities you have observed. Are they simply coincidences or inevitable byproducts of the soaring wage gap?

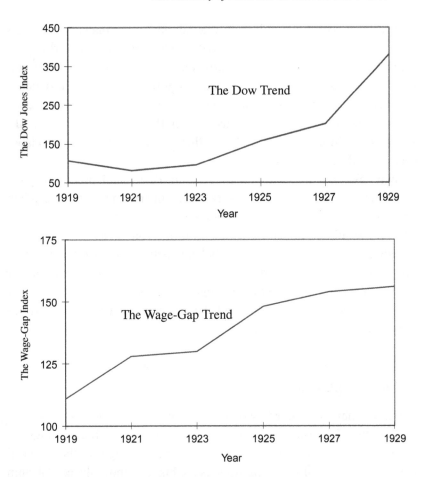

Figure 10.2:   The Dow and the Wage Gap in the 1920s

Source: P. S. Pierce, *The Dow Jones Averages: 1885–1990.*

3. Centrality of the Labor Market

How is the wage–productivity gap related to the macro economy? Stated another way, how are aggregate supply and aggregate demand, which form the cornerstone of macroeconomics, linked to the workforce? Through wages and productivity. You will soon discover that what happens in the labor market is the key to a country's prosperity and stability.

You have seen time and again that supply and demand for workers determine wages and employment. Skilled and motivated workers are the backbone of high productivity and efficiency in any firm; but what is perhaps crucial is that company wages are proportionate to labor productivity. When new technology enhances hourly output, then fairness demands that workers are properly compensated for their hard work and skills. This, as you will see, is not simply an ethical matter, but is crucial to labor peace as well as to general prosperity.

Why? Because wages are the main source of demand, productivity the main source of supply, and if the two are not in sync with each other, aggregate supply and demand cannot be in equilibrium for long. If wages continue to trail output per worker, equilibrium can indeed be maintained through artificial means, but the imbalance between demand and supply only grows over time, and eventually the economy runs into major hurdles. Whenever any country or region suffers a deep depression, or long-term stagnation, you will find the presence of a persistent wage–productivity gap in the background.

4. The Wage Gap

So far, we have examined two popular theories of unemployment — classical and Keynesian. However, both of them have shortcomings, or else they would have ended joblessness a long time ago. In the classical view, job losses occur if the real wage is too high, or above the equilibrium wage, so that if wages fall the problem would vanish. In the Keynesian view, unemployment arises from the deficiency of demand relative to supply, which makes sense, but Keynes did not explain why demand remains stagnant for long. However, the theory of the wage gap explains what classical and Keynesian theories do not.

As an example, let us suppose General Motors builds 50 cars and puts them up for sale. If only 45 are sold, then GM is stuck with five unsold autos, and it lays off some workers to keep profits high. In other words, if a firm does not sell all it has produced, it has to fire some workers and then produce whatever it can sell. It is now a simple matter to extend this idea to the macro economy.

As explained in previous chapters, macro supply means the value of goods and services produced by the nation as a whole, and macro demand signifies the level of spending by consumers and investors on those products. Both concepts are in terms of dollars. For now, let us ignore what the government may do to generate aggregate demand through its fiscal policy. Economic equilibrium requires that

$$supply = demand$$

As you know by now, supply is simply GDP, that is, the value of a nation's output in a year, whereas demand has two components. One is money spent by consumers out of their incomes, and the other is investment, which is spending by firms and people on investment goods, such as capital equipment and newly built residences. Thus,

$$demand = consumer\ spending\ on\ domestic\ goods + investment$$

For now, assume that there is no borrowing of any kind and the government has no budget shortfall. Let us suppose, supply at current prices equals $2,000, consumer demand or spending is $1,500 and investment equals $500. Then

$$demand = 1,500 + 500 = \$2,000 = supply$$

Here the economy is in balance, where supply equals demand, so that there are no layoffs. Now let the wage rate fall in line with the prescription of the classical model. Then consumer spending will also fall, because people's salary is the major determinant of their spending. Suppose this spending declines $300. Therefore, now

$$demand = 1,200 + 500 = \$1,700 < supply = \$2,000$$

Since supply exceeds demand, there will be layoffs; so you see the classical theory is flawed. Instead of solving the problem of job losses, it makes it worse. In fact, investment will also decline because of decreasing consumer spending, and more layoffs will follow. On the other side of the spectrum, the Keynesian model is indeed valid, but it fails to explain why demand may remain deficient for long, as it did during the Great Depression and now since 2007.

Recall that the wage gap is defined as

$$\text{wage gap} = \frac{\text{labor productivity}}{\text{real wage}}$$

where the real wage is the purchasing power of your salary, and productivity is output per employee or what you produce for a business. If productivity grows faster than the real wage, the wage gap goes up. In the classical model, the real wage falls and augments this gap. The other case is where only productivity rises, say, by 10 percent; then at current prices supply also increases 10 percent. Thus, supply is now $2,200. If the wage rate is constant, consumer spending and demand stay constant as well. Recall that initially the economy was in balance, with demand equaling $2,000. After the productivity rise,

$$\text{supply} = \$2,200 > \text{demand} = \$2,000$$

Here again there is overproduction and hence layoffs. The real cause of joblessness must now be apparent. Whenever, the wage gap grows, layoffs become inevitable. This is because productivity is the main source of supply and wages are the main source of demand, and if productivity outpaces wages, supply outpaces demand, and some workers become redundant.

The outcome of our model does not depend on what happens to prices, which will sink somewhat as output rises and the increase in the value of production will be less than 10 percent. However, with stagnant wages supply will still dwarf demand, resulting in layoffs. If prices were to plummet, then there would be massive unemployment, as happened during the Great Depression, because sinking prices demolish profits and lead to widespread job losses. Furthermore, prices may not fall at all if total demand rises to the level of enhanced supply because of society's borrowing.

The aforementioned idea explains why demand may stay deficient relative to supply for a long time. If productivity keeps rising and wages remain stagnant, as has been the case since 2007, then supply sails ahead of demand, so that either there are persistent layoffs or sluggish demand for new entrants to the labor force. And until the wage gap closes, i.e., returns to the pre-recession level, joblessness and poverty will stay.

5. Budget Deficits

The wage gap paradigm presented earlier explains many phenomena observed since 1980. We will now see why the rising wage gap also generates perpetual budget deficits, especially in a nation where elected officials face voters every two or four years. No politician likes to face the electorate in an environment of growing joblessness. Therefore, when the wage gap rises and layoffs begin, the politicians have a painful choice. They either have to adopt a policy that closes the wage gap or face irritated voters and lose their lucrative jobs along with their power.

In fact, we can calculate how much budget deficit is required to avoid layoffs. If Supply = \$2,200 and Demand = \$2000, then there are \$200 worth of unsold goods. In the absence of consumer borrowing, the budget deficit must equal the value of unsold goods or \$200 to close the supply–demand gap. If the budget deficit cannot rise to this level then consumer borrowing is needed to preserve economic balance. Therefore, in order to avoid job losses

value of unsold goods = budget deficit + consumer borrowing

Thus, our theory must be restated: whenever the wage gap goes up, either there are layoffs or debt must rise at the consumer and/or the government level to avoid job losses. If productivity continues to rise and wages remain sluggish, then consumer and government debt will have to keep rising to avert layoffs. This is precisely what happened after 1980, as official policies stimulated productivity on the one hand and led to stagnation wages on the other. During the 1920s, consumer debt soared while the government debt fell slightly, so overall debt grew in society.

6. Concentration of Wealth

There still remains the question of soaring income and wealth disparity that has occurred in the United States since 1981. You will now see how the measures designed to create debt, known as monetary and fiscal policies, add to the affluence of the well-to-do, while offering crumbs to those who are laid off. There are two possibilities, one where the government faces a threat of layoffs and the other where some workers have been already fired. The budget deficit has persisted ever since 1980, frequently in the absence of unemployment. There was only one year, 1999, that saw a slight surplus. Deficits existed even in the 1960s and the 1970s, but because of their tiny levels, they may be ignored.

In the absence of layoffs, the deficit simply raises profits without benefiting the workers. When productivity and output rise 10 percent, business revenue also increases 10 percent, and if wages and hence consumer demand remain stagnant, there is a potential for layoffs, which are averted by the existence of the deficit. This way, the rate of employment and people's incomes stay the same. All that happens is a rise in business revenue of 10 percent, and that increases profits. Thus, in the absence of unemployment the fruit of the budget deficit goes entirely to companies, with no benefit to workers.

In the other case where the government raises its deficit to tackle increasing layoffs, some workers are indeed called back to work, but usually at lower wages. Here the workers do benefit some from official policy, but in this case also profits rise further because of lower wage cost to employers. Here, the fruit of the deficit accrues mostly to producers.

History, past and recent, clearly demonstrates that high deficits increase the incomes of the affluent, and the relevant information comes from many

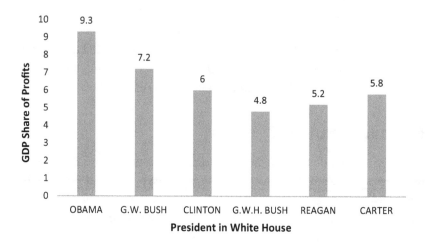

Figure 10.3:   GDP Share of Profits under Various Presidents

Source: Ravi Batra, *End Unemployment Now*, 2015, and *The New York Times*, April 4, 2014.

sources. An article from *The New York Times* reveals that after-tax profits as a share of GDP were the highest in recorded data under President Obama, at 9.3 percent, followed by his predecessor, President Bush, at 7.2 percent. Both Presidents added enormously to federal debt. Thus, high government debt gave rise to vast profits, even though GDP growth in the new millennium has remained low to mediocre (see Figure 10.3).

7. Debt and Destitution

Destitution means extreme poverty, something that separates the Third World from the first. When people are homeless or hungry, they are said to be destitute. Does destitution exist in the United States, still the largest economy in the world? It certainly does, and on a large scale.

According to Lauren Bush, the granddaughter of former President George H. W. Bush and the founder of FEED, an organization that provides meals for needy children and families, "49 million Americans are food insecure. This means one in six people does not know where his or her next meal is coming from." These people clearly live in extreme poverty. Are they unemployed? Most of them are not. The *2015 Economic Report of the President* reveals that out of a labor force of 156 million, fewer than 9 million were jobless. In other words, more than 40 million workers go partly hungry in America, which has a GDP of over $21 trillion.

The Economic Report also shows that poverty is now the worst in almost 50 years. What about America's middle class? A Bankrate.com survey commissioned in December 2014 concluded that 62 percent of Americans, a vast majority, have mere $500 of cash in checking or savings accounts. Even in 2019, most Americans, according to another study, had less than $1,000 in savings (https://www.cnbc.com/2019/01/23/most-americans-dont-have-the-savings-to-cover-a-1000-emergency.html).

Thus, few realize how bad things have become in the United States, where destitution, poverty, hunger and a struggling middle class stalk the land.

All this, of course, is the havoc caused by the Great Recession that started in December 2007 and was declared over in mid-2009. Meanwhile, the highest incomes rise faster than ever. According to Berkeley Professor

Emmanuel Saez, "Top 1% incomes grew by 31.4% while bottom 99% incomes grew only by 0.4% from 2009 to 2012. Hence, the top 1% captured 95% of the income gains in the first three years of the recovery." (See http://eml.berkeley.edu//~saez/saez-UStopincomes-2012.)

8. Macro Equilibrium and Monopoly Capitalism

Why are the well-to-do gaining and others including the middle class getting poorer? The answer will surprise most of you. The real culprit turns out to be government policy since 1981 that fosters monopoly capitalism and creates debt in the economy. Monopoly or crony capitalism is a system dominated by giant firms that charge high prices, pay low wages and extract huge productivity from their employees. High productivity generates high production or supply, whereas low wages create stagnant demand. With supply constantly exceeding demand, there is overproduction that either leads to layoffs or few entrants to the labor force are hired. Thus, the real reason for high unemployment or sluggish recovery is a relentless rise in the wage–productivity gap generated by monopoly capitalism.

However, joblessness not only hurts the workers but also irks the politician, especially the one interested in re-election. Few incumbents wish to face an unemployed electorate. Their jobs are also in jeopardy in times of rising joblessness. They then have two choices: either follow policies that raise wages to the level of growing productivity or do something else that raises demand to the level of supply. Unwilling to raise the minimum wage regularly and thus offend monopoly capitalists who finance their election campaigns, they adopt debt-generating policies. Ever since 1980, the Federal Reserve has slashed interest rates to lure people into debt, so that consumers raise their spending not out of a wage rise but out of increased borrowing. Federal deficits and debt have also risen for the same reason. This way demand increases artificially to match the ever-growing supply. Those laid off are then recalled to work and the incumbents retain their cushy positions of power.

Debt and destitution coexist in the Third World; now they also do in the United States of America. Under the modern version of monopoly capitalism, even the nature of macro equilibrium has changed. For thousands of years, macro equilibrium was defined by aggregated

$$supply = demand$$

But now it is defined by

$$supply = demand + new\ debt$$

where new debt reflects society's total borrowing that equals excess of supply over demand.

New debt has become a part of equilibrium because first, automatic stabilizers raise government spending and second, the government follows expansionary fiscal and monetary policies to raise total spending whenever it falls short of the supply of goods and services. The government action, being as predictable as that of markets, is now a part of equilibrium. This is what explains why there is enormous debt at all levels in the United States. Consumers, students, federal, state and local governments are all sinking in an ocean of debt. In fact, the whole world is drowning in debt. Figure 10.4 offers how equilibrium is established in global economies today.

Figure 10.4: Modern Representation of a Balanced Economy
Source: Ravi Batra, *Commonsense Macroeconomics*, Cover Page, 2012.

If productivity rises every year and wages remain stagnant, then

$$\text{supply} > \text{demand}$$

every year. Therefore, debt must rise every year to create equilibrium. Since productivity grows exponentially, then debt must grow exponentially. According to *2019 Economic Report of the President*, productivity more than doubled between 1980 and 2018 while the real wage remained more or less constant. Since wage income is the main source of demand, supply rose much faster than demand and to raise spending to the level of supply, both consumer and federal debt soared to all-time highs.

9. Debt and Inequality

The debt generating policies, however, make the super-rich richer. This is how the process works. All production is divided between capital income (or profits) and labor income. Thus,

$$\text{profits} = \text{GDP} - \text{wages}$$

However, if some goods remain unsold, then

$$\text{profits} = \text{GDP} - \text{wages} - \text{unsold goods}$$

because the value of unsold goods lowers the real value of profits dollar for dollar. Through debt-creating policies, politicians ensure that consumers and the government borrow enough money to eliminate overproduction. In other words,

$$\text{consumer borrowing} + \text{government budget deficit} = \text{unsold goods}$$

Thus, debt creation means that unsold goods become zero; this way profits rise by the amount of borrowing in the economy. As a simple example, suppose GDP equals \$100, wage income is \$60 and unsold goods are worth \$10. Then

$$\text{profits} = 100 - 60 - 10 = \$30$$

However, if unsold goods vanish as consumers and the government spend an extra \$10 out of their borrowing,

$$\text{profits} = \$40$$

The point is that debt-creating policies followed by the government, including the Federal Reserve, primarily benefit the 1 percenters whose incomes soar from rocketing profits. This analysis explains what Professor Saez has observed: "Hence, the top 1% captured 95% of the income gains in the first three years of the recovery."

10. Rocketing Profits and Share Prices

We have already seen that when debt rises to maintain the demand–supply equilibrium, profits must rise sharply. Herein lies the seed for the stock market bubble.

Share prices depend primarily on profits. People buy a company's stock to participate in its growth, which is fueled by its earnings. Some companies pay an adequate dividend to shareholders; others pay nothing but plough back much of their profit into business expansion, and then grow exponentially. Microsoft is one such growth firm among many others. Both the dividends and company growth are lubricated by high profits. Therefore, when profit soars, the stock market also soars.

Let us suppose, for the sake of argument, that initially the stock market index equals the level of profit, and that, other things remaining the same, share prices increase in proportion to the rise in profits. In our illustration, when the wage gap is constant, the share market will double with the doubling of profit, and it will quadruple when profit grows four times its original level. Thus, when the wage gap and debt grow, company profits rise sharply, and so does the share market.

When some other things change, the stock market escalation can be even sharper. Another factor that stimulates the share price is the fall in the interest rate resulting from the rising wage gap. When the government lowers the interest fee to push the public into increased debt, assets that compete with stocks lose some of their attraction. The public parks its savings into a variety of assets — stocks, bonds, gold, real estate. Some earn interest, some do not. Bonds yield interest income, whereas stocks primarily yield dividends or capital gains from price appreciation. Bonds may also generate capital gains from a rise in their prices, but such gains are relatively small.

Bonds and shares are very competitive with each other. When the rate of interest falls, bonds become less attractive, so more funds flow into share markets. This is then another avenue through which the rising wage gap fuels the stock market bubble, because the gap forces the government to bring the interest rate down in order to eliminate the shortfall in aggregate demand. Thus, share prices outpace even profits in the wake of a rising wage gap. Therefore, after the fall in the interest rate, the stock index will exceed 400. Say, it rises to 600.

The falling interest rate plays a supportive role in the stock market gains. The primary role goes to the rocketing level of profit. When profit falls, then the declining rate of interest may do little to shore up share prices, as occurred during the 1930s and recently from 2008 to 2009.

11. Bubble Economy

The phrase "bubble economy" became popular during the 1980s, when Japan experienced a stock market euphoria, which at the time appeared to be much more potent than the corresponding euphoria in the United States. A bubble economy is born when collectively debt, business investment, business mergers and share prices appear to flout all bounds of rationality. They all exceed productivity rise and GDP growth. Speculation thrives, as the public and financial institutions rush to acquire various assets at exorbitant prices.

In fact, as mentioned above, the law of demand regarding the purchase of assets breaks down. Normally, people buy less of anything as its price rises. However, for a while, the opposite happens in a bubble economy as people buy more of some assets as their prices go up. If the wage gap and debt continue to rise, a bubble economy is the inevitable result.

12. The Inevitable Crash

The speculative bubble is supported by an ever-rising debt, and common sense tells us that debt cannot rise forever. Around such times, experts may come out with various ratios, such as the debt to investment ratio, the debt to GDP ratio, the debt to consumption ratio and so on, and offer pearls of wisdom assuring that these ratios are reasonable. But rationality dictates that the debt binge must come to a halt someday.

When the public is up to its neck in loans, the financial institutions simply slow their lending for fear of defaults by borrowers. Some households and corporations become risky customers. The government can perhaps barrow money indefinitely, but the public cannot, because a time comes when people run out of good collateral and banks reduce their pending. That is when Supply > demand and profits crash along with the share market.

In Japan, the public bought more of some assets as their prices went up; for example, the price of land leaped even faster than share prices. At one point, Tokyo's real estate was valued above the real estate in all of California. The only thing that sinks in the bubble economy is sanity, and the fraction of GDP going into wages and possibly consumption. If the wage gap continues to rise unchecked, a bubble economy is the inevitable result.

However, all this only succeeds in creating a fool's paradise. New dogmas are born. People, and even experts, come to believe, as they did in the roaring 1920s, that everyone can become a millionaire. They equate soaring share prices with a growing living standard for the nation. How is this ever possible? The living standard is not paper profit. It is realized capital gains or profit. Soaring share prices are like distributing a bucket of printed money to every citizen. Does that improve the nation's lifestyle? Those few who sell their shares in time indeed become millionaires and billionaires overnight, but if everyone tries to cash out, the stock market will indeed crash. The entire nation cannot possibly see a jump in its living standard.

The living standard rises with an increase in the production of tangible goods and services. Suppose 100 workers live in only 10 houses. If the number of homes doubles, and people are no longer cramped in living quarters, that is certainly an improvement in lifestyle. But if stock prices skyrocket with little rise in the availability of tangible goods, how can the living standard improve? In the hoopla of the bubble economy, however, rationality gives way to euphoria, euphoria gives way to mania, and the nation gets drunk, until it wakes up one morning, and suffers a mega hangover. Companies begin to fail; some file for bankruptcy, and credit growth slows down. This is the beginning of a chain reaction that unravels the bubble economy.

The seed of the speculative bubble is also the seed of its destruction. The rising wage gap feeds profits on one side and debt on the other. A time comes when the debt growth slows. That is when the demand–supply imbalance, thus far masked by growing debt and overinvestment, comes to the surface. That is when profit begins to fall, and the nation receives a sudden jolt. First, the stock market moves sideways. But as excess supply of goods continues, share prices begin to crash.

Most of the investors then head for the exit, in a stampede that cripples mega fortunes built on the foundation of paper profit or sandy capital gains. Those who were late in joining the bubble party suffer real losses; some even lose their retirement money and lifetime savings.

This is why governments should do all to suppress a speculative bubble. The capital gains may come and go, but debt is there forever, until it is paid off or until the debtor declares bankruptcy, none of which is a happy prospect.

What really matters is the size of the wage gap; if the wage gap rises, the rest follows as a matter of cause and effect. In fact, the speculative process described above happened during the 1920s and later repeatedly from 1982 to 2010. Each time the wage gap leaped high.

When the wage gap remained more or less constant, as in the 1960s, economic growth was stronger than in any other post-WWII decade, yet there was no speculative bubble, and hence no crash.

It may be noted that stock market crashes have become frequent since the early 1970s. Prior to WWII, there was only one crash in the 20th century — the crash of 1929. But since 1972, when the real production wage first began a steady decline, there have been at least four. Between 1973 and 1974, the Dow dropped from 1020 to 616, or some 40 percent. The worst crash is said to have occurred on October 19, 1987 when the Dow plummeted more than 20 percent in one day. However, this collapse in share prices was short lived, as the year ended up with higher stock prices.

The next crash ended the dot-dot.com euphoria of the 1990s and occurred from 2000 to 2002. This was followed by another crash in 2008 and 2009. But as the wage gap and society's debt continued to rise from expansionary monetary and fiscal policies, each crash was followed by another bubble. Therefore, at the time of this writing, another bubble has formed, which means another crash could occur at any time.

13. Reasons for the Rising Wage Gap

Why does the wage gap rise? As stated before, for much of U.S. history wages kept up with productivity, but not during the 1920s, and ever since the 1970s. Therefore, stock market bubbles are rare occurrences, because wages refuse to trail hourly output all the time. But sometimes a variety of institutional changes occur to bring about a growing wage gap. These changes may be described as follows.

13.1. *Regressive Taxation*

In general, anything that generates a decline in labor demand or a rise in labor supply produces a rise in the wage gap. Since the labor force consists primarily of the poor and the middle class, anything that increases their tax burden can force them to work longer hours. Regressive taxation has generally increased the labor-force participation in the United States. People have to survive and feed their families. Their rising tax burden, along with the declining real wage, then induces them to increase their labor supply.

Consider Figure 10.5, which is the standard labor–market graph of the classi-Keynesian model. It displays not only the MPL or the labor

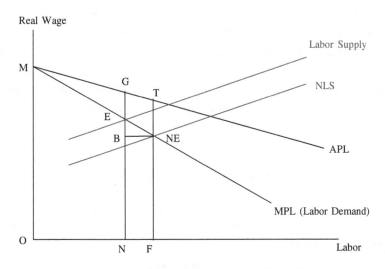

Figure 10.5: Labor Supply and the Wage Gap

demand curve but also the APL (average product of labor) or the labor productivity curve. Starting from point M, the MPL decreases faster than the APL. The initial equilibrium is at point E, with the real wage at EN and employment at ON. At this employment level, the APL is GN, so that the wage gap equals GN/EN.

An increase in the supply of labor caused by a rise in regressive taxes shifts the labor supply curve to NLS. The new equilibrium occurs at point NE, and the real wage falls to FNE. The APL also falls but not by as much. The real wage fall along ENE is steeper than the fall in the APL along GT. Clearly then the wage gap rises. It can be shown that the new wage gap given by FT/FNE exceeds the old level of GN/EN. Thus, one reason for the wage gap growth since the 1970s is the steady rise in the sales tax and the Social Security tax that primarily burden the work force, which responds through increasing family participation in the labor market.

13.2. *Monopolistic Competition*

Market imperfections triggered by the merger mania produce a fall in labor demand and a concurrent rise in the wage gap. When product markets lack intense competition, they become monopolistic. The producers then have the capability to control their prices by controlling their output. They realize that to sell more of their product they have to charge a lower price, which they despise. Therefore, they reduce their output and employment and raise their price. The end result is a lower real wage and a higher wage gap.

Under monopolistic competition the real wage falls below that paid by perfectly competitive firms. When competition declines, profit-maximizing firms hire workers until the money wage is equal to the marginal revenue product of labor (MRPL), i.e.,

$$\text{money wage} = \text{MRPL} = \text{MR} \cdot \text{MPL}$$

where the marginal revenue (MR) is less than the price level. The MR is the extra revenue that a company receives from the sale of a new unit of output. Since each extra unit of output is sold at a lower price, the MR of a monopolistically competitive producer decreases with expanding sales.

For a competitive producer, price is constant, because the firm is so small that it has no influence on the market price. Its marginal revenue is also constant and exceeds the decreasing MR of the firm facing monopolistic or restrained competition. If we divide both sides of the aforementioned equation by the price level, we get

$$\text{real wage} = \frac{\text{MR}}{P} \cdot \text{MPL}$$

or

$$\text{real wage} = m \cdot \text{MPL}$$

where $m = \text{MR}/P$ is a fraction that equals the monopoly markup of the firms operating in the environment of restrained competition. Under intense or perfect competition, the real wage equals the MPL. It then follows that the monopolistic real wage is a fraction of the competitive real wage. Needless to say, the wage gap goes up when competition declines.

Figure 10.6 makes the argument crystal clear. As in Figure 10.5, the MPL curve lies below the APL line, but the $m \cdot \text{MPL}$ line lies even below

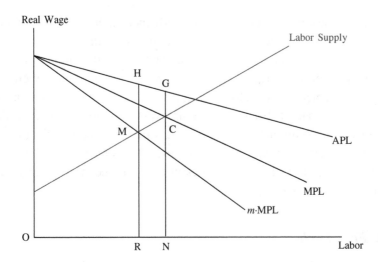

Figure 10.6:   Monopolistic Competition and the Wage Gap

the MPL curve. If the MPL line furnishes the labor demand curve for perfectly competitive firms, the $m \cdot$ MPL line furnishes the labor demand curve of monopolistically competitive firms. The labor supply curve intersects the two labor demand curves at two different points.

Point M is the equilibrium point for monopolistic firms, with the real wage equaling RM, APL equaling RH, and the wage gap being RH/RM. By contrast, point C is the equilibrium point under perfect competition, with NC being the real wage, NG being the APL and NG/NC being the wage gap. Clearly, the wage gap is larger under monopolistic competition.

Business mergers climbed in the 1920s and then again between 1982 and 2019, crimping rivalry among firms. Some markets became monopolistic, even oligopolistic, where just two or three firms dominate the industry. Microsoft in the software industry became a giant, as did some pharmaceutical firms in the field of medicine. The 1996 merger between Exxon and Mobile generated a petroleum-industry behemoth with enormous production, profits and financial clout. Such developments could not but raise the wage gap.

13.3. *Labor Union Decline*

Labor unions normally exert a powerful influence on the real wage of their own members. They tend to offset the negative impact of business mergers. But during the 1920s, as well as since 1970, the union influence, for a variety of reasons, declined. The real wage of union members suffered as a consequence. However, the result percolated throughout the national labor market, because the employers have to pay a wage that competes with the union wage. Otherwise, workers could join the unions, which the producers regard as adversaries. Therefore, when unions lose their influence, the real wage declines in the entire economy, and generates a rise in the wage gap.

13.4. *Free Trade*

Another reason for the growing wage gap is the increasing U.S. reliance on foreign trade. According to the trade theory literature, globalization or free trade tends to raise a country's output and its APL. At the same time its real wage falls if it imports labor-intensive products, i.e., goods that use a lot of labor to produce a dollar of output. Many American imports such as shoes, textiles and autos turn out to be labor intensive relative to American exports such as airplanes, farm goods and computers.

Rising imports create job losses in import-competing industries, whereas rising exports produce job gains in exporting industries. But if imports are labor intensive relative to exports, job losses outpace job gains, and the overall impact is a decline in American demand for labor. With the fall in labor demand comes a fall in the real wage, while the overall productivity of the nation rises with increasing trade. The wage gap then has to rise. This reason applies to the economy since the 1970s but not during the 1920s, when foreign commerce was exceptionally small.

13.5. *The Declining Minimum Wage*

The U.S. minimum wage in 2019 was $7.25 and had remained constant since 1997. By contrast, the corresponding wage in the late 1960s was close to $11 in terms of today's prices. Clearly, the purchasing power of the minimum wage has eroded sharply since 1970. Typically, a minimum wage employee is an unskilled worker, with very little bargaining power. Ten million Americans earn this wage, while another 20 million have their salaries tied directly to it.

The average U.S. wage is far above the minimum. How does the minimum wage then affect the average salary? It serves as a benchmark for the salaries of production workers. Both the employer and the employee look at the minimum wage and add the skill premiums to it in their wage negotiations. The greater the skill the higher the premium.

Thus, the benchmark wage sets the standard for the salaries of most non-supervisory workers, who constitute up to 80 percent of the work force. When the benchmark declines, naturally production workers experience a drop in the purchasing power of their pay, and the wage gap rises.

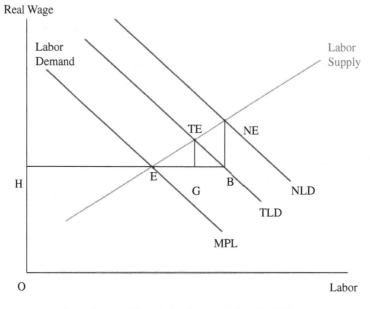

Figure 10.7:   New Technology and the Real Wage

13.6. *Monopolistic Competition and New Technology*

How does improving technology affect the real wage in the wake of declining competition? The answer can be found in Figure 10.7. An improvement in technology increases the MPL and shifts the labor demand curve to NLD, raising the real wage by BNE and employment by BE. Under perfect competition in the economy, the real wage rises to the full extent of the rise in the MPL, and the wage gap remains constant. But with declining competition the new labor demand curve does not shift as far as NLD, so that the real wage rises by a smaller amount.

If the shift is up to only the line TLD, then the real wage rises only by GTE, creating a rise in the wage gap, because improving technology has sharply increased the APL (not shown to avoid the clutter).

14. The Macro Model

Let us now weave the aforementioned analysis into our macro model, where we do not need the simplifying assumptions that we have used to

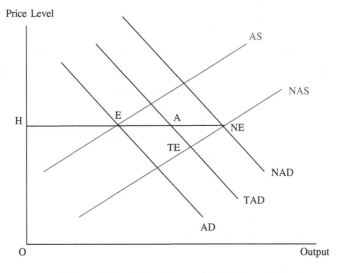

Figure 10.8:   Wage Gap and Debt Growth

avoid numerical complications. Take a look at Figure 10.8, which is the, standard AD–AS graph of the classi-Keynesian model, ignoring the vertical or the horizontal portions of the aggregate supply curve. The initial equilibrium is at point E, with the price level given by OH and output by HE.

An improvement in technology shifts the AS curve to the right to NAS, suggesting that output rises by ENE at the current price of OH. There is also a rise in the MPL and the real wage, which leads to a rightward shift in the AD curve, because at the current price level consumer spending goes up; investment also rises in response to rising consumption and output. If the real wage increases in proportion to productivity, then the consumption rise is strong, and so is the increase in investment. The end result is that the AD curve shifts to NAD and cuts the new AS curve at point NE. Equilibrium output rises by ENE, but there is likely to be no change in the price level.

If the real wage rise falls short of the productivity increase, then the AD curve shifts short of the NAD line, to the TAD line, because both consumer and investment spending then rise less than before. At the current price of OH, there will be excess supply of ANE in the goods market.

If the price level is allowed to fall, a new equilibrium could occur at TE. But this the government would not, and cannot, permit, because deflation could bring back the Great Depression. Instead, it would pursue expansionary monetary and fiscal policies, pushing the nation further into debt. At a constant price level the total rise in the debt has to be ANE to eliminate overproduction and the threat of layoffs.

In most countries, wages have trailed productivity since the 1970s, even as government deficits and debts have skyrocketed. Is it a coincidence that this phenomenon coexisted with the soaring wage gap? Clearly not. In fact, the logic of our argument is that this was inevitable; governments around the globe were forced to do this to maintain superficially healthy economies. Unable and unwilling to eliminate the wage gap, this is all they could do in the name of sound economic policy.

15. The Stock Market Again

Figure 10.9 is the demand–supply graph of the share market. In equilibrium, the share price is OH and the trading volume is HE. GDP is divided into labor and capital income, so that

$$Y = AL = wL + \text{profit, or}$$

$$\text{profit} = AL(1 - w/A)$$

or

$$\frac{\text{profit}}{\text{output}} = 1 - \frac{w}{A}$$

Here "A" is productivity and w/A is the wage gap. If the real wage rises at the same pace as productivity, then the share of profit in GDP is constant. Profit then rises at the same rate as output.

The rising profit level causes the share demand curve to shift to the right to TSD, and the share price rises in the new equilibrium by BTE. However, if the wage gap rises, or w/A falls, then the profit share goes up, and profit increases faster than output. Here then the share demand curve

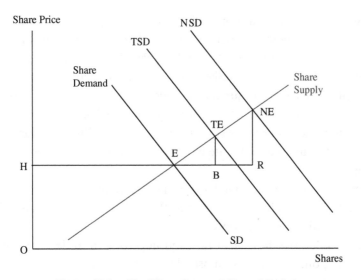

Figure 10.9: The Wage Gap and Share Markets

has a stronger rightward shift, to NSD, and the share price climbs faster by RNE.

If the government adopts the policy of monetary ease to fight the threat of overproduction, then the rate of interest falls and the share demand curve rises further than NSD. The share price would then rise even more. If this process continues, soon there will be a stock market bubble.

Finally, when debt stops growing and AD falls short of AS, then profit falls by the value of unsold goods. Then the share demand curve goes into reverse gear, moving leftward from NSD to TSD and possibly to the original level. The stock market crashes, and the State's frantic efforts to avert the collapse through feverish interest rate cuts prove abortive. Such has been the universal experience of governments all over the world.

16. U.S. Economy: 1962–2019

Let us briefly examine the behavior of the U.S. economy from 1962 to 2019, especially its debt growth over five decades. We can divide this period into two parts, the pre-1980 era and the post-1980 times. Until 1980, the federal debt in America was less than $1 trillion. From the birth of the Republic in 1789 to the fateful year of 1980, there were a total of 39 presidents. And together they had a collective debt of about $900 billion. Then came supply-side economics in 1981 with a promise to balance the budget. What an irony. By now the debt has soared to over $21 trillion and currently rising at the rate of a trillion a year. It took almost 200 years to accumulate a debt of $1 trillion. Now, this is done in just one year.

True, the economy is much bigger now; wealth concentration is at its all-time high. In such a rich economy, there should be no debt at all. But logic and reality do not always mix.

Other countries have also incurred huge debt in order to keep their economies going. In the past, mostly businesses used to borrow money for economic growth. Now, thanks to supply-side economics, governments borrow money as well.

On top of the federal debt, there is also now a vast ocean of consumer debt in America, some $4 trillion. Of this roughly $1 trillion is from the use of credit cards, $1.5 trillion is student debt and the rest is money borrowed for buying a car. In other words, the debt has been incurred mostly to meet necessary expenses. All this is the handiwork of a relentless rise in the wage gap.

17. Summary

(1) Share prices rise in proportion to a rise in profits or capital income.
(2) Keynesian and neoclassical models are unable to explain why stock market bubbles arise and fall.
(3) Normally, the stock market moves proportionately with an increase in productivity, because then both profits and real wages share equally in the fruit of economic growth. But once in a while, the real wage trails the gains in productivity; then profits (or capital income) and share markets soar; if this process continues for long, stock market bubbles are born.
(4) A speculative bubble occurs when the law of demand for certain risky assets break down. People then purchase more of these assets

in spite of their soaring prices. On the other side, they buy less of the assets even as their prices fall.

(5) The wage gap is defined by the ratio of labor productivity and the real wage; when productivity outpaces real earnings, then the wage gap rises, the labor market becomes distorted, and many unexpected things happen in the economy.

(6) The share market mania or any kind of speculative bubble is born when productivity gains are accompanied by a rise in the wage gap.

(7) The increase in the wage gap germinates a rise in the economy's debt, including consumer, corporate and government debt.

(8) There were two periods that experienced share-price bubbles in the United States in the 20th century — first in the 1920s and then from 1982 to 2010. Each time the wage gap went up for at least a full decade.

(9) The wage-gap rise also causes overinvestment and a merger mania, both of which, coupled with soaring debt and stock prices, generate a bubble economy.

(10) Japan's bubble economy occurred during the 1980s, whereas U.S. bubbles took place in the 1920s and then from 1982 to 2010.

(11) Every bubble bursts in the end, because the growing wage gap that creates the bubble also sows the seed of its destruction, which occurs when debt growth slows down.

(12) U.S. stock market bubbles burst in 1929, 1987, 2000 and 2008.

(13) In the aftermath of the bubble occurs a depression or a long period of employment stagnation.

(14) The wage gap may rise because of a fall in the minimum real wage, labor union decline, free trade, rise in regressive taxes such as the Social Security tax and the sales tax, or a persistent decline in market competition.

(15) Once the bubble economy bursts open, economic policy may be ineffective for a while in curing the stagnation.

Chapter 11

Wage Gap, Global
Imbalances and Poverty

In 1964, America declared war. This was no usual war, but a war against poverty. The government decided to spend a lot of money to raise the living standard of the poor and lift them into the middle class. Many laws were passed to introduce several new government programs that would directly give assistance to the needy. Has that war been won? This is a loaded question and the answer is not clear. If you consider the official measure, the rate of poverty is down slightly. On the other hand, if you look at the annual cost of that war, it appears like a totally wasted effort that eventually makes the super-rich richer and breeds inequality in society.

Applying the standard of cost–benefit analysis, the war has miserably failed. Critics assail the programs for their cost which currently runs over $1 trillion per year (Cato Institute). You know a trillion here, a trillion there and pretty soon we are talking real money. For a nation accustomed to mega deficits, this does not matter much, but the price is huge in terms of speculative bubbles and crashes, which, as demonstrated in the previous chapter, are the inevitable consequences of wasting money and enriching the rich.

1. Wage Gap and Poverty: The 1950s

With the relentless rise of the wage-gap, government programs for helping the poor are bound to fail. Let us examine the 1950s, when poverty programs were yet to be enacted. This is one decade when the wage gap actually fell in the United States. Consider Figure 11.1, which clearly shows that as the wage gap declined, the real median income of families soared. In all, this real income went up by as much as 37 percent from 1950 to 1960.

How did the wage gap really fall in a milieu of monopoly capitalism? During the 1950s, mergers occurred not only among large corporations but also between labor unions. In 1955, the American Federation of Labor (AFL) joined with the Congress of Industrial Organization (CIO) to form one giant union — AFL-CIO. Powerful unions became even more powerful to counter the might of big business. This way there was a sort of bilateral monopoly between large corporations and strong unions. Companies were still able to dictate product prices, but they were unable to set wages. Thus, productivity gains resulting from technological advance were more than matched by wage gains, so that the wage gap fell slightly. Such a rare development had dramatic and salutary effects on American society.

First, the rate of unemployment fell to 2.9 percent, a feat never replicated in the long American chronicle. Second, the real median income soared, as illustrated in Figure 11.1. From 1950 to 1960, as the wage-gap index fell from 47 to 41, median income jumped 37 percent. Needless to say, poverty levels plummeted, as the number of families with incomes below a threshold of $3,000 plunged, as displayed in Figure 11.2.

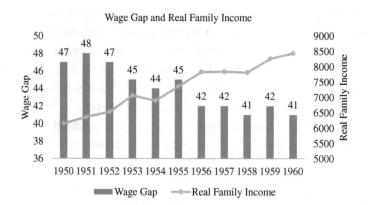

Figure 11.1: The Wage Gap and Real Family Income in the United States: 1950–1960

Sources: The Economic Report of President, 1975, p. 274, and Ravi Batra, *End Unemployment Now,* Palgrave Macmillan, 2015.

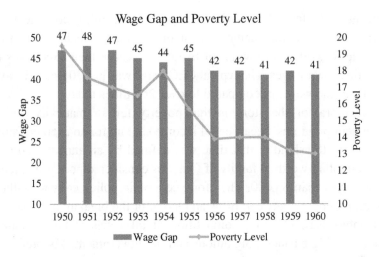

Figure 11.2: **The Wage Gap and Poverty Rate in the United States: 1950–1960**

Sources: *The Economic Report of President, 1975*, p. 274, and Ravi Batra, *End Unemployment Now*, Palgrave Macmillan, 2015.

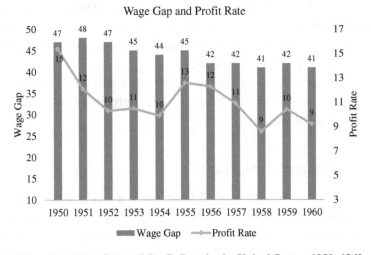

Figure 11.3: **The Wage Gap and Profit Rate in the United States: 1950–1960**

Source: *The Economic Report of President, 1975*, p. 337.

The rate of profit, of course, declined from 1950 to 1960, as in Figure 11.3, but companies did not go bankrupt. They still employed millions of workers, as unemployment varied between 2.9 percent and

5 percent of the labor force, which, as you may recall, is consistent with the concept of natural unemployment or full employment. Giant firms were able to work with low profit margins, because their executives did not set their own wages. The typical CEO wage was just 20 times the average production wage, as compared to over 250 times today.

The moral of the story is that poverty fell dramatically without government programs, because real income shot up for an average family. The poverty threshold at that time was defined by an annual income of $3,000. In other words, a family of four was considered poor if its income was no larger than $3,000. Therefore, economic policy calls for either a bilateral monopoly between firms and labor, or the breakup of all sorts of giant enterprises. Creating competition at all levels is better than an economy of big business, big unions and big government. My preference is for free enterprise wherein intense competition exists among corporations on the one hand and workers on the other. But if that is not possible because of politics, then a bilateral monopoly between producers and labor unions is the best alternative, so that the two parties involved in the process of production have equal bargaining power. This is because when industrial monopoly power is balanced by labor's monopoly power, the real wage keeps pace with the rise in productivity. The wage gap remains stable and the entire nation benefits.

Today, giant companies dictate both wages and prices and workers subsist at their mercy. This is precisely why poverty is growing in America and the rest of the world.

2. Government Programs

Now let us look at the effect of all those government programs. Myriads of government plans support the needy today. They provide food stamps, housing vouchers, tax relief, healthcare and cash assistance. They all serve to lift poor families out of poverty. Without them the indigent would be starving and millions of people would be homeless. But their annual cost is enormous, and they do not do much to remove the root cause of poverty. They create a culture of dependence on these programs, discourage work ethic and encourage a lazy lifestyle. Over the years, such programs have indeed lowered poverty as Figure 11.4 based on data from the U.S. Census Bureau shows.

Systematic records about poverty began in 1959. We have already seen from information provided by *The Economic Report of the President* that poverty fell sharply in the 1950s without the help of government programs. Figure 11.4 extends that message up to a point as it shows that a

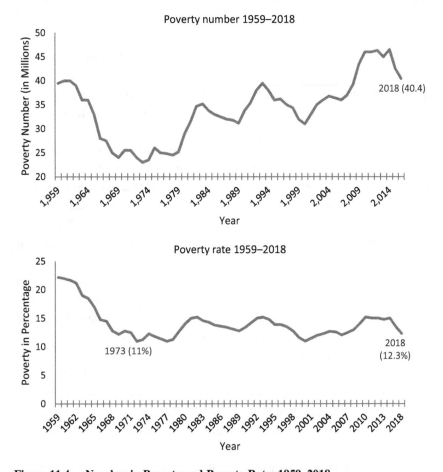

Figure 11.4: Number in Poverty and Poverty Rate: 1959–2018

Source: U.S. Census Bureau, Current Population Survey, 1960–2017, Annual Social and Economic Supplements, and The Economic Report of the President, 2019.

fast decline in poverty rate occurred between 1959 and 1964, when the government declared the war on poverty. In 1965, the poverty rate was about 15 percent and it fell to 11 percent by 1973, about the time the real production wage peaked. That was the lowest it would go as the official poverty figures since that year have varied between 11.3 percent and 15 percent.

You may recall from Chapter 2 that the real production wage peaked in 1972 and then began to decline, slowly but steadily. Since 1973, the year that provides the lowest point for the rate of poverty, the wage gap began to rise slowly but relentlessly and so did poverty in spite of numerous and ever-increasing government programs. It is then clear that government assistance is most productive when wages keep up with productivity. If not, much of the money that the government spends for the needy goes to waste and just enriches 1 percent of the population, as shown in Chapter 10.

Going back to Figure 11.4, the poverty rate in 1993, at 15 percent, was exactly the same as in 1964, which means that government programs had made no dent in poverty in nearly 30 years. But there was a dramatic drop in the rate following 1993 and by the start of the new millennium it came close to its lowest point. In 2000, the poverty rate fell to 11.3 percent, which is close to the 1973 nadir of 11 percent. Did the wage gap fall again? No.

The seeming prosperity of the late 1990s occurred without a drop in the wage gap. It was mostly due to the dot.com boom and an unprecedented speculative bubble that catapulted the stock market to new highs. Such a bubble is an ugly combination of a rising wage gap and government budget deficits. As shown in the previous chapter, it creates an illusion of prosperity in which share prices go sky-high but then crash down to Earth. Soon after 2000, when the stock market crashed, poverty rates began to climb and stayed at 15 percent from 2010 to 2012. Since then they have dropped again and in 2018 the rate was 12.3 percent.

Here we go again. History is repeating itself. Another ugly combination has formed in the form of a rocketing wage gap, growing budget deficit and a stock market reaching new highs. The result will eventually be the same — a stock market crash and an inevitable jump in poverty.

3. Regressive Taxation

Besides the wage gap, there are other causes of persistent poverty such as regressive taxation. Supply-side economics was legislated in 1981 with a major change in America's tax system. The change led to an ultra-regressive revenue system, as income tax rates plunged for wealthy individuals and corporations, and then continued to fall over the years. Another major transformation occurred in 1983 when most taxes that disproportionately burden the poor and the middle class soared. Thus, the Social Security tax, the self-employment tax, gasoline tax, and some excise taxes among others, went up that year. Consequently, the U.S. tax system became ultra-regressive, as taxes fell for rich individuals and corporations and climbed for those paid mostly by poor and middle income groups.

Such developments had to generate the vast imbalances that we find today in the U.S. and global economy. History reveals that unethical policies that benefit the wealthy at the expense of the poor always generate inequality and increase poverty. For they also tend to raise the wage gap, as the after-tax wages fall further behind labor productivity. As we see in the next chapter, GDP growth fell below its historical average after supply-side economics went into effect.

4. Regressive Interest Rates

Another cause of a rise in poverty is the presence of regressive interest rates. When low income people have to pay higher rates of interest than the affluent, the interest rate system becomes regressive. This also tends to raise poverty. Central banks around the world have been trying to lower interest rates and have even made them negative in some countries. At such a time, you may find it difficult to believe that interest rates are still high for some groups. Well, they are high, even onerous, where they should not be. They are low for homeowners, companies and speculative activities, and even wealthy holders of credit cards, but incredibly high for the poor.

Normally, credit card rates do not affect high income groups, because they have a thick cushion of savings and can pay their bills on time. They rarely incur interest penalties and interest charges. Credit card interest rates are normally much larger than other rates such as the mortgage rate, prime rate, etc.; therefore, the poor, who frequently use their cards even to buy necessities and make only a minimum monthly payment for their bills, are at a great disadvantage. They are unable to get out of their debt.

When credit card rates rise, the poor become poorer even if their wages stay constant or rise slightly. Something like this has been happening in America since 2003, when according to the Federal Reserve Bank, the average card rate was 12 percent but rose to a high of 17 percent in May 2019. If the average is 17 percent, low income groups, with low credit scores, may have to pay rates as high as 30 percent, even if they pay their bills on time.

Why have the card rates rocketed when the cost of funds raised by banks has plunged? In 2003, banks paid about 5 percent interest on a 5-year certificate of deposit (CD). By 2019, they paid less than 2 percent. Thus, in 2003, a bank's profit margin on card loans was just 7 percent, but it climbed to 15 percent in 2019. There is no earthly reason for this to occur, except a vast increase in monopoly power of the financial industry because of extensive bank mergers. Only four banks — Bank of America, Citi Bank, Chase Bank and Wells Fargo Bank — now dominate the banking sector in the United States. Official statistics fail to capture the negative effects of regressive interest rates on poverty.

5. Global Poverty

The Great Recession afflicted the whole planet including nations known as underdeveloped economies or developing countries. Of them some such as Brazil, Russia, India and China, the so-called BRIC nations, have made great strides since 1990. They have industrialized and each flow has a big middle class that has been steadily shrinking in the United States but expanding in these so-called emerging markets.

Among the BRIC nations, India and Brazil chafe under the stranglehold of oligopolies, while China and Russia continue to have a regulated economy coexisting with a market-based system. Monopoly capitalism pervades India and Brazil, whereas in China and Russia state enterprises flourish amidst a small but growing private sector. Poverty has declined in emerging markets since 1990 but at an excruciatingly slow pace. The reason is that CEOs in these nations, as elsewhere, insist on grabbing their own pound of flesh from any government assistance offered to the needy. Consequently, progress against poverty has come at a torturously slow pace. Billionaires and multi-millionaires are now mushrooming in BRIC nations. but, as a 2018 press release from the World Bank is entitled, "Decline of Global Extreme Poverty Continues But Has Slowed" (https://www.worldbank.org/en/news/press-release/2018/09/19/decline-of-global-extreme-poverty-continues-but-has-slowed-world-bank).

South Asia has the dubious honor of having the largest concentration of the destitute. There, almost 70 percent of the people are stricken with poverty, living on $1.90 a day. About a quarter of the global population still lives in poverty, while just 85 of the world's richest individuals own as much wealth as 3.5 billion people. Meanwhile, global GDP growth has increased global emission of carbon dioxide by 50 percent. That is the real shame of the system: even as billionaires gobble up the lion's share of production gains, environmental pollution that tends to hurt everyone equally grows apace.

Reasons for a slowdown of progress against poverty are the same as in advanced economies: a rising wage gap, regressive taxation as well as regressive interest rates. For instance, credit card rates in India are about 40 percent; in Brazil, they hover near 100 percent per year. However, there is one additional reason that applies only to economies that are mostly agrarian: their lack of industries. While much of the world is now industrialized, Africa has badly lagged behind. People there mostly live in rural areas, and their cities are highly congested and polluted, even though their GDP growth is low. However, they have great economic potential, and we will discuss what they can do with very little investment to reduce poverty in Chapter 15.

Chapter 12

Long-Run Growth and Growth Cycles

The peaks and valleys that periodically dot the path of real GDP are commonly called the business cycle, which is mostly a short-run phenomenon. All the models you have studied so far are primarily concerned with this question, which explores fluctuations in output, employment and prices. In the short run, capital stock and population are constant, but they vary in the long run, and generate what is called economic growth. The study of the growth process is just as important as that of the business cycle, especially because of the relentless rise in population around the world.

Every year new mouths have to be fed, more people need to be clothed, housed and educated. Factories have to expand, some people retire but more enter the labor force and need to be employed, new inventions and ideas come into being, and so on. All these are basic ingredients of the growth process, which is now a pervasive fact of life.

But fluctuations occur not just in output but also in the rate of output gains, and growth cycles are as frequent as business cycles. In fact, Keynesian "demand management policies" have shortened recessions to the point that some scholars regard the business cycle as obsolete. In their view, growth should take precedence over short-run concerns. Yet the theory of economic growth today is in a state of underdevelopment. It is where macroeconomics was prior to the rise of Keynesian thought.

The classical school dominates growth economics today in the same way it once did macroeconomics. It slights the growth cycle just as it once slighted the business cycle. The legend of Say's law that "supply creates its own demand" now runs through the veins of this literature, which focuses on two supply-side factors — capital and technology — as major determinants of the rise in living standards. Yet there are annual, in fact quarterly, fluctuations in the rate of GDP growth. How, then, can you ignore the demand side in examining this process?

1. Growth Fluctuations

Even a cursory look at Table 12.1, and its graphical counterpart Figure 12.1, confirms that economic growth is subject to short-run fluctuations. The period under study starts from the first quarter of 2016 and ends in the third quarter of 2019. The rate of growth in real GDP in column 2 is the "quarterly growth rate projected at the annual rate." It is obtained under the assumption that the rate realized in the first quarter prevails over the next three quarters.

The table reveals an astonishing variation in quarterly growth. In 2016, for instance, the annualized growth rate varied from a high of 2.3 percent to a low of 1.5 percent. The following year the range of variation was even larger. If in some years, there are negative rates and positive rates, the business cycle applies to that year, which witnesses a recession as well as recovery.

Table 12.1: Quarterly Fluctuations in GDP Growth at Annualized Rates: 2016–2019

(1) Year and Quarter	(2) GDP Growth	(3) Year and Quarter	(4) GDP Growth
2016		2018	
I	1.5	I	2.2
II	2.3	II	4.2
III	1.9	III	3.4
IV	1.8	IV	2.6
2017		2019	
I	1.8	I	3.1
II	3.0	II	2.1
III	2.8	III	2.0
IV	2.4	—	—

Source: The Economic Report of the President, 2019, Council of Economic Advisers, Washington, D.C.

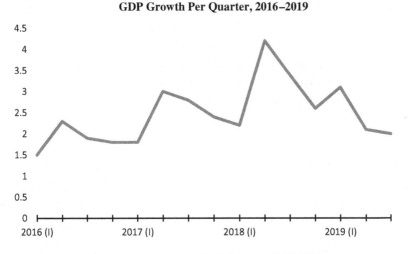

Figure 12.1: **Quarterly Fluctuations in GDP Growth, 2016–2019**

Source: *The Economic Report of the President*, 2019.

Clearly, the fluctuations are not just limited to the business cycle. The growth cycle can be even more explosive.

Figure 12.1 brings out the cycle visually and is therefore more persuasive in the matter of growth fluctuations. It displays the up and down movement of quarterly growth rates around their trend line. So, what creates these cycles? The same forces that generate the business cycle. In this respect, the theory of economic growth and the business cycle are two sides of the same coin. But before we jump to an analysis of growth cycles, let us see what conventional ideas have to say in this matter.

2. Professor Solow's Growth Model

The most popular theory of economic growth is offered by Professor Robert Solow, an MIT Economist, who won a Nobel Prize for his contribution. His thesis explains an economy's long-run growth experience, something like average growth prevailing over a few decades. For instance, since 1950, the U.S. economy has expanded at an average rate of 3.5 percent per year. The Solow model, also known as the neoclassical theory of growth, identifies the various factors that have made this possible.

One factor, of course, is the rate of population growth that approximates the rate of growth in the labor force, which has been around 1.5 percent per year. Since output depends on employment, labor growth then explains 1.5 percent of the average growth. What about the other 2 percent? That obviously comes from productivity growth. Let us rewrite our familiar AS equation as follows:

$$Y = AL$$

where Y is output, A is labor productivity, and L is employment. "Assuming full employment," as in the classical model, the growth in employment equals the growth in labor force. From this relationship, we can write the following:

$$YG = PG + LG$$

where the "G" around a variable indicates its rate of growth. Thus, YG is the rate of growth of output or real GDP, PG is productivity growth or the growth rate in the average product of labor, and LG is the growth rate of labor force. Thus, if YG is 3.5 percent, and LG is 1.5 percent, then PG is 2 percent per year.

One measure of a country's living standard is per-capita output, which has been increasing in many countries for a long time. The growth in per-capita output allegedly tells us how fast the gain is in the standard of living. By definition, such gain equals the rate of output expansion minus the expansion of the workforce,

$$YG - LG = PG$$

Thus, productivity growth defines a nation's growth in per-capita output. With PG equaling some 2 percent per year, per-capita output has also grown at this rate. Growth works like the formula for compound interest rate. At the 2-percent rate, the living standard doubles every 35 years. This comes from the so-called "rule of 70." Dividing 70 by the rate of productivity growth approximately gives us the number of years it would take to double per-capita output. Therefore, if productivity growth is 7 percent per year, a rate that prevailed in Japan for almost 25 years, the living standard doubles in just a decade.

The Solow model also tells us how a country can enhance its growth rate. Productivity growth depends on capital accumulation as well as technological progress. Capital stock in turn derives from investment, which in turn equals savings in equilibrium. In fact, real business investment minus depreciation of capital defines the "change in capital stock," i.e.,

$$I - \text{depreciation} = \Delta K$$

For simplicity, we assume that depreciation is zero. Then dividing both sides by K gives us the following:

$$\frac{I}{K} = \frac{\Delta K}{K} = \text{KG}$$

which is the growth rate of capital. When companies purchase plant and equipment, they make a down payment in advance but get delivery for these goods sometime in the future. Factories take a while to build, so capital stock remains constant at the time firms spend money for future delivery of capital goods. The initial payment for plant construction constitutes the current period's business investment. Capital stock increases by the amount of this investment, when capital goods are delivered.

In the Solow model business investment equals savings, which are assumed to be a constant fraction of output, i.e.,

$$\text{investment} = \text{savings} = sY,$$

so that

$$\text{KG} = \frac{\Delta K}{K} = \frac{sY}{K}$$

where s is the economy-wide saving rate. The growth rate of capital, from this formula, equals the rate of saving times the average product of capital, i.e., *Y/K. In equilibrium the growth rate of capital equals the growth rate of labor*, that is,

$$\text{KG} = \text{LG} = \frac{sY}{K}$$

and output grows at the same rate as either capital or labor, provided we assume constant returns to scale. *Returns to scale are constant, if equal rises in capital and labor raise output by the same amount. In other words, if capital and labor double, output also doubles*, and so on.

From the above formula, a rise in the rate of saving clearly raises the growth rate of capital, and hence output.

3. Productivity Growth

An improvement in technology raises the efficiency or productivity of labor, which, for analytical convenience, may be defined in terms of efficiency or technology units as TL. Here, T is the index of technology and equals one initially. Each time technology advances, there is a rise in T. Labor growth then becomes

$$\text{effective labor growth} = \frac{\Delta L}{L} + \frac{\Delta T}{T}$$

In equilibrium

$$\frac{\Delta K}{K} = \text{effective labor growth} = \frac{\Delta L}{L} + \frac{\Delta T}{T}$$

In other words, in equilibrium capital grows at the same rate as labor and productivity. This, with constant returns to scale, means that output grows at the same rate as labor and productivity, or

$$\frac{\Delta Y}{Y} = \frac{\Delta L}{L} + \frac{\Delta T}{T}$$

or

$$YG = LG + PG$$

We are back to the formula we first stated in Section 2. From the formulas it is clear that in equilibrium output grows at the same rate as the labor force and the rate of technical improvement, which is the same thing as the rate of productivity growth. Clearly, an increase in productivity growth raises the growth rate of output.

Thus, Professor Solow's model tells us that a country's growth rate depends positively on its rate of saving and technology. The faster the growth of technology, the faster the rise in per-capita output.

4. Population Growth

Some countries like China and India have huge populations; others like Canada and Australia have fewer people relative to their natural resources. How does population influence growth in the Solow model? To answer this question let us note that from the capital formation formula KG = *sY/K*.

This shows that capital growth depends on the average product of capital (*Y/K*). An increase in capital stock, with labor employment constant, lowers the marginal and average product of capital. Just like the law of diminishing MPL, there is also the law of diminishing MPK, which comes into play when the labor input is constant. But if labor is constant then capital per worker (*k*) rises with an increase in capital stock (*K*). Thus, a rise in capital per worker has the same impact on the average product of capital as the rise in *K*. This idea also holds when capital grows faster than labor, so that *k* rises.

Let us now utilize this relationship in Figure 12.2, where KG, the capital growth curve, has a negative slope, suggesting that the growth rate of capital falls with a rise in capital per worker. LG, the labor growth line, is horizontal, implying a constant growth rate of labor.

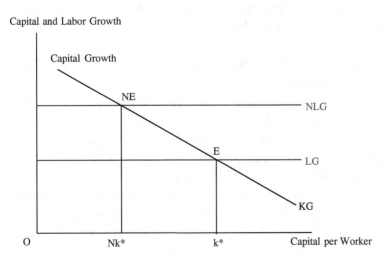

Figure 12.2: Population Growth and Capital Stock

Equilibrium occurs at point E, where the growth rate of capital equals the growth rate of labor, furnishing an equilibrium capital–labor ratio at k^*. Now suppose there is an increase in the growth rate of population, so that the labor growth line shifts up to the NLG line. Equilibrium now shifts to point NE, and the capital–labor ratio falls to Nk^*. Therefore, high population growth leads to a fall in the level of capital per worker in the new equilibrium. The end result is a fall in output per worker, because one property of the constant returns to scale production function is that output per worker is positively linked to per-capita capital or k.

This is another interesting feature of the Solow model. All in all, Professor Solow's growth theory predicts that *nations have a high per-capita real GDP if they have*

(a) *a high savings rate,*
(b) *a high rate of technical advance, and*
(c) *a low rate of population growth.*

5. New Growth Theory

A problem with the neoclassical growth model is that *the rate of technical improvements is independent of economic growth.* The model is silent on what determines this rate; it seems to appear like manna from heaven, and nations accept it gratefully. It may go up and down on its own, and nothing can be done about this.

A new growth theory has recently emerged to erase this flaw. The Solow model predicts that the living standard grows at the constant rate of technical progress. The new growth theory, pioneered by a Berkeley expert, Professor Paul Romer, argues that our unlimited wants generate ever-rising productivity and perpetual economic growth. In this view, per-capita output grows because of the choices people make in pursuit of profits, and nations make in pursuit of growth.

Technology does not just descend from the heavens like raindrops, but depends upon choices people and firms make in enhancing their incomes. People themselves determine their years of schooling; they may quit studying after high school or go on to receive a college education. They may stop at the level of a B.A. or go to a graduate school. Others may go for technical training and post-doctoral research. These are all the choices that you and I make, and upon them depends the pace of technical advance.

Similarly, firms may allocate their investment spending between physical capital and the invention of new technology. Technology gains will accelerate if more is invested in inventions rather than the acquisition of capital stock. Investment in technology, frequently called "research and development," may be more significant than business spending on capital goods. Technological advances may have "positive externalities" in the sense that they benefit all, not just their inventor. New inventions and ideas spread quickly from one industry to another. This way they have a greater beneficial outcome than investments in capital stock.

The Internet revolution is a case in point. When one company benefits from setting up a website, other companies follow. When one firm opens an Internet store, others in the industry imitate. Therefore, investment in technology may have a much greater impact on productivity than investment in capital goods.

However, people would not spend time and money in new discoveries, if there were no patent laws protecting the fruit of their research. Here comes the profit aspect underlying new ideas. If inventors did not have a monopoly, however temporary, over their patents, their profits would quickly disappear as others rush to duplicate their inventions. Once a patent expires, competition trims its profit, so people try to find new discoveries. *Thus, profit is the chief motivating force behind novel ideas and products.*

As long as new discoveries continue to flow — and because of our unlimited wants, there is no reason for them to ever stop — productivity will keep rising, and in fact accelerate due to their externalities. Thus, the new growth theory stresses two main points. First, technology arises from individual and national choice, not from heaven; second, productivity growth itself may accelerate, thus improving living standards at a faster pace.

6. A Critique of the Growth Theory, New and Old

You may have already noticed that neither the old growth theory nor the new one addresses the central question of economic development: Why do growth rates vary so widely from quarter to quarter? They neither explain the growth cycles nor do they have any active role for aggregate demand (AD) in their frameworks. The ghost of classical economics has revived. Growth rates are entirely determined by supply factors — capital, labor, technology, education, the nature of the production function. How is that possible, especially when GDP growth fluctuates so widely?

The Solow–Romer growth models try to explain some fictitious numbers that exist in the averaging process but not in reality. The U.S. growth rate over the half-century after 1950 may be 3.5 percent, but actual growth rates, quarterly or annual, are very different. In fact, Table 12.1 reveals a remarkable slowdown below U.S. average growth.

The Solow–Romer framework offers a variety of policy implications to nations to stimulate their growth rates and per-capita GDP. Desirable economic policies range from increasing the savings rate, levels of education, research and development to the control of population growth. Yet you may wonder what advanced economies such as the United States and Japan, both mired in stagnation, would gain from increasing their saving rates today.

Increased thriftiness works in a developing economy, where people's basic needs have not been fully satisfied, so that all sorts of investment projects are profitable. If an economy lacks the infrastructure of electric and water plants, sewage facilities, roads, bridges, railways, airlines, telephone lines, and so on, there are plenty of undeveloped industries that can absorb the high level of savings. Raising the rate of saving in such deprived areas provides precious funds for investment, so that, with investment matching the rise in savings, there is no deficiency of AD. Otherwise, the Keynesian paradox of thrift will overcome the economy and push it into a recession.

Japan is usually cited as an example where miraculous growth took place because of its spectacular rate of saving. But that was when the Japanese were hungry for all types of goods and services. They had a pent-up demand for practically everything, because their basic needs were not satisfied after the devastation of WWII. However, once their economy matured by the 1980s, their high savings rate became a liability. Japan's savings rate climbed higher after 1990 and has stayed high ever since. What is it accomplishing? The country is trapped in the quicksand of stagnation along with an upward creep in unemployment.

The neoclassical growth model, encompassing both Solow and Romer's contributions, predicts that the real wage rises at the same rate as productivity growth, whereas the real return to capital is constant over time. In fact, in all neoclassical models, as you have seen time and again in previous chapters, the real wage rises in sync with productivity. But that has not happened in the United States, where real earnings have fallen since 1972 for as much as 80 percent of the labor force, while the CEOs roll in affluence. How can the Solow–Romer advice ever benefit the American worker?

7. Factors in Demand Growth

What we need is a growth model that can explain why quarterly growth can vary from 6.1 percent to 2 percent in a single year, as occurred in 1999. Once we solve this mystery, we will also know what the prescription is for stimulating economic growth. And remember that a one-sided analysis will not do. Our answer should also be compatible with other developments in the economy, such as falling real wages, rising capital income, rocketing income and wealth inequalities, and so on. Let us start anew with the concept of AD, which is given by

$$AD = C + I + G + (X - M)$$
$$= C + I + G - TD$$

As before, C is consumer spending, I is business and household spending on investment goods, G is government spending, X is exports, M is imports and $TD = M - X$ is the trade deficit, all expressed in terms of constant or base year's dollars. In the growth setting, the concept of AD has to give way to another idea, one involving demand growth (DG). What determines DG?

One factor is, of course, the population pressure that raises consumer spending; the other is the rise in profits and real earnings, both of which spring from improving technology. Rising profits and earnings raise investment and hence AD. As consumer spending grows, investment follows, followed in turn by increases in government spending, and changes in the trade deficit. Thus, DG is a weighted average of the growth in consumption, investment, government expenditure and the trade deficit, which incidentally enters negatively into AD. In other words,

$$DG = c.CG + v.IG + g.GG - z.TDG$$

where the addition of "G" to a variable indicates its rate of growth, i.e., $DG = \Delta AD/AD$ is the rate of growth in AD; CG is the growth rate of consumption, with c being its weight or share in GDP; IG is the rate of growth of investment, with v being its weight in GDP, GG is the growth rate of government spending, with g being its weight in GDP, and TDG is the growth in the trade deficit, with z being its weight in GDP.

7.1. *The Demand Growth Curve*

DG is then the weighted average of the growth in consumption, investment, government spending and the trade deficit, which may also be negative or zero. The weights respectively are the shares of each variable in GDP. Thus, c is the share of consumption in output, and is approximately 66 percent, or two-thirds of the economy. Similarly, v is the investment share that approximates 16 percent of GDP, g is the government share approximating 22 percent, and z is the corresponding share of the trade deficit. This can be zero, positive or negative.

DG is subject to a variety of influences. Each year the price level goes up, so that the rate of inflation is positive; AD also rises year after year simply because of population growth and some other factors. The first question then is how is DG related to the rate of inflation? DG is negatively linked to the rate of inflation, for the same reasons that AD is negatively related to the price level.

Suppose you have a proud addition to your family, but your income is constant. Your family's spending increase or DG will then come from your cash holdings in your checking or savings accounts. If inflation heats up, the fall in the purchasing power of your money balances will accelerate. Your family's DG will then decline.

Suppose the current rate of inflation is 3 percent, and, at this rate, because of your family's expansion, you plan to increase your nominal spending by 10 percent. Your DG is then 10 minus 3, or 7 percent. If the inflation rate jumps to 4 percent, then your DG will be only 6 percent. Of course, this concept of DG assumes a positive rate of population growth that would normally cause the growth in real consumption.

Higher inflation, as you have seen in Chapter 9, generates a rise in the nominal rate of interest, although the real interest rate falls. This will dampen any plans you have to buy durable goods, and lower your consumption growth, because your spending is negatively linked to the actual or the nominal interest rate that you pay. Thus, consumption growth tends to fall for two reasons — the "accelerated decline in the value of money," and the rise in the nominal rate of interest. *A falling inflation rate, by contrast, stimulates consumption growth.*

As regards investment, let us recall that it has two main components — business spending on plant and equipment, and household spending on new homes. Rising inflation, up to a point, is a great spur to business investment, even if the nominal rate of interest rises. Much of this spending comes from a company's own savings, and not from borrowed money. Post-WWII history shows that there are two instances when capital spending soared in the United States. First, this occurred from 1975 to 1985, the decade of high inflation, when investment growth rose above its level prevailing in periods of subdued inflation. Second, this happened from 1995 to 2000, amidst a speculative bubble.

Thus, history reveals that capital spending soars in a bubble economy, or in an inflationary milieu that reflects the high pressure of aggregate demand (see Chapter 6). However, household spending on new homes tumbles because of a rise in the nominal rate of interest. Such was the case in the late 1970s and the early 1980s. The end result is that the effect of rising inflation on investment growth is uncertain, because while business investment rises, the household investment falls. *We will assume the investment growth effect of inflation to be zero.*

A rising inflation rate also has a negative impact on the rate of growth in net exports. Suppose net exports were poised to rise by 5 percent, say, because of a sharper increase in foreign DG. Then if inflation heats up, and American goods become sharply expensive, the net exports growth will fall below that level. Conversely, growth in the trade deficit accelerates from rising inflation. *For all these reasons, we conclude that rising inflation dampens DG, and falling inflation stimulates it.*

8. Supply Growth

The other concept that we need to develop is the idea of supply growth, which may also be impacted by the rate of inflation. We know that by definition

$$SG = PG + EG$$

where SG = YG is supply growth. Here EG is employment growth that under full employment equals LG (or labor growth). LG is exogenous and constant, but PG or productivity growth depends on two forces — capital accumulation and the rate of technical advance. Both these forces are linked to developments in the past, as they take time to materialize. Capital growth of today was decided by business investment in prior years; similarly, the rate of technological progress also depends on research and development spending in the past.

The question of relevance is as follows: How does the current rate of inflation influence supply growth? If inflation accelerates, what happens to output growth in the current period? There are many factors that could cause supply growth to rise. With inflation heating up, companies could ask their suppliers to accelerate the delivery of capital goods they had ordered in the past. In return, they could increase the delivery price, which they can well afford because of accelerating inflation. As a result, the growth of capital would rise.

Further, escalating inflation also raises a firm's rate of capacity utilization, just as a price increase did in Chapter 9. The effective rate of capital growth is

$$CU.KG$$

where, as before, CU is the capacity utilization rate with an upper limit of one, and KG is capital growth. Thus, the "effective rate of capital growth" rises with inflation until capacity utilization reaches its upper limit. There are then two reasons why accelerating inflation raises the effective growth of the capital stock and hence PG. First, it increases CU; second, it raises KG itself through speedier delivery of equipment. A rise in CU may also increase EG if it is less than LG. Thus SG may rise from an increase in PG as well as EG.

9. Growth Equilibrium

Growth equilibrium occurs when

demand growth = supply growth

The growth process is described in Figure 12.3, where the DG and SG lines intersect at point E, generating a GDP growth rate of OM and an inflation rate of OH in equilibrium. The supply growth line becomes vertical at the point of full capacity, setting an upper limit for growth in the current period, which may be a quarter or a year.

In the graph both inflation and growth are positive, as is normally the case nowadays. In the past, however, positive growth coexisted with zero or negative inflation. During the 1920s, for instance, inflation was zero while growth was positive. By contrast, from 1870 all the way up to 1910, prices fell along with torrid growth. Here growth coexisted with deflation. Figure 12.4 describes these two cases, depending on the position of the supply curve. At point E, GDP growth is OE, but inflation is zero, whereas at point AE, output growth is ON but the rate of inflation is a negative NAE.

Growth can also be negative as in a recession or a depression. In that case, equilibrium occurs in a negative quadrant for real GDP, which is not

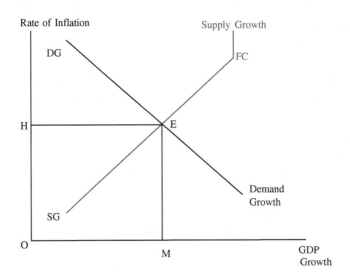

Figure 12.3:   Growth Equilibrium with Inflation

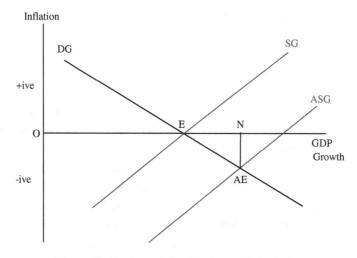

Figure 12.4:   Growth Equilibrium with Deflation

shown, but which you can easily draw. Thus, our model describes the entire spectrum of economic growth and inflation in U.S. annals.

10. Growth Cycles

Armed with these ideas and figures, you can now easily see what causes the growth cycles. The answer obviously lies in the position of the demand and supply growth lines. If DG expands and the DG line shifts to the right for any reason, then for a given SG curve, growth and inflation will accelerate. This happens in Figure 12.5, when the DG line shifts rightward to the NDG curve; so inflation accelerates from OR to OG, while GDP growth rises from ER to GNE. On the other hand, if DG sinks then the DG line moves to the left to ADG; so both growth and inflation decline.

Lest you think that the ghost of the Phillips curve has returned, take a look at Figure 12.6, where the SG curve shifts for any given DG line. If the supply growth line shifts to the left because of a sharp increase in the price of oil, then inflation picks up but GDP growth falls and could even be negative for a while. When the SG line shifts to the left to the NSG curve, inflation rises from OH to OR, while GDP growth tumbles from HE to RNE. On the other side, if the SG line shifts to the right because of, say, bountiful weather, then inflation falls but growth picks up.

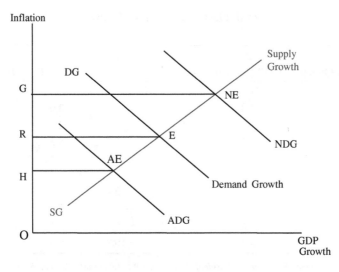

Figure 12.5:   Demand Factors and Growth Cycles

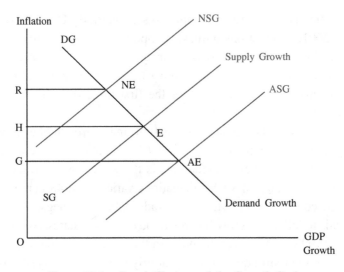

Figure 12.6:   Supply Factor and the Growth Cycle

Figure 12.6 describes the experience of the 1970s, when the SG line shifted to the left. We have discussed this in detail in Chapter 9 and will not repeat it here. How fluctuations in DG have caused fluctuations in output growth in recent years is displayed in Table 12.2.

Table 12.2:   Demand Growth Fluctuations and the Growth Cycle (in percent), 1999 and 2001

(1)	(2)	(3)	(4)	(5)	(6)
Year and Quarter	GDP Growth	C-Growth	I-Growth	G-Growth	TD-Growth
1999					
I	3.0	4.7	7.7	3.0	16
II	2.0	5.7	7.9	2.9	20
III	5.2	4.6	7.7	5.3	15
IV	7.1	5.0	3.0	7.1	48
2001					
I	−0.6	2.4	−5.4	5.7	27
II	−1.6	1.4	−14.5	5.6	0
III	−0.3	1.5	−6.0	−1.1	−15
IV	2.7	6.0	−10.9	10.5	10

Source: *The Economic Report of the President*, 2003, Council of Economic Advisers, Washington, D.C.

The table lists the various components of quarterly DG in two years, 1999 and 2001. Fluctuations in these components cause DG to expand or contract and thus generate variations in quarterly growth rates. In 1999 consumption growth, listed in column (3), is remarkably stable; so is investment growth (in column 4) for the first three quarters, but in the fourth quarter it sinks.

A big surprise is the extent of fluctuations in the growth of government spending (column 5), which ranges from 7.1 percent to 3.0 percent. By far the biggest source of these fluctuations is the growth in the trade deficit (column 6). The range of such fluctuations varies from 48 percent to 16 percent. Of course, the growth of the trade deficit is a negative for DG, which tends to fall as the growth in the trade deficit escalates. Annual GDP growth in 1999 was 4.1 percent, and even though the trade deficit grew by 48 percent in the fourth quarter, the quarterly growth rate was still as high as 7.1 percent. The reason was a big jump in government spending, which constitutes 22 percent of GDP, and has a much greater impact on the economy than the trade shortfall, which is now about 5 percent of GDP.

It is clear that the character of the U.S. economy has changed significantly. *Investment may no longer be the chief culprit in growth fluctuations. The government has become a large presence in the economy and its size may now be adding to instability. The trade deficit is also destabilizing.*

When it comes to a recession, as in 2001 with three quarters of negative growth, investment seems to play the same role as it did in the past. It is the sharply negative growth of investment that caused the downturn that year, while government spending also made its contribution. But for the negative growth in government expenditure, the GDP recession would have ended in the third quarter of 2001, when the 9/11 massacre occurred. The surprising part is that government spending fell somewhat just when it was needed the most to reassure the public and restore consumer and business confidence. This is the biggest surprise of the data, which reinforces the idea that the government's large presence may now be destabilizing.

11. Economic Policy

Is there any role for economic policy in minimizing growth fluctuations? More specifically, can monetary and fiscal policies be used to spur economic growth or lower unemployment, which rises when EG falls short of LG? The answer is yes. Expansionary policy can be used to spur growth and reduce unemployment until productive capacity is fully utilized, but not beyond that point.

You may note that the jobless rate can rise in a growing economy, and even layoffs may continue. This happens when output growth approximates the rise in productivity, so that job creation or EG is too low to absorb new entrants to the labor force. Such a state is sometimes described as a "growth recession," in which new jobs are created but the rate of unemployment still rises. In this case, the government can adopt expansionary monetary and fiscal policies to raise the rate of GDP growth and stabilize the rate of unemployment around the natural rate. However, such policies should not aim at taking the economy beyond the natural rate of unemployment, for they will become inflationary, and joblessness will return eventually.

So long as the jobless rate declines, even if slowly, expansionary policies should not be used just to raise the rate of growth. This rule may be scrapped if inflation stays low for some time and seems to be well under control.

12. Summary

(1) According to Professor Solow's model, a country's rate of GDP growth depends positively on its rate of saving and technological progress that springs from some unknown source.

(2) Per-capita GDP growth equals labor productivity growth.

(3) High population growth reduces the standard of living.

(4) New growth theory says technological progress depends on choices people and firms make about education and spending on research and development.

(5) According to new growth theory, associated with Professor Romer, investment in new technology may be more important to economic growth than investment in physical capital, because new ideas and inventions may have positive spillover effects that move from one industry to another.

(6) Both the Solow model and the Romer model slight the demand side of the economy.

(7) The Solow–Romer model is unable to explain the growth cycles that now occur every year.

(8) A growth cycle describes the fluctuations that occur quarterly or annually in the rate of GDP growth.

(9) Such fluctuations can be properly explained only by a theory that gives prominence to both demand and supply growth.

(10) Recent growth fluctuations in the United States have been caused mostly by variations in government spending and the trade deficit.

(11) Expansionary monetary and fiscal policies is desirable if growth is too low to provide employment to all job seekers.

(12) If growth is too low to absorb all job seekers into the economy, then a growth recession occurs.

Chapter 13

The Supply of Money

There is an oft-cited phrase: money makes the mare go. Others say money rules everything, not just the mare; it even runs the economy. It certainly runs the CEOs, some of whom in recent years have run amuck with other people's money. But what is money? Everybody knows what it is, yet economics offers a precise definition for it.

Money is anything that is commonly accepted as a "medium of exchange." That is right. Anything can serve as money, as long it is generally accepted by people. These days, stores exchange their goods for paper bills, bank checks, credit cards and traveler's checks. All these have some properties of money.

However, paper currency became popular only in the 19th and 20th centuries. Until then some commodities used to serve as the media of exchange. In early America, tobacco and furs were used to carry out transactions. Gold and silver, of course, have been used for ages as money in all civilizations. In India, rice was once accepted routinely for the exchange of goods and services. Thus, anything can be money if people find it trustworthy in their transactions.

The general acceptability is only one property of money. Another is that it is a "store of value," that is, it can be used to preserve wealth over the long run. The medium of exchange must be durable, otherwise wealth would depreciate over time. That is why perishable goods have rarely been money. Precious metals are particularly suitable to serve this purpose. There are some other stores of value as well — stocks, bonds, real estate — but they lack the quality of general acceptability. Money has something that other assets lack. The ease with which goods and services can be converted into money is sometimes called "liquidity." No other asset has the same degree of liquidity.

Credit cards are also liquid and generally acceptable, but they are not the stores of value. If you have 15 plastic cards in your wallet, it is a sign of your indebtedness, not wealth. Therefore, credit cards are not money, although they do come handy in transactions.

Another property of money is that it is a "unit of account." Prices of various goods are expressed in terms of dollars and pennies. This function of money enables us to compare the value of various goods. It also enables us to estimate different aggregates like the GDP, investment, consumption and so on.

The most popular form of money today is "fiat money," which has the backing of governments. One side of the dollar bill says: In God we trust. However, that is not the reason why the whole world accepts dollars for transactions. It is the backing provided by the American government that makes them generally acceptable. The greenback is fiat money, because the federal government so decrees it.

1. Money Supply

What is the supply of money in the United States? The answer depends on what is included in the definition of money supply. The most basic concept of such supply today is known as "M1."

$$M1 = \text{cash in the hands of the public} + \text{checking accounts} \\ + \text{traveler's checks} + \text{OCDs}$$

This category includes those forms of money that the public, including some government institutions, uses most often for spending, and readily accepts for exchange. Cash, which includes currency and coins, has the highest degree of acceptability for most transactions. When large amounts are involved, people generally use checks, which are backed up by money held in checking accounts. If you buy a car, for instance, chances are that you will write a check, rather than pay cash. You will certainly do this when buying a house. If you go abroad, you generally use traveler's checks to pay your routine bills. Thus, cash, ordinary checks and traveler's checks comprise the most basic definition of money supply. It also includes OCDs or other checkable deposits. Both traveler's and OCDs are rather small amounts and are generally ignored in the formula used to estimate M1.

Currency held by banks in their vaults is not included in M1, as it is not available for general spending. Checking accounts are also called "demand deposits," because money can be withdrawn from such deposits on demand. In other words, M1 includes the most spendable and accessible forms of money.

At the end of 2019, M1 stood at about $4 trillion, of which about $1650 billion, or about 40 percent, was in the form of currency.

There is another concept of money supply, called "M2," that includes M1 and other types of deposits, such as savings accounts, small certificates of deposits (CDs) and money market mutual funds. Small CDs are time deposits with less than $100,000, which pay a higher interest rate than savings accounts. But unlike savings deposits, they cannot be cashed before maturity without a penalty. (The Fed calls these CDs small, but for "lowlies" like myself they are quite large.) Thus,

$$M2 = M1 + \text{savings accounts} + \text{small CDs}$$
$$+ \text{money market mutual funds}$$

In 2019, M2 stood at $15 trillion. A still broader concept of money is called "M3" that mainly includes M2 and large time deposits, equal to or greater than $100,000. Thus,

$$M3 = M2 + \text{large CDs} + \text{some other items}$$

2. The Missing Money

In 2002, the amount of paper currency in circulation was $624 billion, presumably held by some 200 million adults in the United States. This means that the average cash holding of an adult is about $3,120, which is large enough to stuff any one's wallet. Few Americans handle this much cash. So, where have all the dollars gone?

There is no clear-cut answer because no one reveals how much cash they carry in their wallets. One possibility is that a large number of dollar bills are being held abroad. Residents of many countries prefer to hold dollars rather than their own unstable currencies. Hundred-dollar bills are especially popular. Brazil, Argentina and some other Latin American countries are particularly fond of the greenback. In fact, the dollar is the currency of choice in Argentina.

Criminals — drug dealers, smugglers, money launderers, tax evaders — also hoard their wealth in hundred-dollar bills. They are afraid to leave a paper trail of transactions through banks. If these explanations are correct, then the size of M1 inside the United States is much smaller than believed. Recently, after the American victory in the war against Iraq in April 2003, some $750 million in cash were discovered in one of Saddam Hussein's ornate palaces. Apparently, the Iraqi dictator hated the United States but loved the greenback.

3. Money Supply or Money Demand

You may recall from Chapter 7 that Keynes had introduced various concepts of money demand to determine the rate of interest. His transactions and precautionary demand for money included the components of what we now call M1. Is M1 then money demand or money supply? It is both. From the viewpoint of the public it is money demand. From the viewpoint of the government and the banking system, it is money supply. The public uses the components of M1 to carry out daily transactions, whereas the government looks upon this aggregate as a determinant of economic activity. Therefore, M1 can be construed as both money demand and money supply.

Cash held by the public is certainly the transactions demand for money, whereas checking accounts are mostly for transactions and precautionary purposes. The context in which the concept is used decides whether M1 is money demand or money supply. If income and prices increase, there is no reason to think that money supply should change, although money demand must go up as the public spends more for transactions. In this context then, M1 is money demand.

On the other hand, if the government or the banking system takes action to change M1, then M1 becomes money supply.

4. The Banking System

The very definition of M1 indicates that the banking system is heavily involved with the level of money supply, because, ignoring the usually miniscule amount of traveler's checks and OCDs,

$$M1 = currency + demand \ deposits$$

and once you mention deposits, banks come into play. Initially, let us assume that there are no banks, and hence no deposits. Then cash and coins are the only form of money. If the Treasury has printed $100 for the public, then that is the total amount of money circulating in the economy.

One problem with the absence of banks is that everyone has to take safety measures to keep their cash away from thieves and muggers. A man of means may then seek a haven for his money. In fact, this is how banks started out, as havens for safekeeping. During the Middle Ages, some persons even used to charge a fee to safeguard other people's cash held in the form of gold. Such havens later evolved into banks.

Let us begin with such an elementary banking system that accepts cash deposits, stashes them away in vaults, but does not use them to make loans. The deposits that are not used for making loans are called "bank reserves." They are part of assets that banks hold to fulfill their obligations to their customers. In the absence of loans, the only function of a bank is to enable its depositors to write checks against their accounts for routine transactions. Banks then use their reserves only to support the transactional needs of the public. Such a banking system may be called "100-percent reserve banking."

As long as banks make no loans, the money supply is unchanged. Suppose the public deposits $60 in Safebank, keeping only $40 as cash. The money supply is still $100, which the Treasury has printed and put in circulation. The only difference is that the public now holds $40 in currency and Safebank holds the remaining $60 in its vault. In the absence of any loans, money supply is not affected by the banking system.

5. Fractional Reserves and the Money Tree

Over time Safebank may discover that, on any given day, the depositors need only a small portion of their funds to make transactions. If on average its customers use only 20 percent of their deposits to withdraw money or to write checks, then the bank may feel justified in lending out the remaining 80 percent, and earn interest in the process. Banks have a strong incentive to seek borrowers for their unused funds. A system in which banks make loans and keep only a fraction of their deposits in reserve is called "fractional reserve banking."

Assuming that Safebank can find a borrower for all it wants to lend, it makes a loan for $48, which is 80 percent of the original deposit of $60. A bank typically lends money by opening a checking account in the name of the borrower. Therefore, $48 must be added to the total supply of money, even though no new greenbacks have been printed. Now money supply is $40 of public's cash, $60 in public's checking account and $48 in the checking account that the borrower has obtained in loan. M1 has increased to $148. Clearly, *under fractional reserve banking, the banks have the power to create money.*

If ever there was truth to the dictum that money grows on trees, the fractional reserve banking system is the one that makes it possible. Modern banking system is thus a money tree. Unfortunately, this tree is a Scrooge because it expects more money back than it lends out. If loans are not paid back with interest, the bank will repossess the borrower's collateral — car, house, factory.

Money creation continues apace. The borrower is not going to let her loan sit idle and just pay interest on it. She has obviously borrowed money to buy something, a car, house, even a factory. She will write a check to someone else, spending her loan of $48. That check could come back to Safebank or be deposited in some other bank, which in turn keeps 20 percent of the new deposit in reserve, lending out the remaining 80 percent or $38.40 in the form of another checking account. Therefore, money supply climbs further by $38.40. Thus, with each deposit and a fractional loan, money supply rises a notch. Clearly our money tree has many green branches for the spread of the greenback.

You may note that with each new loan, the loan amount declines. First, it was $48, then $38.40; in the next round it will be 80 percent of $38.40 or $30.72, and so on. Thus, the money tree is not unlimited. Its generosity ends someday.

The end point comes when the new loan is close to zero. If we were to add up all these loans along with the "original deposit" of $60, we will obtain a sum equaling $300, which turns out to be the sum total of all the demand deposits created by the original deposit of $60. This is because whenever a bank makes a loan, it opens a checking account or a demand deposit in the name of the borrower. *Thus, demand deposits are opened in two ways. The public may open an account, or a bank may open an account for the borrower.* In general, demand deposits (DDs) can be estimated through the following formula:

$$DDs = \frac{BR}{rr}$$

where BR stands for bank reserves, which the banking system keeps in reserve to meet the customers' needs for daily withdrawals, and rr is the reserve ratio, which is a fraction of the banks' total demand deposits. Since the reserve ratio is assumed to be 20 percent, and the original deposit from the public is $60,

$$DDs = \frac{60}{0.2}$$

or

$$60 \times 5 = \$300$$

In all, banks keep $60 in reserve because they need only 20 percent of total DDs of $300 on any given day to meet the cash needs of their customers, which include the public and the borrowers. The formula for M1 is then

$$M1 = \text{public's cash holding} + DDs = \text{public's cash} + \frac{BR}{rr}$$

In our example,

$$M1 = 40 + 300 = \$340$$

6. The Required Reserve Ratio

You can easily see that the volume of bank loans depends on the reserve ratio. When rr is 20 percent, the original deposit of $60 enables the banking system to lend out $240, so total DDs add up to $300. But if rr were kept at a low level of just 5 percent, then the same $60 would generate total deposits of 60/.05 or $1,200, out of which bank loans would be $1,140. Banks would then make bushels of money from interest earnings.

Thus, the system has a built-in incentive to set its reserve ratio as low as possible and lend money out to the maximum. However, maximum lending often requires relaxing the loan requirements, for without borrowers such activity is not possible. Therefore, the fractional reserve system is potentially reckless.

Some nation-wide panics resulted in the past, because the banks were loaned out to the maximum, and had insufficient cash on hand to meet the needs of their customers. In booming times, hordes of borrowers would apply for loans, which the banks were happy to make to earn lofty incomes.

Then a large and reckless borrower would be unable to pay his loan back and throw the entire system into a tailspin. If one bank could not meet its customers' cash needs, rumors of its insolvency would spread, the public would make a run for its money, and several banks would be forced into bankruptcy. This way bank failures were common in the 19th century and created panics and recessions.

A severe banking panic occurred in 1907, and finally woke up Congress, which passed the Federal Reserve Act in 1913, establishing a central-banking system, called the "Federal Reserve System," or "the Fed" in short. The Fed was started in 1914, mainly to be the banker of last resort to banks in need of help, and to regulate the supply of money. The country was divided into 12 districts, each with a Federal Reserve Bank of its own, and a Federal Reserve Board was put in charge of managing the system. Such banks now exist in New York, Washington, D.C., St. Louis, Dallas and San Francisco, among others.

Most nations have a central bank. Britain has its Bank of England, Japan has Bank of Japan, while Europe is regulated by the European Central Bank. The United States, by contrast, has a system comprising 12 such banks, because some states, especially in the southern farm belt, were afraid of vesting vast economic powers in the hands of one centralized institution. The Fed is an independent agency of the federal government but is overseen by the Senate.

Congress empowered the Fed to set up a reserve requirement ratio (rrr) to make sure that banks were not stretched out in the lending process. Therefore, now the Fed sets legal reserve requirements to ensure that each bank holds a certain percentage of its demand deposits in vault cash or as a deposit with a regional Federal Reserve Bank. Under this constraint, the reserve ratio of each bank can be no less than the reserve requirement ratio, i.e.,

$$rr \geq rrr$$

The reserve ratio can, of course, exceed the required ratio, but cannot fall short of it. In uncertain times, banks may not feel comfortable in making too many loans and may set a reserve ratio larger than the required ratio. At present, the required reserve ratio is approximately 10 percent of demand deposits.

7. Money Multiplier

Since banks seek to maximize their profits, it is reasonable to assume that in normal times their reserve ratio equals the required ratio. They have no incentive to keep reserves higher than those dictated by law and lose out in earned interest in the process. The simple formula for determining demand deposits presented earlier is as follows:

$$DDs = \frac{BR}{rr}$$

which in reality sets the upper limit for such deposits, assuming that banks can lend all they want. Thus, demand deposits equal bank reserves times a multiplicand, called the "money multiplier," which is equal to 1/rr. With rr = rrr in normal times, the money multiplier is 1/rrr. Thus, if rrr is 10 percent, then the money multiplier is 1/0.1 or 10. If rrr is 20 percent, then the money multiplier is 1/0.2 or 5. In uncertain times, where rr > rrr, the money multiplier is smaller than these figures.

In practice, the money multiplier is not as large as 10 or even 5, mostly because the borrowers withdraw a part of their loans in the form of cash. At the same time, they may not spend every penny of their loans. Every cash leakage withholds some money from the banks and reduces their ability to generate money. The actual value of this multiplier lies between 2 and 3.

Over time, with increased use of credit cards and growing crime, people have been reducing their cash holdings in their wallets. How does this affect the supply of money? You know that normally

$$M1 = \text{public's cash} + \frac{BR}{rrr}$$

Suppose the public reduces its cash holding, and bank reserves rise to that extent. Does M1 remain constant? No, assuming that banks are already loaned out to the maximum. Money supply actually increases, because banks can do more with their reserves than what the public can. They can generate money, which the public cannot.

Let us revert to our numerical example in Section 4, where M1 turned out to be $340. Suppose cash in public hand falls from $40 to $30, and rrr is 20 percent. Then BR rises from the initial $60 to $70. Demand deposits now become

$$DDs = 70 \times 5 = \$350$$

so that the new level of

$$M1 = 30 + 350 = \$380$$

which is larger than the old M1 value of $340 obtained previously. Note that when M1 increases by $40, so does M2, which includes M1.

Thus, *a decrease in the public preference for holding cash tends to increase the supply of money, and vice versa.*

8. The Regulation of Money Supply

One of the most important functions of the Fed is to regulate the nation's supply of money. Upon this regulation may rest the fate of all Americans and increasingly of the whole world. During the 1930s the Fed's inaction is said to have deepened and prolonged the depression. During the 1970s, our central bank appears to have contributed greatly to inflation by printing oodles of money. Recently, in 2002 and again in 2008, the Fed was extremely active in expanding money growth to counter the potential harm of the stock market crash.

Money supply or its growth is under the supervision of the "Board of Governors" of the Federal Reserve System. The board consists of seven people appointed by the president of the United States under the watchful eyes of the Senate. Each member serves a term for 14 years, with one person's term expiring every two years. The Fed is supposed to be an independent body, free from political pressures. This is one reason the Board's members are appointed for a long period, so that their decisions are not colored by the interests of the party in power.

The president is also empowered to appoint one board member as a chairperson, whose term lasts four years, after which the chair holder may be re-appointed or replaced by someone else. One of the most illustrious chairmen was Paul Volcker, who single-handedly tamed the monster of inflation in the early 1980s. He took great courage in restraining money growth at a time when neo-Keynesian thought dominated the halls of Congress and major media, including the newspapers.

Volcker was replaced in 1987 by Alan Greenspan, who continued to be the Fed chairperson until 2006. With the Dow and the Nasdaq stock index kissing the sky, the American investor, especially the CEOs with all their stock options, came to worship Greenspan as a demi-god, but then came the Great Recession, which was blamed on Greenspan's policies. The current chair is Jerome Powell, who followed Janet Yellen, who was the first female Fed chief.

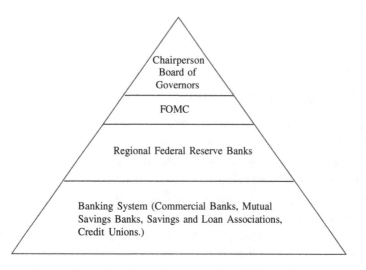

Figure 13.1:   The Pyramid of the Federal Reserve System

The regulation of money supply is in the hands of yet another body called the "Federal Open Market Committee" (FOMC), which consists of the seven members belonging to the Board, plus the president of the New York Federal Reserve Bank, and presidents of four other district banks. In all, the FOMC has 12 members, who keep a watch on the nation's supply of money.

Figure 13.1 furnishes a bird's eye view of the Federal Reserve System, which can be portrayed by a pyramid. Perched atop this pyramid is the chairperson, followed by six other members of the Board of Governors. Then comes FOMC with 12 members, who oversee the activities of the pyramid's base, comprising commercial banks, mutual savings banks, savings and loan associations and credit unions. The base has the power to create money, and the upper echelons of the pyramid topped by the chairperson have the powers to regulate it.

9. Changing the Reserve Requirements

How does the Fed regulate the nation's supply of money? The basic money supply formula is as follows:

$$M1 = \text{public's cash} + \text{demand deposits}$$
$$= \text{public's cash} + \frac{BR}{rrr}$$

assuming that rr = rrr. The central bank can control money supply by changing cash in the hands of the public, or by influencing demand deposits, which are linked to bank reserves and the reserve requirement ratio. However, the public's preference for cash is beyond the influence of the Fed. The central bank is not supposed to tell the people what to do with their money, whether to hold it in cash or in terms of deposits. But the Fed can regulate the level of demand deposits, the other component of M1.

One way this can be done is through the change in rrr. The Fed may want to expand or contract the supply of money, depending upon the state of the economy. Facing a recession or its threat, the Fed may seek to open the money pump; faced with inflation, the Fed may seek to lower the supply of money.

If the Fed raises the reserve requirement ratio, banks will have to set more cash aside in their vaults and reduce their lending, which in turn will trim the creation of demand deposits. The supply of money will then fall. On the contrary, if the rrr goes down, the banks can lend more out of their current reserves, and thus expand money supply.

Suppose the public cash is $40, bank reserve is $60 and rrr is 20 percent. Then you know that M1 is $340. But if rrr falls to 10 percent, then demand deposits rise to 60 × 10 or $600, and M1 becomes $640. Thus, a high value for rrr lowers the supply of money and a low value raises it.

A change in the reserve requirement ratio exerts a powerful influence on money supply but is rarely tried. It is usually regarded as a heavy-handed way of doing things, because it compels banks to do something about their loans. If they were operating close to the official ratio, then raising the ratio will force banks to abruptly call in some loans or to borrow money to raise their reserves. Lowering the rrr does not create much trouble but raising it does. The last time the Fed changed the required reserve ratio was in 1992, when the ratio fell from 12 percent to about 10 percent of demand deposits.

10. Changing the Discount Rate

The Fed was set up mainly to be the lender of last resort in order to prevent bank failures and financial panics. Commercial banks and savings institutions, when facing shortage of funds, can come to the Fed and borrow money. For this privilege they have to pay an interest fee, which is called the "discount rate." Banks are usually reluctant to exercise this privilege because they may have to answer awkward questions or open their books to official scrutiny, but when all else fails and cash is needed, then they do borrow money from the Fed. The Fed does not mind lending them money, but it charges them a fee. *The interest fee that the Fed charges for its loans to banking institutions is then the discount rate.*

The Fed can change the discount rate to alter the supply of money. If its objective is to trim money supply, the Fed can raise the discount rate and try to discourage bank borrowing. Bank reserves will then fall, and so will money supply. If the Fed wants to adopt a policy of monetary ease, it can trim the discount rate to encourage bank borrowing. As the banks obtain more funds from the Fed, their reserves rise and more money can be created.

The discount rate is changed more often than the reserve requirement ratio, because it does not force the banks to take some action. The discount rate is more a device of persuasion than compulsion. In fact, some banks do nothing different when the discount rate is altered. For this very reason, this instrument of monetary policy is a blunt instrument that may not be very effective in fulfilling the Fed's goal. Its efficacy relies on banks' activism or cooperation, which may not be forthcoming.

Changing the discount rate may not encourage or discourage the banks from borrowing from the Fed. The reason is that the market interest rate usually rises or falls with the discount fee. If the market rate of interest rate rises in sync with the discount fee, banks may keep borrowing as much as before, because their profit from such borrowing remains unchanged. A bank's profit rate from such activity equals the difference between the market interest rate and the discount rate, and if the change in the Fed's policy leaves this profit level unchanged, there may be no reason for banks to adjust their behavior and conform to the objectives of official policy.

The discount rate has proved to be a rather ineffective instrument of monetary policy. Why is it then used at all? Mainly to signal the Fed's intentions to financial institutions. Paul Volcker raised the discount rate in 1980 and 1981 to demonstrate that the central bank was serious in its fight against inflation. More recently, Ben Bernanke, the Fed chief immediately following Greenspan, repeatedly lowered the discount fee to show his resolve to stabilize the stock market. As a signaling device, the discount rate is quite useful, but not as an instrument to regulate the supply of money.

11. Open Market Operations

Congress has empowered the Fed to buy and sell federal government bonds openly in the bond market. When the Fed engages in such activity, it conducts what are called open market operations. This is the most important task facing the FOMC, or the Federal Open Market Committee, which usually meats every six weeks in Washington, D.C. to decide whether or not the state of the economy warrants any new action.

Open market operations are the most flexible instrument of monetary policy; they can be conducted with ease, and at the same time they do not compel the banks to take drastic action. Yet they offer a potent tonic to accelerate or slow the growth of aggregate demand. In the normal state of an economy that grows because of increasing population, capital stock and technology, the supply of money also grows automatically, and sometimes independently of the Fed's action. With the rise in employment, loan demand rises, and more paychecks are written and deposited with banks. This way, money supply tends to rise automatically with rising economic activity.

The total amount of cash, held by the public and by banks, is called the "monetary base." Up to a point, money supply can rise with employment, even if the monetary base remains constant. However, this is only possible if banks are not fully loaned out, and if the monetary base is not replenished, the economy could face a shortage of money, or a credit crunch.

One function of the Fed today is to ensure an adequate level of money growth to lubricate a growing economy. The quantity theory of money, introduced in Chapter 5, tells us that

$$MV = PY$$

where M is the supply of money, V is velocity, which normally remains constant in the short run, P is the price level and Y is aggregate supply or output. You can easily see that if Y rises and M and V do not, then P has to fall. In other words, if output grows, but the supply of money and its velocity are constant, then the price level has to decline. This, as the world saw during the 1930s, can devastate an economy. Therefore, the Fed must allow money to grow in a growing economy. In fact, this is where the monetarist preaching, first studied in Chapter 8, comes in handy. *Monetarism argues that money growth should match the rate of growth in real GDP, so that there is neither inflation nor deflation.*

Among bonds, the Fed is authorized to purchase federal government bonds, foreign government bonds, or those offered by the banking institutions, but not state and local issues, nor corporate bonds. The Fed also cannot buy company shares. The Fed normally expands money supply by buying federal bonds in the bond market. The central bank is not authorized to buy them directly from the government.

The sellers of these bonds may be the public or institutions, including banks. When someone sells these bonds to the Fed, bank reserves go up, as the Fed writes a check to pay for its purchase, and the bulk of this payment ends up as bank deposits. If you sell a bond to the Fed and then convert the proceeds into cash, then of course the bank reserves are unchanged. But that rarely, if ever, happens. *Therefore, an open market purchase of bonds by the Fed quickly raises bank reserves.*

A rise in bank reserves then translates into a multiple rise in the supply of money via the process of credit and loans. Suppose the Fed buys one bond and writes a check for $50 to the seller, who deposits it in a bank. Using the formula for M1, since the public cash does not change, demand deposits will rise by

$$50 \times 10 = \$500$$

given that the reserve requirement ratio is 10 percent. The money supply will also increase by this amount, which will raise the rate of money growth. On the other hand, if the Fed sells federal bonds in the open market, then bank reserves decline, and so does money supply or its growth.

When the central bank conducts open market operations, the supply of funds available in money markets changes quickly, and almost immediately there is a change in the rates of interest. The rate that responds first is called "the federal funds rate." This is the rate that a bank charges when it lends money to another bank for overnight loans.

Banks usually borrow funds from each other to meet their shortage of cash and pay a certain fee. This fee is the federal funds rate, which is a misnomer, because it indicates that it is set by the federal government. In December 2007, the funds rate stood at 4.25 percent, but was repeatedly brought down until it sank to 0.25 percent in 2010, where it stayed till 2015. Another rate called the prime rate also fell sharply because of the action by the Fed.

In reality, the federal funds rate is determined in the money and bond markets by the forces of supply and demand. The Fed can influence this rate but cannot dictate it. Most other rates of interest — the prime rate, the mortgage rate, etc., — are linked to it. The "prime rate" is the fee that banks charge their most credit-worthy borrowers. This is the rate that companies like Microsoft, IBM, Toyota would pay. "Lowlies" like myself pay a premium above this rate. The rate on credit card purchases usually responds sluggishly to variations in the prime rate.

12. Margin Requirements

The fed can also set margin requirements for trading in the stock market. Some investors trade on margin, that is, they pay only a fraction of the share price, borrowing the rest from their broker. The broker collects a fee and interest for this service and retains the right to sell the stock if its price falls below a certain level called the margin call. The power to regulate margin requirements is a particularly effective device to control stock speculation, but it was not used in the share-price mania of the 1990s. If the Fed had raised the margin requirement, the bubble would not have been the worst in history, and the crash might have been avoided.

13. Monetary Policy and the Interest Rate

The change in the supply of money works through the money or bond market, as in Figures 13.2 and 13.3. In the money market, the money supply curve shifts to the right to NMS if the Fed buys bonds, equilibrium shifts from E to NE, and the market rate of interest falls by BE in the new equilibrium.

The money supply line may be positively sloped, provided banks increase their lending to maximize their income from a rising interest rate. When the interest rate rises, banks double up their effort to find new borrowers for their unused funds.

You students may have received bank solicitations to apply for credit cards or loans, even before you have graduated. They want to hook you before you wise up and shun borrowing. This way rising interest rates induce banks to find more borrowers, and thus increase the supply of money. This is why the money supply curve in Figure 13.2 has a positive slope, while the money demand curve has its usual negative slope.

Similarly, in the bond market portrayed in Figure 13.3, the intersection point of the bond demand and supply lines determines the bond price in equilibrium,

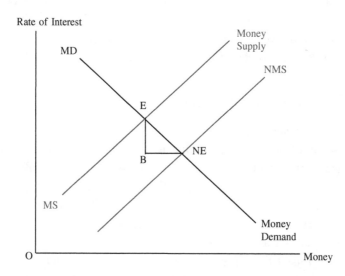

Figure 13.2:   Open Market Purchase and the Money Market

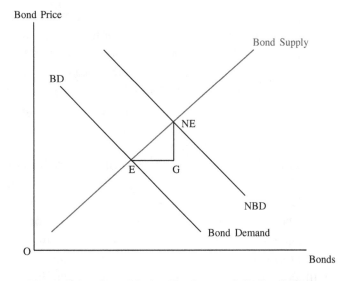

Figure 13.3: Open Market Purchase and the Bond Market

where bond demand equals bond supply. The bond price determines the rate of interest simultaneously, because the two are mirror images of each other.

This point was emphasized by Keynes, and is explained further in Chapter 14, Sections 7 and 8. The open market purchase of federal bonds by the Fed shifts the bond demand curve to NBD and raises the bond price in the new equilibrium by GNE. As explained in Chapter 14, the bond price rise is the same thing as the fall in the rate of interest. Therefore, both graphs lead to the same answer. This is how monetary policy impacts the economy. It first alters the rate of interest in bond and money markets, and then the components of aggregate demand, such as consumption and investment.

14. How Effective is Monetary Policy?

How effective is monetary policy in regulating the supply of money? A related question is: Does the Fed succeed in its real objective, which is to repair a faltering economy? The supply of money is not the goal but a means to some goals. It all depends on how sensible the Fed chairman and his policies are. Does he follow common sense or his pre-set ideology?

In the short run, there is little doubt that money supply is somewhat under the Fed's control, but the long run is another matter. Even if money supply behaves in accordance with the Fed's wishes in the short run, that does not mean that other desirable goals of the economy are accomplished. Sensible and timely action is crucial in steering the economy toward high growth with low inflation.

Take for instance the case of Arthur Burns, who presided over the Fed from 1970 to 1978. He believed in the Phillips curve, as did much of the economics profession at the time. However, that theory blatantly flouted common sense, because it required ever-increasing doses of monetary injections to maintain high employment. Yet the Fed chairman persisted with high money growth, because his ideology and econometric models conflicted with common sense. The end result was double-digit inflation and panic in the nation.

In came Paul Volcker. He faced the same politics as his predecessor; he was vilified by the media for his persistence with monetary restraint. But he stood his ground, talked common sense that inflationary expectations had to be broken first before sanity could return to people's behavior and the economy. Eventually, he succeeded in taming inflation.

Take another case. In the 1920s, the nation came to believe that money would grow on the stock market tree. Everybody could be wealthy just by investing in shares, a view shared by the most celebrated economist of the time, Irving Fisher, among others. What nonsense? How can people become prosperous without the expanded production of goods and services to fulfill their needs?

Some raised doubts about the get-rich-quick-sentiment flying high in the 1920s, but their voices were muffled by the rising chorus of optimism from economists and politicians, including prominent members of the Board of Governors. What they failed to see was that the progressive decline in business competition had been sharply increasing the wage–productivity gap, and worsening the level of income inequality, which tends to subdue aggregate demand, output and employment. But they were trained or inclined to belittle such worrisome developments. They did nothing to reverse the growing tide of inequality and the share-price bubble. The end result was a stock market crash, followed by years of misery and poverty for the world.

History repeated itself during the 1990s, when Alan Greenspan became a cheerleader for Wall Street. At first the share-price boom bothered him and he even coined a new phrase, "irrational exuberance," to describe the stock market behavior at the end of 1996, but turned into its defender, when speculators howled. He argued that a new economy had been born with the aid of a computer-technology explosion that had permanently lifted productivity and profit. This reminds you of Irving Fisher's immortal words in 1929: "Stock prices have reached what looks like a permanently high plateau."

To Greenspan the permanently high plateau of productivity and profits justified rocketing share prices; but he ignored the problems arising from the increasing wage gap. He forgot that wages are the main source of demand, and productivity the main source of supply, and if the two fail to rise together then the demand–supply equilibrium can be only maintained by rising debt. Therefore, he mistook the ever-growing level of debt-supported profit for tangible and lasting prosperity.

Alan Greenspan is the Jean Baptiste Say of the modern world, with a firm belief that supply creates its own demand. It was from his prodding that the Social Security tax was vastly increased in 1983, starting a massive transfer of the tax burden from the affluent on to the backs of the poor and the middle class, as if the tax would not limit demand growth and hence output growth. William Greider, formerly with the Washington Post, puts it aptly: "… Alan Greenspan recommended the tax increase and other 'reforms' to ensure the soundness of the retirement system far into the century …. The terms were now established in the way that the government is financed."[1]

Actually, the Social Security system was not in dire straits when the tax hike was legislated. It was completely solvent and needed no infusion of funds. However, Greenspan, along with some others, created the myth that the system would soon go bankrupt, and that a massive tax hike was necessary to create a big and growing surplus in the trust fund, so future retirees

---

[1] William Greider, *Who Will Tell the People*, New York: Simon and Schuster, 1992, pp. 93–94.

would have a cushion waiting for them. Thus, Mr. Greenspan invented a cure for which no known sickness existed in 1983. *The same economic theory that had looked upon high income taxes as destructive of growth was now silent about the proposed increase in taxes on the destitute.* Supply-siders had absconded because the new tax burdened mainly the poor.

However, the tax legislation turned into a fraud. Soon after the enactment of the massive tax hike, the growing Social Security surplus was used to finance the federal deficit that had resulted from the huge income tax cut of 1981. Therefore, now that vaunted trust fund mostly has the IOUs of the federal government, but not enough cash to meet the State obligations to future retirees. Thanks to Mr. Greenspan and other branches of the government, the poor and the middle class have been paying the massive Social Security tax since 1983, but there is little money in the trust fund that was supposed to build a trillion-dollar nest egg for future needs of the handicapped and the elderly. Therefore, the tax will have to be raised further when baby boomers start retiring in large numbers in a few years.[2]

Suppose the Social Security system and income tax rates had been left alone at the levels prevailing in the 1970s. Then demand growth, GDP growth, employment and real wages would have been higher. The tax revenue would also have been higher without any increase in Social Security rates. All the suffering that people have undergone because of this tax hike could have been averted. Therefore, you see again that *a little knowledge of economics is a dangerous thing.*

It is Greenspan's understanding or misunderstanding of economics that catapulted the nation into lower growth, the accelerating wage gap, the stock bubble of the millennium, and eventually a horrendous crash in the Nasdaq market, where the stock index fell by as much as 75 percent over two years. Millions of unsuspecting shareholders lost trillions of dollars, and the nation entered a long period of employment stagnation. Greenspan thus played a major role in creating the bubble economy in the 1990s, and in the ensuing stock market collapse.

To his credit, the Fed chairman moved with alacrity whenever share markets crash. He did this in October 1987, when the Dow suffered the biggest one-day decline in history — 22.5 percent — as he lowered

---

[2]Ravi Batra, *Greenspan's Fraud*, Palgrave Macmillan, New York, 2006.

the federal funds rate immediately. In 2001, he broke his own record of speedy reductions in the federal funds rate, which fell at the fastest pace in memory. By the end of 2002, the chairman had engineered 12 such reductions. His goal was to expand money growth to fight the ongoing recession; money growth did pick up smartly, as M2 grew 10.5 percent in 2001 and another 6.5 percent in 2002.

Money growth indeed soared just as the Fed wanted, but the economy continued to stagnate. Thus, even though the Fed met its monetary objective, it failed in its economic objective because of years of flawed economic policies.

During the Great Recession of 2008, the Federal Reserve took the policy of monetary expansion to another extreme. As a result, the unemployment recession was over in a few years, but the poverty recession continued as explained in Chapter 11. By now the Fed has exhausted much of its arsenal with which to tame the jobless rate and poverty, leaving the nation highly vulnerable to a new shock.

15. The Cycle of Money Growth

In Chapter 3, you first met the long-run cycle of money growth in the United States. It revealed an amazing pattern, easily discernible from the money growth data. The cycle is presented again as Figure 13.4, which shows that under normal circumstances money growth per decade has peaked every 30 years, going as far back as the 1770s. Only the catastrophe of the Civil War could disrupt this cycle; otherwise its resilience is truly remarkable.

The money growth cycle has survived phenomenal changes in the economy and society. It has lived through two industrial revolutions, breath-taking technological change, two world wars, waves of regulations and business mergers, the Great Depression, the New Deal, discovery of the atom, the hydrogen bomb, the computer revolution, the fall of the Berlin Wall and numerous social movements. Now the question is: What did the creation of the Fed in 1914 do to the cycle?

The Federal Reserve System constitutes a milestone in banking annals of the United States. It was established to erase a number of flaws that had

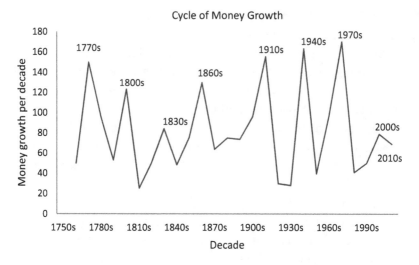

Figure 13.4:   The Long-Run Cycle of Money Growth in the United States

Note: Except for the aftermath of the Civil War, money growth peaked every third decade in the United States.

Source: Historical Statistics of the United States, 1975; The Economic Report of the President, 2019.

plagued the economy since the birth of the Republic. Prior to the Fed, money supply responded only to changing conditions in money and bond markets. Since the Fed was created precisely to control the supply of money, you would think that the central bank would have at least tamed, if not eliminated, the money cycle. Instead, it had just the opposite effect. Figure 13.4 reveals that the decade-wide fluctuations in money growth were of smaller magnitude in the 19th century than in the 20th century. Thus, the creation of the Fed simply augmented the long-run oscillations of money growth without disrupting the cycle.

Yet it is true that fluctuations in the annual growth of money have declined since the 1940s. All this suggests that the Fed can leash the money supply in the short run but not in the long run. While the exactness of the money cycle remains a mystery, it can be used to make a variety of forecasts for the current decade, which, according to the cyclical pattern, is likely to see a big jump in the growth rate of money, with all the consequences for the real and nominal variables of the economy. Are we poised to see a return of the 1970s?

16. Summary

(1) Money is anything that serves as a medium of exchange, store of value and unit of account.

(2) Three definitions of money supply are widely used in the world — M1, M2 and M3.

(3) M1 includes cash in the hands of the public, checking accounts or demand deposits and traveler's checks.

(4) M2 includes M1, savings deposits, small CDs that are less than $100,000, and money market mutual funds.

(5) The very definition of M1 indicates that banks are heavily involved in the creation of money.

(6) In a 100-percent reserve system, money supply equals cash in public hands plus that held in bank vaults.

(7) In a fractional reserve system, banks lend their excess reserves and open demand deposits in the name of the borrowers. This way, banks create money.

(8) Demand deposits can be computed with a formula that

$$DDs = \frac{BR}{rrr}$$

which means that

$$M1 = \text{public's cash} + \frac{BR}{rrr}$$

(9) The reserve requirement ratio (rrr) is a legal requirement that the Fed imposes on banking institutions, which currently have to set about 10 percent of their demand deposits in reserve to meet the public's needs for spending.

(10) The Fed, consisting of 12 regional banks, is the nickname of the Federal Reserve System, which was established in 1914. The Fed acts as the nation's central bank.

(11) The Fed can regulate the supply of money in three ways — by changing the reserve requirement ratio, the discount rate, and the federal funds rate. The federal funds rate changes when the Fed buys

or sells federal bonds openly in the bond market — a practice called open market operations.

(12) The discount rate is the interest rate that the Fed charges for making loans to banks, whereas the federal funds rate is the interest fee that banks charge each other for loans.

(13) Even if the Fed succeeds in controlling money growth, the policy objective of the Fed may be thwarted if the Fed chairperson adopts faculty policies.

(14) The cycle of money growth shows that the Fed has no control over money supply in the long run.

Chapter 14

An Open Economy

On August 1, 1990, President Saddam Hussein of Iraq invaded Kuwait out of the blue and took control of its oil. The world would never be the same again.

The U.S. President, George Herbert Bush, afraid that Saddam could dictate the petroleum price to the globe, quickly organized an international military coalition, and attacked the Iraqi army on the outskirts of Kuwait and Saudi Arabia. The United States won a swift victory with minimal loss of life but stopped short of dethroning the Iraqi dictator.

Finally, in April 2003, with the 9/11 massacre in the background, in which nearly 3,000 people died in New York and Washington, another American President, George W. Bush, finished what his father had left undone. This time global terrorism was the primary trigger for the war, but some parts of the world, especially Europe, saw it as an American ruse to take control of Iraqi oil.

U.S. daily consumption of crude oil is about 19 million barrels, of which nearly 50 percent or 9 million barrels comes from abroad. Like it or not, oil is a crucial ingredient in the American standard of living. It is a symptom of the country's vulnerability and reliance on foreign trade. Another such symptom is the giant American trade deficit, some $500 billion per year, nearly 5 percent of the GDP. Today, America imports as well as exports oil, which suggests that foreign trade is crucial to the health of its economy.

The United States now is an open economy, one that welcomes foreign goods and money with open arms. But it was not like this just 50 years ago. For much of its history, for all practical purposes, America was a "closed economy." Today, without oil and cheap imports of other goods and raw materials, the American economic engine would come to a screeching halt. The United States has now become a "natural importer," one that cannot prosper without foreign trade. Japan, Canada and Saudi Arabia are also natural importers.

In theory, a closed economy is one that imports and exports nothing. In practice, it is a system that can live and thrive without much foreign trade, which is then a tiny fraction of its GDP. For much of its history, the United States imposed giant taxes on foreign goods, with an import dependence falling short of 5 percent of its GDP. Its exports also were close to 5 percent of GDP. Thus, foreign commerce hovered around 10 percent of output, a paltry figure when compared to the 25-percent level prevailing today.

Figure 14.1, which starts from 1930 and ends in 2000, highlights America's dependence on trade in recent years. Until 1970, GDP's share of international commerce hovered around 10 percent, but following that

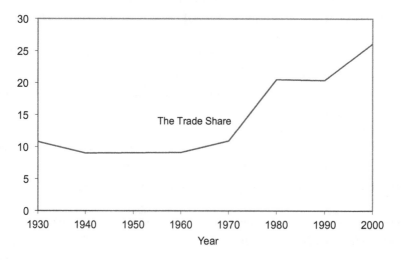

Figure 14.1:   The Trade Share of GDP, 1930–2000

Source: The Economic Report of the President, 2003 and Historical Statistics of the United States.

year, it took off, never to return to the earlier days. Now the nation's reliance on foreign trade is the largest ever.

1. Why Do Nations Trade?

There must be a solid reason why nations engage in foreign commerce. There is. It is called gains from trade. The simplest example of such gains comes from the well-known Ricardian analysis of international trade. The model assumes two goods but only one factor of production, such as labor. One of the goods is exported and the other is imported. In a closed system, both products have to be produced at home, but with the opportunity to trade, each nation specializes in the production of only one good and obtains the other from abroad.

Suppose the United States produces corn and autos at home, using labor in both industries. Let us assume that the cost of production for a dollar of output is constant in both sectors. A graph based on a numerical example illustrates how America gains from trade. Suppose there are 100 fully employed workers; if all work in the auto industry, they produce 100 autos, generating a point such as B in Figure 14.2; and if all work in corn

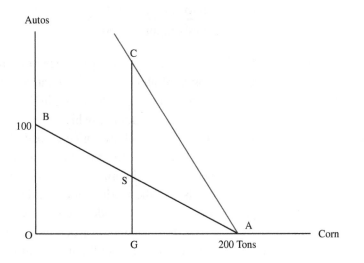

Figure 14.2: The Consumption Gain from Trade

fields, corn output is 200 tons, generating a point such as A. Joining the two point gives us what is known as the "production possibilities curve" (PPC). The PPC represents all efficient and feasible points of production in the economy. The points are efficient because they are generated by a fully employed labor.

The PPC tells us that, with labor fully utilized, the output of one industry can only expand at the expense of the other industry. To produce more of corn, the nation must give up something of autos. For instance, starting from point B where 100 autos but zero corn are produced, a movement to a point such as S requires auto output to fall to GS so that corn production rises to OG.

The slope of the PPC furnishes a ratio of exchange between the two goods. Since labor produces a maximum of 100 autos or 200 tons of corn, then the value of 100 autos equals the value of 200 tons of corn, because both values equal labor's income. Since labor is the only factor of production, labor's income equals national income or GDP. Therefore,

auto price · maximum auto output = corn price · maximum corn output
= nominal GDP

or

$$\frac{\text{corn price}}{\text{auto price}} = \frac{\text{auto output}}{\text{corn output}} = \frac{100}{200} = \frac{1}{2}$$

The slope of the line AB is then ½, which is the relative price of corn, i.e., the price of corn relative to the price of autos. Thus, the relative price of corn is one-half, or the relative price of autos is 2. Suppose, in the absence of trade, America produces and consumes at point S, which stands for self-sufficiency. If autos are produced at a lower relative price abroad, then the United States will find it beneficial to import cars in exchange for its corn.

As home farming tries to meet increased corn demand, domestic and foreign, the relative price of corn rises in the world market, and corn producers expand their output at home. On the flip side, the relative price of autos falls. Since the cost of production per dollar of output is constant, the auto output will cease altogether and will take the nation all the way to point A, where all workers are employed in corn. Unit cost in auto, being constant, will exceed the auto price and produce a loss to auto firms at any positive level of output. Therefore, the country will end up specializing completely in the production of corn.

Let us assume that transportation costs are relatively small. Then under free trade, where the equilibrium relative price of the two goods is the same in both countries, America will produce at point A, and exchange goods in accordance with the price ratio prevailing in the world market. Since the relative price of corn has increased, the new exchange line will not be the same as AB, but something steeper than AB, such as the line AC. The consumption point will then lie anywhere on this line.

Suppose the consumption point coincides with point C. Then the United States has clearly benefited from trade. In the self-sufficiency equilibrium, America consumed OG of corn and GS of autos, but after the opening of trade, the country can consume the same amount of corn, OG, and the GC number of autos. The gain from trade is then CS number of cars.

2. The Production Gain from Trade

What you have explored in Figure 14.2 is the "consumption gain" from trade, equaling the CS number of autos. But trading partners also derive production gains when they import raw materials, whose prices then fall. This tends to lower production cost for each dollar of output, so firms can produce more at the old price. In other words, the short-run AS curve shifts to the right in any country that imports raw materials from abroad.

The United States is among the largest importers of oil in the world; it also imports many unfinished goods and other intermediate products, such as steel. The fall in the price of such goods shifts the AS curve to the right to the NAS line, as in Figure 14.3, producing a fall in the general price level of BE and a rise in output of BNE in the new equilibrium. Of course, output will rise only up to the limit of productive capacity, as first explained in Chapter 9. This is the production gain from trade.

3. The Growth Gain from Trade

If a country imports capital goods from abroad, then capital stock grows faster for the same level of investment. For instance, suppose a company

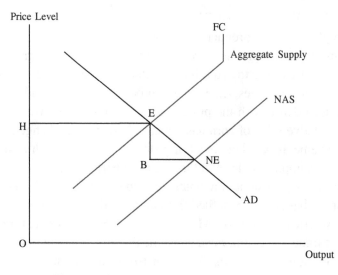

Figure 14.3:   The Production Gain from Trade

seeks to invest $100. If machines cost $50 each, it can then buy only two such goods, but if their cost falls to $25 through imports then it can buy four machines. Thus, the same level of investment spending adds more to the stock of capital. This increases supply growth (SG), because you may recall from Chapter 11 that

$$SG = PG + LG$$

where PG is productivity growth and LG is labor growth, which equals employment growth in a fully employed economy. A pickup in the growth of capital stock spurs productivity growth and SG.

Importing capital goods also adds to productivity in another way, as they embody the latest technology. Thus, international trade in machines stimulates productivity gains in two ways. First, cheaper machines raise the growth of capital stock, and second, imported machines embody new technology. Both spur productive efficiency.

In Figure 14.4, capital goods imports cause a shift in the supply growth curve to the right to line NSG, generating a fall in the rate of inflation and a rise in the rate of growth. In the figure, the growth rate rises by BNE, whereas the inflation rate falls by BE in the new equilibrium.

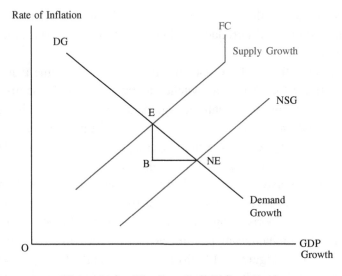

Figure 14.4: The Growth Gain from Trade

Here, because of enhanced growth of capital stock, GDP growth can accelerate sharply, and not be unduly constrained by the limit of productive capacity.

This is how Japan and South Korea grew apace in their early days of development after WWII. They imported capital goods from Europe and the United States to enhance their capital stock, and, for a long time, grew at close to 10 percent per year. Such imports also helped Germany in the development process. However, the tide turned in the 1980s, as America itself began importing capital goods in large quantities, principally from Japan and Germany, but also from Korea. The U.S. growth pickup from 1995 to 2000 arose partly from imported capital goods, and partly from imported components assembled at home to make finished products.

You may like to raise a skeptical note at this point about the growth gain from trade, because the U.S. growth rate actually fell soon after 1970 just when trade started to rise and continued to fall in the 1980s and the early 1990s. Rising trade was then associated with declining growth. You have already seen that this is also the period when the tax system became regressive, and that tends to decrease output growth. However, the United States did not become a substantial importer of capital goods until the early 1980s, so that the growth gain from trade did not start until later. Then why did the 1980s produce the lowest rate of growth since the Great Depression?

The answer lies in the worsening distribution of income that occurs when a country like America switches to free trade and imports labor-intensive goods. You may recall the argument, first established in Chapter 10, that the real wage falls in such a nation, while the profit level rises. This increases inequality, which in turn reduces aggregate demand and demand growth and hence output growth in equilibrium. Thus, for a nation that imports labor-intensive capital goods free trade has two influences on GDP growth — one negative and the other positive. The positive effect arises when the nation imports inexpensive machinery from abroad; the negative impact stems from increasing income inequality. You can see this by shifting the DG line in Figure 14.4 to the left. The two effects may offset each other and leave practically no imprint on the rate of economic growth.

However, for a nation like Japan that imported capital goods from America and Europe in the 1950s and the 1960s, both effects worked in the positive direction. This occurred because Japanese imports at the time were capital intensive relative to exports. Trade itself increased Japan's real wages, and inequality declined. This is another reason why Japan turned out to be among the fastest growing nation in history.

4. The Key Currency Gain from Trade

The gains from trade explored earlier are available to any trading nation. But the United States benefits from foreign connections in yet another way, because its currency, the dollar, is accepted as a medium of exchange throughout the world. The greenback is what you may call a key currency. Nations are happy to accept paper dollars in exchange for their tangible goods. This enables Americans to run huge trade deficits and enjoy high-quality and cheap foreign goods without having to pay higher interest rates to trade-surplus nations.

Normally, a trade-deficit nation has to offer higher interest fees to attract loans from abroad so as to pay for the deficit. Brazil is a case in point. If it runs a big trade shortfall with, say, Europe, it needs euros to finance its deficit. If Europe accepted the Brazilian currency without limit,

Brazil would not have to raise its interest rates. However, because of its constant need to attract foreign money, Brazil's interest costs are among the highest in the world.

There are other key currencies in the world as well — the Japanese yen, the euro, the Swiss franc, the British pound. But their acceptance is not as widespread as that of the dollar. The United States is in a unique position in this respect, because it has been able to run unprecedented levels of the deficit without much cost to its global respect and growth. Nothing like this has ever happened in world history and deserves a careful examination.

5. The American Business Empire

A plausible explanation for the unique position of the dollar is that for a few decades now the United States has run a business empire, which is reminiscent of the British colonies or the Roman Empire. A national business empire may appear to be worlds apart from a colonial empire, but in reality, it has many similarities. While America does not have political dominance over other nations, it has commercial dominance.

In a colonial empire, the victorious country has the highest living standard; it collects gifts and taxes from the conquered people; its ideas, values, culture and language spread to captured areas; it obtains cheap labor from those under its dominance; and above all, it has military supremacy over imperial territories. In all these respects, the American business empire of today has the features of a colonial empire.

Indeed, the United States has one of the highest living standards in the world. Instead of gifts and taxes, it receives tangible goods like cars, cameras, TVs, VCRs, oil, from abroad in exchange for paper dollars, which practically cost nothing to produce. Its ideas in the form of books, movies and TV productions circulate around the world; its language is avidly taught everywhere; it gets cheap labor from illegal immigrants from Mexico and Latin America, and since the fall of the Soviet Union, it dominates the planet militarily. The world seems to be addicted to McDonald's hamburgers, American movies and TV shows, and American youth culture. Thus, America indeed has a business empire, though clearly not a colonial empire.

How did the United States manage to amass the largest business empire ever in history? Following WWII, the United States was the strongest economic power on earth, its industrial might unmatched, its technology envied and in demand all over the globe. What is interesting is that the country then relied so little on foreign trade. In 1950, U.S. exports were just 5 percent of GDP, whereas U.S. imports were 4 percent of GDP. In the lingo of economics, the country was nearly a closed economy, not open to foreign competition, with a small trade surplus.

By contrast, the war had devastated the economies of Russia, China, Japan, Germany, Italy, France and Britain. In order to contain the rising tide of communism, the United States launched what is known as the "Marshall Plan" as well as a policy of globalization. The idea was to enable Western Europe to grow rapidly through financial aid as well as freer trade. The United States also helped Japan through export of technology embodied in capital goods and by opening its markets to imports. This way America hoped to build up its allies to counter the threat of communism from the Soviet Union and China.

Powered by U.S. aid and trade, Western Europe and especially Japan grew apace and turned into unexpectedly strong competitors. American businessmen never foresaw the challenge that was to emerge from war ravaged nations. By 1970 the U.S. trade surplus had turned into a trade deficit. The world was now awash in dollars.

6. From Fixed to a Flexible Exchange Rate

Unlike today, other nations at the time were not ready to accept the greenback indefinitely for their trade surplus. The world wanted payment in gold, which the United States had in plenty, but not enough to finance a persistent trade deficit.

After protracted trade negotiations among G-7 countries (America, Canada, Britain, France, Germany, Italy and Japan), the link between the dollar and gold was severed in 1973, and the world moved from a fixed exchange standard to a flexible rate system. Until that year, the international price of gold was fixed at $35 per ounce, and all other currencies were linked to the dollar. The yen, for instance, was set at the rate of 360 to one, but in 1973 and thereafter the dollar began to fall and the yen began to rise. Currency values were no longer fixed but were determined by the market forces of supply and demand.

The idea was that flexible exchange rates would eliminate trade deficits and thus the U.S. need to export gold. In fact, this is what happened in the 1970s, and the U.S. import surplus all but disappeared. This occurred in spite of the global turmoil caused by the rocketing price of oil that America imported in abundance.

Economic conditions changed dramatically in the 1980s. High inflation along with the need to curb it through restrained bank lending sharply raised the U.S. interest rates. Foreign money poured into the United States to earn high yields. This raised the global demand for dollars and caused an appreciation of the currency. Expensive currency means expensive home goods abroad and cheaper foreign goods at home. Consequently, U.S. exports fell, but imports rose, and the trade deficit made a return, this time to stay forever.

7. Rising Wage Gap in Japan

What had altered the world's willingness to hold paper dollars for goods and services? The main change had occurred in Japan, where, because of the rising wage gap, consumer demand could not grow as fast as before. In order to grow at the old high rates, Japanese companies began to sell more and more of their products abroad, especially the United States. They earned vast sums in dollars and kept their factories humming, but American factories started to shut down.

In the meantime, the U.S. government needed to borrow large amounts of money to finance its growing budget deficit. Japanese companies and the bank of Japan used a part of their surplus dollars to buy U.S. government bonds. Another part went into the purchase of American factories and real estate.

The reinvestment of Japan's surplus foreign exchange into American assets prevented the depreciation of the dollar, which would have normally followed the U.S. trade deficit. This suited Japan fine, but in the process created growing dependence of the nation on foreign demand.

After 1985, the G-7 countries collectively adopted a policy of the dollar's depreciation to bring the U.S. deficit down. The dollar's value declined sharply relative to other currencies, but the deficit fell sluggishly, mainly because several years of the U.S. policy of globalization had resulted in a vast inflow of manufactured imports in American markets. In the process, the domestic industrial base had shrunk and did not offer enough product variety to expand exports sharply.

Several sectors of production had been in full retreat — autos, consumer electronics, machine tools, textiles, shoes, etc. Some major industries vanished altogether. In spite of the dollar depreciation, the home production of goods and services was not high enough to match home demand, and the difference between the two equaled the trade deficit.

8. Developments in China

Japan had experienced phenomenal growth after 1950. For 40 straight years, with few exceptions, the country kept growing at an average rate of 8 percent per year. It served as a model for the neighboring countries of South Korea, Taiwan, Singapore, Hong Kong and even China. They sought to emulate Japan first by creating a vast industrial base at home and then by exporting their goods abroad, mainly to the United States. If, in the process, they had to accept paper dollars or reinvest them in U.S. government bonds, then so be it. Japan had done this with great success, and so could they.

While Japan had started the process of deindustrialization in the United States during the 1970s, China took it to another level during the 1980s and beyond. As with Japan, China imported large amounts of capital and technology from America. The U.S. multinationals were invited to open new factories and share their latest innovations with their Chinese partners. The nation offered cheap, disciplined and highly skilled labor, which attracted companies like Apple, Microsoft and IBM, among many others. For instance, Apple discovered the iPhone but chose to produce it in China.

There are two types of technologies — new process technology and new product technology. The first replaces labor but the second creates new jobs, provided the new product is produced in the home country, not abroad. Innovations have been occurring in America for over two centuries; some were labor saving and eliminated jobs, while others generated new products and absorbed those who were laid off by labor-saving innovations. Thus, technological advance kept employment and GDP growth high, and sharply raised the production wage and hence the living standard for over 200 years.

This salutary process of new product technology was shattered once China entered the U.S. market. In the past, high American tariffs made sure that American innovations not only replaced labor but also provided new jobs, because new products were made in USA. Once the United States switched to free trade and tariffs all but vanished, innovations still occurred in America, but their output materialized in China, which offered cheap but skilled labor. With tariffs gone, goods made in China by American firms could be imported without any duties. Tariffs would have discouraged such imports but they were no longer there. American multinationals frolicked in profits, but the real production wage kept falling, especially after taxes.

This is how the U.S. trade deficit with China rose year after year. But there was another reason as well — the rising wage gap. New technology sharply raised Chinese productivity but Chinese wages stayed low; so, there was a huge jump in China's wage–productivity gap. Since productivity is the main source of supply and wages are the main source of demand, supply outpaced demand year after year. China then had to ship its surplus production abroad to maintain its demand–supply equilibrium. *The soaring Chinese wage gap made it necessary for the nation to manage its currency and ditch free trade.*

While the world followed free trade, China retained its tariffs on manufactured goods and regulated its currency — the yuan. When the world moved from fixed to flexible exchange standard, the Japanese currency, the yen, appreciated sharply while the dollar fell. This is what usually happens when a nation has a trade surplus. A dollar once bought 360 yen, but it now buys about 110. This means the dollar has sharply depreciated.

But China's regulation of the yuan ensured that its export surplus with the U.S. kept growing every decade since the 1980s. The nation did this by buying U.S. government bonds. China exported goods to the United States in exchange for a meager amount of goods from America plus American treasury securities. This strategy kept the Chinese demand for dollars high enough to prevent the dollar depreciation with respect to the yuan. Therefore, the U.S. trade deficit kept rising. *Here then is another example of why a rising wage gap is responsible for global imbalances.*

9. Foreign Bond Holdings

Many countries own U.S. government bonds but China and Japan are the ring leaders. At present, the two Asian nations each hold about $1.2 trillion of Treasury securities. In all, according to the Federal Reserve the world had $6.5 trillion of such bonds in 2019. Fortunately, for the United States this is foreign debt in name only, because the debt is in terms of its own currency.

10. The Rate of Exchange

The rate of exchange (R) is the relative price between any two currencies. We define it the way it is listed in the business section of daily newspapers. It is the number of units of foreign currency you can get for each dollar. Suppose you can buy two euros for one dollar, then

$$R = \text{no. of euros/dollar} = 2$$

There are as many exchange rates as there are currencies, but most of them rise and fall together. Therefore, one exchange rate can represent most other rates. The dollar is said to appreciate when it buys more units of foreign currencies.

When a dollar buys 90 yen rather than 80, it appreciates; if it buys 70 instead, then it depreciates. Note that the dollar depreciation amounts to a fall in the exchange rate as just defined.

In a fixed rate system, exchange rates are set by national governments. In a flexible standard, the one that prevails today, they are determined in the market for foreign exchange, as usual, by the forces of demand and supply. In this market the exchange rate is the price, and foreign currency is the commodity bought and sold. The dollar is the principal foreign currency for the rest of the world, so Figure 14.5 examines the forces that influence global supply and demand for the dollar and determine the foreign price of the greenback.

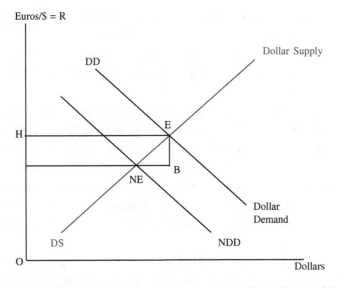

Figure 14.5: The Market for Foreign Exchange and the Global Value of the Dollar

The global demand curve for dollars has a negative slope and the global supply curve has a positive slope. The world demand for dollars comes from a variety of sources — importers of U.S. goods and services, tourists visiting the United States, and foreign investors ready to park their funds into American financial institutions.

As the exchange rate declines, or the dollar becomes cheaper abroad, the foreign demand for dollars rises. A fall in the value of the dollar means that American goods, priced in dollars, become cheaper to foreigners, who then want to increase imports from the United States and need additional dollars to do so. Similarly, the cheaper dollar attracts more foreign tourists into the United States, and they also want extra dollars. Finally, foreign investors find American assets more attractive than before, pursue U.S. bond and share markets and seek more dollars. For all these reasons, the decline in the rate of exchange, as defined, increases the global demand for the dollar.

By contrast, the U.S. supply of dollars to the globe increases with the rise in the exchange rate, which marks the appreciation of the dollar relative to foreign currencies. Rising dollar means cheaper foreign goods and services to American importers, tourists and investors abroad.

Therefore, Americans spend more on such goods and services and supply more dollars to generate a positively sloped dollar supply curve. Equilibrium occurs in the foreign exchange market, when the two curves intersect at point E, setting the rate of exchange at OH. At this rate dollar supply equals dollar demand.

When the U.S. stock market crashes, usually the dollar depreciates. For instance, following the stock market crash in 2001 the dollar's value fell in world markets. The dollar bought 1.2 euros prior to March 2001, but less than a euro by early 2003. The reason is the flight of the foreign investor away from American assets, especially company shares and federal bonds. This serves to shift the dollar demand curve to the left to NDD; so the dollar falls by BE in the figure. On the flip side, the euro appreciates to that extent.

On the other hand, in 2019 the U.S. stock market appreciated sharply; the foreign demand for the dollar went up and so did the value of the dollar.

11. The Stubborn Trade Deficit

There is a well-known theory in the area of international economics, namely, currency devaluation eliminates a nation's trade deficit, at least after a while. Indeed, this is what happened during the 1970s, when the dollar's fall took care of the American shortfall in trade. *Since 1983, however, the dollar has waxed and waned, but the U.S. trade deficit is as persistent as ever.*

Let us take another look at the basics of aggregate demand and supply. American aggregate expenditure (AE) or national demand equals

$$AE = C + I + G$$

whereas in equilibrium

$$AD = C + I + G + X - M = AS$$

Therefore,

$$TD = M - X = C + I + G - AS$$
$$= AE - AS$$

Thus, the trade deficit (TD) is the difference between AE and aggregate supply or GDP. Why does the American deficit not respond to economic policy anymore? A number of explanations have been offered.

During the 1980s and the early 1990s, the most popular hypothesis was one of "twin deficits," wherein the unprecedented federal budget deficits coexisted with an escalating trade deficit. The idea was that the big jump in government spending and deficits caused AE to exceed AS year after year. But then the government budget deficit began to decline after 1992, while the trade shortfall kept climbing. At the same time, the budget deficit rose in Japan along with its trade surplus. This was the end of the twin deficit hypothesis.

12. The Price Level and the Trade Deficit

The chief reason for the deficit headache is described in Figure 14.6, which displays the AE curve and the AS curve. The AE curve is negatively sloped in the price–output space for the same reason as the AD curve is (see Chapter 8). In both cases, consumer spending responds negatively to a rising price level, while the investment effect is miniscule. The AE curve cuts the AS curve at point BT, which is the point of balanced trade.

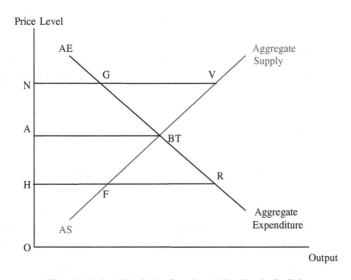

Figure 14.6:   The Price Level and the Trade Deficit

Both AE and AS then equal ABT, and the trade deficit is zero at the price level of OA.

However, this may or may not be the equilibrium price level, which arises when AD equals AS. If the equilibrium price lies above OA, as at point N, the country has a trade surplus of GV, which is the difference between AS and AE at price ON. Such is the case with Japan and China. If the equilibrium price is below OA, as at H, then the nation has a trade deficit equal to FR, which is the difference between AE and AS. Such is the case with the United States. Thus, *a trade imbalance occurs when the equilibrium price is not the same as the one that would produce balanced trade.* The price is either too high or too low.

Let P^* be the price level in the foreign country; P^* is linked to the domestic price level (P) through the medium of trade. Under free trade, assuming that transportation costs are negligible,

$$P = P^*/R = P^*\$/euros$$

Suppose a BMW costs 10,000 euros, and it takes two dollars to buy one euro, then the dollar cost of BMW is $20,000. That is why P equals P^* times $/euro. If the country imposes tariffs (t) on foreign goods, then

$$P = \frac{P^*(1+t)}{R}$$

Thus, the tariff raises the domestic price level above the foreign price level. Now the question is why the U.S. price level is so low that it produces a large deficit in trade. There are three reasons.

One reason is that the U.S. tariff has all but vanished because of the policy of globalization. Clearly, if the tariff declines, so does P. The second is that there is tremendous competition among foreign exporters to capture the American market, which is the largest in the world. Therefore, goods flow into the United States at very low prices, keeping P^* and hence P extremely low. The third reason is that America's trading partners do not allow R to decline, so P could rise. Normally, a rising trade deficit would cause the country's currency to depreciate enough to eliminate the shortfall. But China and to some extent Japan and other trade-surplus nations have ploughed their dollar hoards back into American financial markets, kept the dollar demand high and thus prevented the decline of the dollar.

Why does a low-price level generate a deficit? First, it raises the level of aggregate expenditure; second, it tends to lower the size of aggregate supply, and both combine to increase the trade deficit.

In China and Japan, barriers to free trade are still high. Their tariffs may be coming down, but they have many non-tariff barriers, especially the attitude that prosperity depends on a trade surplus. They try their best to assist exports and resist imports. Their price level is thus higher than the one compatible with balanced trade. This way, the dollar waxes and wanes, but the U.S. trade deficit flies ever higher.

How is our theory linked to another popular thesis that the American savings rate has been sinking lately, so consumer spending has increased consistently to raise AE above AS and thus generate a perpetual deficit? There is some validity to this view, although it must be pointed out that the U.S. rate of saving has been substantially below that of its trading partners through much of history, even when America had a long period of trade surplus with the rest of the world, as from 1900 to 1965. The aforementioned price explanation of the persistent deficit is more complete than any other.

13. The Foreign Trade Multiplier

In Chapter 7, you were first introduced to the concept of the GDP multiplier, which links autonomous spending to equilibrium GDP. That is,

$$GDP = A^*/mps$$

where A^* is autonomous spending, mps is the marginal propensity to save, and 1/mps is the GDP multiplier. The mps captures the leakage that savings cause from the spending stream. In an open economy there is another source of leakage, namely, imports (see Chapter 5). Imports tend to rise with national income in a proportion given by the marginal propensity to import (mpi). Thus, mpi is the fraction of new income spent on foreign goods. The total leakage then becomes

$$leakage = mps + mpi$$

so that the multiplier becomes 1/leakage or 1/(mps + mpi). If the mps is 0.1 and mpi also is 0.1, the closed economy multiplier is 1/0.1 or 10, whereas the open economy multiplier is 1/0.2 or 5. Thus, *the value of the multiplier declines in an open economy.*

Lest you think that an open economy creates a negative impact on GDP, please note that exports tend to raise the size of autonomous spending, as they are not linked to home country's GDP. They may be treated as exogenous or independent of the home economy. Therefore, the rise in the size of A^* offsets any negative impact of the enhanced leakage from the spending stream.

The foreign trade multiplier points to the element of economic and financial interdependence present among nations in a global economy. Because of its addiction to foreign goods, a large economy such as the United States, through its growth, can pull the rest of the world with it. The U.S. trade deficit works as a powerful tonic for the trading partners. It is a locomotive that can make a big difference between high and low growth abroad. This is precisely why the world wants to keep the American economy humming, continues to pile up the dollars, and does not dump them on the foreign exchange market. If the dollar ever lost its appeal, then it could go into a free fall, with unimaginable consequences for the global economy.

There is a well-known saying: when America catches cold, the world catches flu. In order to avoid that flu the world tries to keep the United States free from the virus. American economy is a goose that lays a golden egg for the world. However, the growing trade deficit could kill that goose and devour everyone's egg.

14. Effectiveness of Economic Policy

In an interdependent world, economic policy works only partially. Suppose the United States seeks to combat unemployment and adopts expansionary policy by enhancing its budget deficit and/or money supply. In an open economy, the resulting expansion in AD is subdued because a part of increased spending filters into increased imports. Output and employment still go up but not as much as in the closed economy.

Conversely, if America trims its budget deficit and/or money supply to fight inflation, the resulting fall in AD is again smaller than in the closed economy, because reduced home spending bites into imports. Therefore, the inflation fight must go on a bit longer in an interdependent world. Thus, *increased openness dampens the effectiveness of economic policy.*

15. President Trump's Tariffs

As suggested previously, the relationship between American multinationals and China was extremely cozy and served the interests of both parties. China got its foreign investment and new technology, while the multinationals and their CEOs made enormous incomes by exploiting Chinese low-wage labor. Since money rules politics in the United States, politicians, backed by their economists, sang melodies of free trade. The CEOs made sure that both political parties were in their pockets through generous campaign donations.

In came a maverick President like Mr. Trump, a businessman himself, elected unexpectedly by the American worker in 2016. It was mostly the production worker, sickened by years of falling wages, rising taxes and low employee benefits, who supported Mr. Trump and gave him a narrow victory.

Mr. Trump knew about China's long-term plans, which were to dethrone the United States as the preeminent economic power, ironically with the help of American CEOs. The free trade rhetoric did not fool him. He called upon China, in fact the whole world, to really follow free trade or face American tariffs. The world did not take him seriously, and the President began to impose import duties in 2018. Single-handedly, he shook the world order that had been making money for the multimillionaires and billionaires all over the planet, while creating poverty for millions of people.

The long-term effects of these tariffs cannot but be good for the United States, but the short-term results may lead to a slowdown of global economic growth.

16. Tariffs and Prices

Most people consider tariffs to be inflationary, but this is not always true, especially in the case of the United States. If you recall from Chapter 2, the consumer price index in 1940 was almost the same as in 1820, even though high tariffs existed all through the 19th century. When the president-imposed import duties on Chinese goods, he was denounced by several experts. But the dreaded price increase failed to materialize.

This happened because the effects of tariffs on prices are not as straightforward as may appear at first glance. Indeed, until the pioneering contribution by the late University of Chicago Professor, Lloyd Metzler, the question was not even explored. It was taken for granted that tariffs automatically raise the prices of imported goods. But Metzler's article changed, known in the literature on international economics as the Metzler Paradox, finally clarified the answer. Let us analyze the problem without hysteria. Tariffs have two effects on prices, one tending to raise them, the other tending to lower them. The overall impact depends on which effect is stronger.

It all comes down to supply and demand for goods in China. The United States is a very large importer of Chinese products, so American tariffs should cause a huge fall in American demand for Chinese goods because of the initial rise in prices. But as demand falls substantially, prices of exportable goods inside China will also decline substantially. Assuming that transportation costs are minimal, as they are nowadays, the American price of a Chinese product is determined as follows:

$$\text{American price} = \text{Chinese price} \,(1 + t)$$

where t is the rate of tariff. From this formula, it is clear that there are two countervailing effects on the U.S. price of a Chinese good. A rise in the tariff rate initially tends to raise it, whereas the resultant fall in the Chinese price tends to lower it. The final effect depends on whether the Chinese price declines more or less than the rate of tariff.

As a simple example, suppose Walmart imports a shirt from China for $20, and then faces a 25-percent tariff on that import. If China's price is constant, then the same shirt will now cost $25. But the Chinese price cannot stay constant. Since the United States imports a vast number of Chinese shirts, the demand for Chinese shirts will fall sharply, and that will lower the Chinese price. Say, this price declines to $18, then a 25-percent tariff will raise its U.S. cost by one fourth to $22.50, which is still higher than its free trade cost of $20.

At a Chinese price of $16, the tariff-inclusive price will be the same as the free trade price. But if the Chinese price were to fall below $16, the cost to Walmart will be less than $20. Thus, it all depends on the forces of supply and demand inside China.

The extent of the Chinese price decrease depends on the cost of producing a shirt. If this cost is low, then the price fall can be large in the wake of declining demand, because a producer can still make some profit. Since Chinese wages are much lower than American wages, the Chinese cost of producing a shirt is likely to be very low, in which case the Chinese shirt price can fall substantially. If that happens, American prices of goods imported from China could actually decline.

Indeed, this may explain why so far the U.S. tariffs that were imposed on Chinese exports in September 2018 have not been inflationary.

Large trade deficits with China have decimated American manufacturing and wages. The U.S. industries need a revival, and tariffs are indispensable for this purpose. In 1800, barely 5 percent of the U.S. labor force was employed in manufacturing; today, according to *The Economic Report of the President*, 2019, the share is about 9 percent, vastly below the 30-percent figure that prevailed in the 1960s. The situation is very close to where it was in 1800; clearly, the manufacturing sector needs a lot of support.

Note that under Abraham Lincoln tariffs were as high as 60 percent. As a result, following the Civil War, American manufacturing became the envy of the world. By 1900 the United States was among the nations with the highest living standard. Even though the tariff was so high, prices fell or remained stable for several years. And such price behavior helped raise the overall standard of living. When a 60-percent tariff rate could not harm the American consumer, how can a mere 25 percent? Free trade has been the holy grail of international economics for decades, but historically, the fastest growth in the American living standard has occurred under tariffs.

17. Summary

(1) Through much of its history, the United States was practically a closed economy, as both imports and exports were miniscule relative

to GDP. The GDP share of each hovered around 5 percent, so that trade as a percentage of GDP was close to 10 percent.

(2) Since 1970 the nation has become an open economy and seen its GDP share of total trade rise slowly but steadily. Today, this share exceeds 25 percent. This is a remarkable transformation for the country in barely three decades, with momentous consequences.

(3) Countries open up their economies because they obtain a variety of gains from trade, including a consumption gain, a production gain and possibly a growth gain. The consumption gain arises from a rise in the availability of goods from a constant level of output. The production gain arises from the availability of cheaper raw materials from abroad. Finally, the growth gain stems from access to inexpensive imports of capital goods.

(4) The United States reaps yet another gain, because the dollar is a "key currency," which is widely used for transactions throughout the world. There are some other key currencies as well — the euro, the yen, the pound, the Swiss franc — but the dollar is the most sought after.

(5) Ever since WWII, America has amassed a business empire, which confers certain privileges to the nation that only imperialist countries enjoyed in the past. The colonial masters used to collect taxes and free gifts from their colonies. The United States has no colonies, but since 1983 a portion of its imports has essentially come free, because the world is content to exchange its surplus goods for paper dollars, which cost practically nothing to produce.

(6) Most nations have to offer "high interest rates" to attract foreign funds and finance their trade deficit, but its business empire enables the United States to avoid this discomfort. In fact, foreign countries, in their self-interest, park their dollar hoard back into American financial assets to keep their currencies undervalued and to enjoy the fruit of their trade surpluses.

(7) The rate of exchange is the relative price between any two currencies. The dollar rate may be defined as the units of a foreign currency needed to buy one dollar. This way the foreign exchange value of the dollar can be explored in terms of the usual forces of demand and supply.

(8) Normally currency depreciation eliminates a country's trade shortfall, at least after a while. But such has not been the case with the American deficit since 1983. The dollar has waxed and waned, but the deficit is forever.

(9) The open economy multiplier is smaller than the closed economy multiplier, because imports add another leakage to the spending stream.

(10) The foreign trade multiplier creates economic interdependence in the world, so that growth in one major area spreads across the globe.

(11) The open economy multiplier reduces the effectiveness of economic policy.

(12) Finally, tariffs do not always raise prices.

Chapter 15

Economic Reform

There is only one litmus test for a variety of doctrines that have appeared on the landscape of macroeconomics since 1936, when John Maynard Keynes, the most celebrated economist of modern times, wrote his *General Theory*. This is the test of common sense, which almost every thesis should pass, but few do in entirety. However, some ideas are more sensible than others. When theories lose their rationality, they turn into dogmas, which in the past seem to have created depressions or inflation.

After all, it was the classical gospel of *laissez faire* that prevented the U.S. government from intervening in the economy, as the State even failed to rescue depositors, while bank after bank collapsed in the 1930s. It was the classical thought that engineered a big rise in the income tax rate amid a deepening slump. Few dispute that the gospel eventually turned possibly a routine downturn into the disaster of the Great Depression.

Similarly, obsessed with the Phillips curve, the neo-Keynesians departed from common sense, and clung to their belief that constantly printing money can cure poverty and unemployment. Their obsession caused untold suffering for millions of people around the world in the form of "stagflation," where high joblessness coexists with high inflation. If printing money is all you need to cure economic ills, there should be no poverty anywhere on earth.

1. New Dogmas

Unfortunately, we economists tend to fritter away our hard-won lessons. It seems that as soon as common sense prevails and old dogmas are discarded, new ones crop up. The classical dogma was once despised in the profession; the Phillips curve was also scorned in the early 1980s, but then a new dogma, as perilous to the world as classical theology, appeared in 1981 in the garb of "supply-side economics," and has mostly ruled U.S. economic policy to this day. The consequences are now there for all to see — sluggish growth, rocketing debt among consumers, corporations and the government, horrendous inequality with attendant social and economic ills, and, above all, repeated stock market bubbles and crashes, followed by recessions, rising unemployment and trillion-dollar losses in wealth.

2. Ethical Economic Policy

The verdict of history is that ethics works, and deception designed to foster the interests of the few does not. Ethical policies start out with direct benefits to the poor and the middle class, whereas deceptive policies directly favor the affluent in the name of benefiting the poor and the middle class. Ethical actions generate a trickle-up of prosperity, whereas deceptive actions offer a trickle-down. "Trickle-up" means that the poor benefit the most, followed by the middle class and the affluent. "Trickle-down," by contrast, signifies that the wealthy reap maximum reward, possibly followed by the middle class and the destitute.

Ethical prescriptions keep the tax burden low on the poor and those in the middle, while unethical policies transfer the tax burden from the wealthy to the poor and the middle class. Ethical ideas keep aggregate demand high through high wages stemming from free enterprise, whereas deceptive practices try to revive demand in the name of free enterprise by generating debt. *Ethical measures work for the benefit of all, while unethical measures benefit the few and harm the most.*

Let us take another look at the 1950s and the 1960s, when high economic growth coexisted with confiscatory income tax rates, as high as 90 percent on top incomes, but never below 70 percent. Those were the halcyon days of ethical economic policy. The sales tax rate hovered around 2 percent, whereas the Social Security tax barely averaged 3 percent, on the first $5,000 of wages. The tax system was "ultra-progressive" in the 1950s and the 1960s. In addition, the minimum wage in the period averaged $1.25, which is about $10 in 2019 prices. The economic policy was highly ethical; it was designed to provide a living wage to the unskilled and minimize the burden on those who could least afford to pay taxes. It produced vast benefits for society. Growth averaged 4 percent in the 1950s and 4.4 percent in the 1960s; real wages soared for all, at the average rate of 2.5 percent per year, and consumer, corporate and government debt was extremely low. Unemployment fell to as low as 3.5 percent in 1969.

3. The Legacy of Unethical Policy

Now let us see what unethical policies, such as supply-side economics, have accomplished. Between 1981 and 1983, the tax system became "ultra-regressive," and has remained so to this day. Had the Social Security tax remained constant, it would still be 3 percent with a wage base of about $30,000, which is the equivalent of $5,000 in 1960. However, in 2019 the tax was 7.65 percent on a wage base of $132,900. *Overall, the Social Security tax burden is now about seven times its average burden in the 1950s and the 1960s.* You can see what an enormous weight this tax places on the poor and middle income groups.

Today, the sales tax averages between 7 percent and 8 percent in most states, compared to 2 percent in the 1960s; in addition, the excise tax on gasoline is much higher than in the past. The top-bracket income tax rate is now just 37, whereas the corporation income tax is a flat rate of 21 percent compared to over 50 percent in the 1950s.

What did supply-side economics have to show for itself in the year 2019? A trade deficit exceeding $500 billion a year? A federal budget deficit in excess of $1 trillion? A federal debt over $23 trillion, compared to just $365 billion in 1969? An overall debt level that is twice the level of GDP? Net foreign debt in excess of $6 trillion, compared to a surplus in 1969? A capacity utilization rate of just 78 percent, compared to 90 percent in 1968. An after-tax production wage, earned by 80 percent of working Americans, that is just three-fourths of its level in the 1960s? And, of course, a CEO wage that is 250 times the production wage, compared to just 20 times during the 1960s? *It is abundantly clear that the CEO club owns the government and economic policy.*

The fall in the after-tax minimum wage is really unbelievable. In 1968, the hourly minimum was $1.60 per hour. Assuming that a full-time employee worked 2,000 hours a year, he earned a salary of $3,200, which was subject to the Social Security tax of 4.4 percent. About half of this income was subject to a sales tax of 2 percent. He then paid a total tax of $173, assuming that his low income exempted his family from the income tax. Therefore, his after-tax income was $3,027 which in terms of 2019 prices that are at least 7 times higher is $21,189.

Now the minimum wage earner makes just $14,500 and pays a 7.65-percent Social Security tax. In addition, he pays about an 8-percent sales tax on half his earnings or a 4-percent sales tax on all his income. Therefore, his total tax rate is 11.65 percent, or $1,690, with an after-tax income of $12,810, which is just 60 percent of his after-tax real income in 1968.

Such is the legacy of supply-side economics — an effective minimum wage less than two-thirds of the level in the 1960s. There are 20 million Americans whose wages are directly tied to the minimum pay; the remaining production workers of 80 million have their earnings indirectly tied to the lowest wage. The effective wages of all these employees have plummeted beyond imagination. No wonder the average consumer is up to her neck in debt, saves a miniscule 2 percent of her income and, despite record indebtedness, does not generate enough demand to absorb the production of all factories.

In the 1980s, the supply-side idea was called voodoo economics; now some have called it déjà voodoo, as the ghost of this dogma makes a strong comeback.

The idea miserably flunks the common sense test.

4. The Legacy of Neo-Keynesian Economics

Neo-Keynesian policy started out with an emphasis on fiscal expansion and budget deficits. That part has been taken over by supply-siders, who favor income tax cuts for individuals and corporations along with spending restraint by the government, regardless of the nature of the economic ailment. However, neo-Keynesians were belatedly converted to monetary expansion in a sluggish economy, and that belief has survived. This is what moved Fed Chief Alan Greenspan to open up the money pump and lower the federal funds rate 11 times in 2001 and 2002.

In fact, since the early 1980s the economists have come to believe that monetary ease, within limits, can heal our economy whenever there is a downturn. But, see what it really does. It creates a nation of debtors. In the 1990s, the experts frequently lamented the rising consumer debt. Then when the recession hit in 2007, some of them applauded, even demanded, a quick fall in the interest rate, so consumers could go more into debt.

The Fed indeed obliged them, hoping to lure people into increased borrowing. Even in 2019, the Fed along with other central bankers began to cut interest rates, once again. Is this a sign of sound economic policy, which will work only if people succumb to the debt temptation? Is this not just a way of postponing the problem to the future? The cumulative effect of the repeated adoption of monetary ease since the 1980s and the 1990s is that now aggregate American debt is almost twice the level of gross domestic product. Such is the legacy of neo-Keynesian economics that it has left the nation and the world vulnerable to a new economic shock. Oscar Wilde once said, "The only way to get rid of a temptation is to yield to it." This is what fiscal and monetary policies do: they create the debt temptation, and the public, oppressed by low wages and high taxes, cannot but yield to it.

Whether it is fiscal or monetary expansion, it puts the nation into debt — creating either government debt or private debt. When such prescriptions are used repeatedly over time, their cumulative effect is a "debt mountain," which can become a big burden on the economy. This is why such policies are only short-run panaceas, not lasting cures. A time comes when they no longer work. They fail to cure unemployment or create high-wage jobs. This has happened in Japan since 1990, and now in the United States since 2000.

The government has exhausted neo-Keynesian and supply-side remedies to fight a recession, yet wage stagnation continues. Something new has to be tried — something based on common sense, something ethical, truthful and straightforward.

5. Short-Run Reforms

What can we do immediately to revive the U.S. economy? Let us start by exploring a simple idea: if you want the prosperity of the 1950s and the 1960s, then you have to adopt the economic policies, especially the wage structure, of that period. This sounds like a sensible view, because such policies will revive demand, which is not only at the center of any advanced economy but is also our main problem today. What do such policies call for?

(1) Raise the minimum wage in steps to the 1968 level, which in 2019 prices was about $11 per hour, to $10 immediately, followed by a dollar rise the next year. Thereafter, the real minimum wage should be linked to national productivity.

(2) Enforce "anti-trust laws" to break up giant conglomerates like Exxon-mobil, General Electric, AOL, AT&T and other profitable companies that absorbed their rivals through mergers since the 1980s in violation of such laws. Alternately, either enforce the anti-trust laws to create free enterprise or strengthen the labor unions to create equal bargaining power between corporations and unions. This will lower the wage gap that is responsible for a variety of imbalances prevalent in most nations.

(3) Persuade other nations to adopt free trade, so that the trade deficit is eliminated, and America has "balanced free trade," or impose tariffs to achieve that balance. Expecting the United States to run trade deficits so other trade-surplus nations can prosper is both naïve and dangerous for the world economy. In the long run, it could lead to another Great Depression.

(4) Cut the credit card rates through the government offering competition to banks.

(5) Start industries based on the putting-out system in rural areas and small towns.

These reforms are illustrated in terms of the U.S. economy, but they apply to all countries, although the fifth reform is especially suited to developing economies that lack industries. They are what nations need to raise wages, employment and reduce poverty with minimal investment.

All industrialized nations should offer a minimum wage that fulfills minimum human needs of food, shelter, clothing, education and health-care. Some nations do while many do not. The U.S. real minimum wage has been decreasing for a long time and needs to be raised above the subsistence level.

Europe and Japan generally have minimum wage laws. Additionally, they have strong labor unions so wages in each industry are set by collective bargaining between the employer and the union. In such nations, the minimum wage is just a guidepost, because usually the negotiated wage is higher than the nation-wide minimum. Other countries that have a similar setup are Canada and Australia. In fact, Australia and Luxemburg get the honor of having the highest minimum wage.

China has its states set up their own minimum wages, which are low to mediocre, because it does not have a nation-wide minimum wage. India does have a minimum wage law, but it is poorly enforced, and many states set their own minimums. All in all, except in Europe, Australia, Japan and Canada, the minimum wage is not sufficient to meet the minimum daily requirements, and that needs to change.

The second reform is self-explanatory. Free enterprise powered by intense competition among firms and industries ensures the availability of high-quality goods at prices close to marginal cost of production. No company can then make shoddy products or charge high prices for its goods if it wants to retain its customers. Mergers should be prohibited among large firms; they should also be prohibited among labor unions. This way competition exists among firms on the one hand and workers on the other.

Business mergers lead to layoffs and an increased workload for the remaining employees. Wages tend to fall, while productivity goes up, so that the wage gap rises, and that, as we have seen time and again, creates all sorts of problems for the economy. Mergers should be permitted only among small firms, especially if a company is failing and merging with another firm is a way to avoid bankruptcy.

The third reform is about free trade among nations. Tariffs are the best way to ensure that production occurs where the demand is. Transporting goods to far-off nations creates a vast amount of oceanic and atmospheric pollution but does not add to production of goods. For this reason, economic policy should not encourage transportation but production near the centers of demand. Free foreign investment is preferable to free trade.

In other words, a nation should be free to invest and produce goods in other nations, but not bring goods from elsewhere. This way pollution would be minimized, while production goes up, because capital and labor engaged in intercontinental transportation will become available for localized production.

5.1. *An FDIC Bank*

The fourth reform is to reduce credit card rates and requires a detailed explanation. High card rates generate long-term indebtedness among the poor and keep them under the grip of poverty. Let us first see how the United States can bring them down through government action by providing competition to various banks and credit card agencies.

FDIC, or Federal Deposit Insurance Corporation, is an agency under the executive branch of the government. It insures a bank deposit for up to $250,000 against a bank's failure. In return for deposit protection, the agency charges a fee from insured institutions, and has a large fund worth billions of dollars.

The agency also protects consumers and ensures that banks and savings institutions remain solvent. When banks charge up to 30-percent interest on credit card loans, they are engaged in price gouging and the FDIC should protect consumers against such a rampant abuse of monopoly power. How can the agency stop this gouging?

The FDIC, which in 2019 had a capital of $50 billion, can cut the card rates in three simple and quick steps:

(1) The FDIC takes over an insolvent bank, infuses some capital into it to make it solvent, but does not sell it to another bank. Instead, the FDIC keeps the bank open and by a 1987 law it can do so for up to three years. Such an enterprise is known as a bridge bank. Let us call the new bank the FDIC bank.
(2) Once solvent and fully capitalized, the FDIC bank can raise funds just like any other bank by offering savings accounts and certificates of deposits (CDs), and by borrowing from the Federal Reserve. Suppose the cost of such funds is a lowly 2 percent, thanks to years of quantitative easing by the Federal Reserve.

(3) The FDIC invites people with credit card loans to transfer their balances to the FDIC bank, charges them 7-percent interest and makes a profit of 5 percent. Presto, the credit card rates fall to 7 percent from the 2019 average of 17 percent. It will take about a week to do the whole thing.

I suspect this will be the lowest rate of interest in the history of credit cards. In the spirit of anti-trust laws, all the government has to do is to create competition in the financial markets. Of course, politics stands in the way of breaking up large banking conglomerates. But the agency works for the President and he can easily provide competition to financial behemoths. No new legislation is needed, because a 1987 law authorizes the FDIC to open a bridge bank.

What about commercial banks that issue credit cards? Will they not go bankrupt with the FDIC just charging 7 percent? The answer is an emphatic "NO." Take a look at Figure 15.1, which offers a big surprise to an analyst. The figure details the profit margin on credit cards, which is

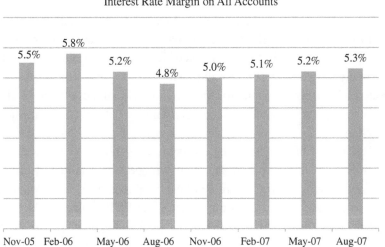

Figure 15.1:   Interest Rate Margin on All Accounts from November 2005 to August 2007

Sources: Federal Reserve, U.S. Bureau of Labor Statistics, and Liana Arnold, CardHub.com.

the difference between interest paid and interest received, from November 2005 to August 2007. Recall that, according to the National Bureau of Economic Research, the Great Recession started in December 2007. The banks' profit margin about that time, i.e., August 2007, was 5.3 percent and had been as low as 4.8 percent a year before.

According to Federal Reserve, banks' collective profit was $414 billion in 2006. If the financial industry that offers multi-million dollars of pay packages to their CEOs made such a large profit at an interest rate margin of just 4.8 percent, competing with FDIC with a profit margin of 5 percent will not hurt them.

Then why are the US banks raising their card rates? You already know the answer — greed. They do it because the poor people are helpless. According to an already cited CNBC report issued in 2019, 40 percent of Americans have less than $1,000 in savings. Even a slight emergency can wipe their saving nest egg out — a car breakdown, an illness, etc. They then have to use a credit card to pay for their bill. And once they borrow money at, say, 20–30-percent annual interest, their monthly payments usually stay forever.

Figure 15.2 gives a vivid example of the avarice of the financial industry. Soon after the start of the Great Recession, banks raised their interest rate margin to more than 11 percent in November 2009. And at this point in 2019 their profit margin is even higher — in fact much higher.

In 2019, the credit card debt exceeded $1 trillion and the average card interest rate was 17 percent. This means that consumers paid at least $170 billion to banks for the privilege of using credit cards. If the card rate drops to 7 percent, consumers will save at least $100 billion in bank charges.

Most of the borrowers using cards are very poor. When their minimum monthly charges plummet, there will be a substantial decline in poverty, almost overnight. It will be like a big rise in everyone's wage, but it will really help the production worker. The FDIC bank can be established in three days, and with the backing of the agency's large capital fund, it could start offering its services to the public in less than a month. Therefore, poverty will fall very quickly.

Credit cards are now used all over the world. In other nations, card rates are even higher, in fact confiscatory, especially in India and Brazil.

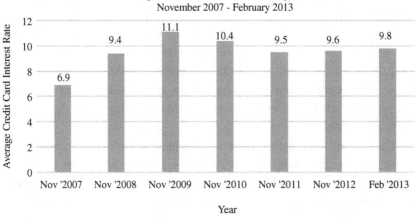

Figure 15.2:   Average Credit Card Interest Rate Margin from November 2007 to February 2013

Sources: The Federal Reserve; US Bureau of Labor Statistics; Liana Arnold, Cardhub.com.

Just imagine what a tonic it will be for economic growth in these nations, if they were to establish FDIC type of banks. Aggregate demand and GDP growth will shoot up without the governments and people getting into new debt.

5.2. *The Putting-Out System*

So far, we have outlined reforms that mostly apply to an industrialized economy such as the United States, China, India, Japan and Europe, among others. These reforms will work wonders in reducing poverty and reviving economic growth. But they will not do much for a developing economy, which just does not have enough factories to employ people.

A developing economy mostly produces raw materials and farm prod-ucts, where wages are low because of low labor productivity and savings are non-existent, so there is not much scope for capital formation. Furthermore, this economy lacks skilled and educated labor. Consequently, the nation is unable to acquire a modern-day factory system without foreign investment.

Conventional thinking is that if such a nation seeks to grow fast and improve the living standard of its citizens, then it should invite multinational firms to exploit its natural resources and export its raw materials to other nations. This is what resource-rich nations like Brazil and South Africa have done with little success in alleviating their poverty. In fact, Brazil and South Africa have both seen a rise in the number of poor people, while the multinational firms operating there have made handsome profits.

The modern-day factory system is the least suitable way to jump-start the rural economies of developing countries, because it requires enormous capital investment to build offices and factories to provide employment opportunities at decent wages to people. It also calls for workers and their families to migrate to cities, because that is where most large corporations are located. This creates new problems in the cities such as urban congestion, traffic jams and pollution.

The best way to lift rural poverty in South Africa and BRIC nations such as Brazil, India and China is to create small-scale cottage industries through a modified version of the old putting-out system that was popular in Europe before large-scale industrialization and in early American towns soon after independence. In this system, a merchant, known as a putter-out, provided raw materials and hand tools or simple machines to workers to produce goods at home. For instance, in textiles, the workers did everything by hand from weaving to making shirts. Later the merchant collected finished or semi-finished products and marketed them to other workers or consumers.

As technology advanced, workshops were built around homes and artisans worked there in groups in cities and small towns. These workshops evolved into modern factories, which coexisted with cottage industries for a while.

The putting-out system was a precursor to capitalism, worked for centuries and prevailed in many industries in almost all countries that are industrialized today. In India, according to Navin Doshi, an economic historian, it has been prevalent since ancient times under the inspiration of an olden economist named Chanakya, who wrote *Arthashastra*, which means, the *Science of Wealth*. Chanakya anticipated Adam Smith's *Wealth of Nations*, and even Keynes's *General Theory*.

Even today the system exists in most nations in the form of small businesses and cottage industries. India has a large cottage industry, employing some five million people. But the problem in India, as in other emerging markets such as South Africa and Brazil, is that the prices that these cottage industries receive from merchant middlemen for their goods are very low, insufficient to make a decent living. Their productivity is also low because of obsolete technology. For these reasons, these small companies are barely able to make a living. They need government assistance to establish a modified putting-out system.

5.3. *A Modified Putting-Out System*

A modified putting-out program can be established by the government in the following steps.

(1) The government provides raw materials and new high-tech machines to individuals and families that can be used at home to fabricate finished or semi-finished goods.
(2) Workers should also be properly trained in the use of advanced technology embodied in the new machines so as to raise labor productivity.
(3) Finally, the government should offer marketing help and eliminate the merchant middlemen who currently pay low prices to artisans working at home but sell goods produced by them at exorbitant prices to consumers. This way they gobble up a large share of profits, while paying only pennies to artisans.

This system will have a number of advantages absent in modern-day factories. The main problem that small businesses face in developing economies is their inability to market their products without a middleman, who gobbles up a lion's share of the profit. A modified putting-out system will raise worker productivity and the prices received by them, because the government will offer them fair prices, while selling goods at a lower markup. The lower markup will reduce prices to consumers and thus increase market demand for goods produced by artisans. At the same time, people could work at home or nearby workshops, and not require a high level of investment.

Furthermore, families need not move to urban centers, thereby avoiding urban congestion, traffic jams and pollution. As their incomes rise, the artisans should be given the choice of buying the machines that the government provides them through installments. This way workers will own their capital and enhance their income, because they will no longer have to pay a rent to the government for the use of equipment. The putting-out program will then become a system of mass capitalism.

6. The Impact of Other Measures

The enforcement of anti-trust laws will expand business competition and improve the quality of goods made in the United States. It will also enhance the demand for labor; therefore, unemployment will fall and the real wage will rise. *The irony of the current economic policy is that it expands foreign competition through increased trade but permits the decline of competition through mergers.* The two contradict each other and tend to crush labor demand. Mergers directly trim labor demand, while growing imports of labor-intensive goods do this indirectly.

We need "true free enterprise," not free markets in name only. Declining business competition is one of the main reasons for the rise in the wage gap, inequality, stock market mania and the inevitable crash, followed by a prolonged downturn or stagnation. Raising business competition to the level of the 1950s will be a step in the right direction. With the return of intercompany rivalry, product quality will improve and Americans will turn to homemade goods, reviving domestic industry in the process. This will also raise labor demand, employment and wages.

6.1. *A Balanced Economy*

In addition to balanced free trade, we should have a balanced economy. On its face this statement appears naïve, for everyone likes the idea of balance. However, as we saw in Chapter 10, global economic ills have sprung from what may be called unbalancing economic policies that are periodically supplemented by fiscal and monetary expansion. Specifically, poverty, hunger, recessions, inflation and depressions result when the government and private behavior create an imbalance in the labor market in the form of the rising wage gap. Once the labor market slips into imbalance, so do other sectors of the economy.

An important feature of a balanced economy is diversification, as opposed to specialization. Diversification tends to mitigate the labor–market distortion, which is a measure of the chasm between real wages and labor productivity. There is a well-known saying: prudent investors do not store all their eggs in one basket. This is because if the basket were to fall, the eggs could all break at the same time. Instead, savvy investors diversify by parking their funds in a variety of assets. They purchase stocks, bonds, real estate and gold; they buy shares and bonds of different companies and entities, and so on. By spreading their funds into a variety of assets, wise investors minimize their risk. If one asset declines in value, the other could rise, cut their losses and maximize their gains.

A balanced economy operates in much the same way and maximizes the living standard from the use of available resources. A diversified economy is far more stable and freer from the scourge of speculative bubbles, market crashes, inflation, recessions and depressions than a specialized economy. The United States today has become a highly specialized economy, especially with the help of its trade deficit. The country hardly produces any manufacturing goods. In the 1960s, our benchmark for a healthy economy, nearly 30 percent of the labor force worked in manufacturing; today only 9 percent does. The American economy was optimally diversified. It produced TVs, VCRs, shoes, fax machines, all sorts of spare parts and industrial raw materials in vast quantities and exported some of them. Today, they are mostly imported.

The mushrooming trade deficit is destroying the dynamism of American industry and the high-paying jobs. Balanced free trade, with enhanced business competition, will go a long way to restore America's economic balance. The United States is extremely vulnerable to troubles arising in its trading partners. If for some reason international commerce is disrupted and other nations are unable to supply the industrial raw materials and spare parts, the American economy will come to a halt and face severe inflation.

7. Economic Democracy

In the long run, the nation must control the wage gap, switch from the current factory system and move into what may be called economic democracy. At present, major stockowners run the companies. Such shareholders usually become CEOs or company chairpersons. They hire a group of executives, who in turn hire managers and production workers. There are thus two groups of employees in a firm — management and laborers — with diametrically opposite interests.

Management wants to squeeze the maximum effort out of employees, paying them the going wage set by the labor market. If the market is tight, that is, if qualified workers are in short supply, then their salaries are consistent with their MPL. However, if joblessness is high or work can be outsourced abroad, productivity considerations are set aside, and employees are usually paid less than their MPL to the company.

When it comes to managerial salaries, labor market tightness matters little. They are set by executive cronies, who, as you have seen, simply scratch each other's backs. The result is that CEO salaries have been as high as 300 times the production wage in the United States. Such inequalities are not only unfair but they also help create economic imbalances. Pervasive inequality leads to insufficient product demand, forcing the government to resort to budget deficits that raise interest rates, may be inflationary and waste resources. The Fed also has to lure the consumer into high debt. It is better to create a system where the consumer as a worker earns a wage high enough to meet basic requirements. There should be no need for the government and the households to borrow to the hilt so that the economy functions smoothly.

In order to create a fair and efficient system, economic democracy should be established to supplement free enterprise resulting from high competition. In this system, company workers own the majority of shares; management is still in the hands of experts and professionals, but the board of directors is answerable to employees, not the CEO and outside shareholders. In fact, the board consists mainly of representatives elected by the workers. Such a body is not likely to approve of anything that increases the gap between wages and labor productivity.

7.1. *Low Inequality*

Because of the democratic nature of this structure, the gap between worker and management salaries is likely to be reasonable. *Inequalities are automatically low in any democratic setup.* In the United States, the president earns $400,000 a year. He has perks similar to those of the CEOs, but receives a fraction of what some company officers make. This is because there is democracy in politics, but "autocracy in corporations." Why else would top executives earn huge bonuses even when profits of their companies plunge? A non-performing chief executive in a democracy is usually booted out by the voters. He is not showered with privileges and outlandish severance packages, unlike what happens with Big Business today.

Not only is economic democracy inherently fair, it is also innately more productive. Knowing that their efforts will be rewarded, self-employed persons work extremely hard. So will factory-owning workers. Wages will also be higher, although management salaries will be lower. Each employee will be paid a certain wage and a year-end bonus depending upon their efficiency and company profits. The same formula will apply to management salaries as well.

With companies still run by experts, productive efficiency will be at least as high as before. In reality, with employee ownership of the majority shares, productivity will be higher. Another advantage of economic democracy is its low level of unemployment. It is normal for all economies to go through ups and downs, but the ups and downs of capitalism occasionally get out of control, and produce catastrophic inflation or depressions, culminating in high joblessness and despair.

7.2. *Fair and Efficient*

Today, when people are laid off, government spending increases to feed the unemployed. The government in turn raises taxes, so those employed end up supporting the unemployed. *Under economic democracy, no hardworking person would be laid off because all employees jointly own the company or at least its majority shares.* In a downturn, working hours and wages would be reduced for all. This way, everybody would share the pain, and no one would feel the psychological trauma of being unemployed.

The current system is wasteful and debilitating for the jobless. Even today, the employed assist the unemployed through higher taxes. Therefore, the pain is shared even in the current system, although not equally, but there is a wasteful middleman collecting taxes to aid the jobless. This function will be unnecessary under economic democracy. There will be no wastage of resources, nor the stigma of being without a job.

7.3. *Stability*

With economic democracy, inequality is automatically low, so that consumer spending and aggregate demand are high. The government does not need high deficits to support high output levels and employment. A democratic system is inherently stable. When wages keep pace with productivity, both GDP and real wages grow apace, because consumer demand then keeps up with supply. With producers assured of a growing market, business investment also then expands rapidly; so does new technology, which in turn ignites productivity growth and real wages. In economic democracy, workers and hence consumers are in a win–win position, although stock markets and speculative manias are mercifully subdued. *A democratic economy is innately a high-growth and low-inequality economy.*

Economic democracy is practical only in large companies, such as General Motors, Walmart, Microsoft, Sony, IBM, AT&T, Toyota, Mercedes-Benz and so on. In big firms, at least 51 percent of the shares should be in the hands of employees, with the rest belonging to outsiders. The board of directors will then come mainly from workers. Medium-sized firms may also operate in this way.

In small companies, this system may or may not be practical. Those with less than a thousand workers may be individually owned or run as co-operatives, where shares may or may not be employee owned. In a consumer co-op, some investment by employee members may be necessary. Otherwise, co-ops are run on the same democratic principles as medium and large companies.

Economic democracy will require state aid and commitment, just as political democracy once did. The federal government can bring this about by targeting an industry's major firm, buying 51 percent of its shares in the stock market and then selling them at subsidized rates to the firm's employees. The workers can buy the shares in installments, that is, a small fraction of their salary can be deducted every month to pay for their purchases. A model is then created in each industry. Once the model firm reveals its natural superiority in terms of efficiency, employee morale and wages, other companies in that industry will follow suit and sell out to the employees.

The government could also use its tax revenue to buy shares from many firms and transform an entire industry into a democratic setup. The action may not involve huge outlays in a depressed stock market. This way, one by one, little by little, economic democracy will spread to all large and medium corporations.

When workers are majority owners themselves, there is no need for unions. Labor cannot strike against labor. Every employee will be paid a need-based minimum wage, plus a premium, depending upon education, experience and skill, including a year-end bonus in proportion to profit. Hard work, innovation and intelligence will be rewarded with extra bonuses, whereas lethargy, dishonesty and inefficiency will be penalized through the loss of bonus, and, as a last resort, the loss of job. In short, there will be true free enterprise. In the rare case of job loss, the company will buy back the worker's shares at the current market price.

8. Mass Capitalism

We should not confuse worker management and ownership with socialism. The system is more like mass capitalism, because shares of Fortune 500 corporations will be majority owned by a vast number of people. Unlike in socialism, in an economic democracy the state is not engaged in the production of goods and services. Once the new system is established, government intervention in the economy would be, and should be, minimal. In fact, the system will materialize the ideals cherished by most macroeconomic theories.

Economic democracy should please the classical and neoclassical economists because of its small government. The neo-Keynesians will be elated because of its low unemployment and inherent stability. Socialists will be ecstatic because of its low inequality. Even the chief executives will like it in the end because of its tendency to produce steady growth in profits and share prices without the ballyhoo and hoopla of the speculative bubble, followed by the inevitable crash. *In short, there is no economic ill on earth that a democratic economy cannot heal.*

Bibliography

Batra, R., Non-traded goods, factor market imperfections and gains from trade, *American Economic Review*, **63**(4), 706–713, 1973.

Batra, R., *The Myth of Free Trade, New York*, Macmillan, 1993.

Batra, R., *The Great American Deception*, New York, John Wiley, 1996.

Batra, R., *The Crash of the Millennium*, New York, Random House, 1999.

Batra, R., Neutrality and non-neutrality of money in a classical type of model, *Pacific Economic Review*, **7**(3), 489–503, 2002.

Batra, R., Economics in crisis: severe and logical contradictions of classical, neo-Keynesian and popular trade models, *Review of International Economics*, **10**(4), 623–644, 2002.

Boskin, M., Tax policy and economic growth, *Journal of Economic Perspectives*, **2**(4), 71–97, 1988.

Feldstein, M., Reducing poverty, not inequality, *The Public Interest*, **137**, 33–41, 1999.

Fite, G. and Reese, J., *An Economic History of the United States*, Atlanta, Houghton Mifflin, 1973.

Friedman, M. and Schwartz, A., *A Monetary History of the United States*, Princeton: Princeton University Press, 1963.

Mulay, A., *Mass Capitalism*, New York, Book Publishers Network, 2014.

Mulay, A., *New Macroeconomics*, New York, Business Expert Press, 2018.

Romer, P., Increasing returns and long-run growth, *Journal of Political Economy*, **94**(5), 1986.

Solow, R., A contribution to the theory of economic growth, *Quarterly Journal of Economics*, **70**(1), 65–94, 1956.

U.S. Council of Economic Advisers, *The Economic Report of the President*, Various Years, Washington, D. C.

U.S. Department of Commerce, *Historical Statistics of the United States, Colonial Times to 1970*, Washington, D. C., 1975.

U.S. Department of Commerce, *Historical Statistics of the United States, Colonial Times to 1945*, Washington, D. C., 1975.

Index